THE PRODUCER'S PERSPECTIVE

A THEATRE PRODUCER IN NYC GIVES HIS
OPINION ON EVERYTHING RELATED TO
BROADWAY AND BEYOND.

YEAR 1: IS THERE A DOCTOR IN THE THEATER?

BY
KEN DAVENPORT

WWW.THEPRODUCERSPERSPECTIVE.COM

Davenport Theatrical Enterprises
250 West 49th Street, Suite 204
New York, NY 10019

ISBN 978-0-578-00475-4

DEDICATION

This book is dedicated to my Father for two reasons:

1) He taught me to always speak my mind.

2) He still doesn't have a computer, so publishing a book is the only way I could get him to read my blog.

CONTENTS

A NOTE FROM KEN

I have to admit it. When I first joined the blogosphere, I felt like one of those crazy people on the subway who talk to themselves. I never imagined that one day I'd be typing a preface to a book of a year's worth of entries, especially since I found myself staring at my screen at 3 AM so many times wondering, "What the &#@$ am I going to write about?"

A year later, I'm still rambling and ranting about the state of the commercial theater and offering my ideas on how we can take it into the 21st century (yes, I realize we're already in the 21st century, but the theater tends to be behind every other industry by at least 10 years). A bunch of smart people helped get me through the year including my staff: Matt Kovich, Jamie Lynn Ballard, Ryan Lympus, and David Gersten, as well as my various blog editors, Michael Roderick, Nicole Brodeur, Ronald E. Hornsby and Tracy Weiler.

And of course, I have to thank my readers. Without you, I would be one of those crazy people who talks to themselves.

Ken Davenport

P.S. All of the text in this book is taken directly from my blog. If a word is underlined it means that there is a hyperlink or a photo or video on the entry on the website. If you wish to check out the link or the photo/video, just visit www.TheProducersPerspective.com and search for that specific entry (you can find it by date in the archives section). While you're there, sign up to receive the blog via email and next year, you won't have to buy Volume #2 of the book.

OCTOBER 2007

October 13, 2007

If a Producer talks out loud in his office and no one is there to hear it ...

. . . he'll blog instead.

Hi everyone. Ken Davenport here, and I like to talk. A lot.

Lately, I've found that my staff is either too busy with all the other work I give them to listen to my latest random thoughts, or they just aren't in the office at 3 AM when I come up with them.

So that brings me (and you) here.

Stay tuned, sign up for the feed and it'll be like you're in my office with me at 3 AM.

Fun times and lots of Red Bull.

October 14, 2007

My office isn't big enough for a Water cooler.

So, we built a virtual one instead.

www.BroadwaySpace.com

Special props to Seth Godin for the inspiration.

October 15, 2007

A buffet, a reclining seat, air conditioning, and, oh yeah, a movie too!

Two nights ago, I went to see The Heartbreak Kid.

The movie wasn't that great.

But my seat reclined and I had more than enough legroom. I had more options for food than I do at some NYC restaurants: chicken fingers, nachos, popcorn, hot dogs, Sour Patch Kids, ice cream, you name it. Even healthy options! And get this - they *encouraged* me to eat in the theater! They even built a drink holder right into the seat. One woman didn't want to pay the concession prices, so she brought in her own Chinese food and the usher didn't even stop her. The temperature in the theater was perfect and my feet didn't stick to the ground when I left.

The movie wasn't that great.

But I guarantee it would have been a helluva lot worse if all of the above didn't add to the experience.

Last night, I went to see a Broadway show.

I was chewing on my knees for the entire show because the theater was recently renovated and they stuffed more seats into the place. They refused to let me bring my Coke to my seat. I had to hide my Sour Patch Kids in my jacket. And the air conditioning was on the fritz (and the guy next to me, whose arm was already in my lap, was not very "fresh").

The show wasn't that great.

But I'll bet you the price of the ticket that it would have felt a helluva lot better if the overall experience was better.

A performance event doesn't begin or end at the rise or fall of the curtain. It's not just about the performance. It's the overall experience - from buying the ticket at the box office to dealing with the ushers to whether or not your a$$ hurts after sitting for 2.5 hours.

As the movie business lost traffic to people staying home to watch TiVo or surf the Internet, they invested in making the "experience" better and more unique.

And when you improve the overall experience, individual elements look better as a result. Win x2.

I mean, aren't you happier when you're eating popcorn? Having a cold beverage? Sitting on a cushioned seat? And of course that feeling transfers to whatever else you are doing at that time.

Happier customer . . . leads to positive feeling about product . . . leads to customer buying more product . . . leads to healthier industry.

The theater has got some catching up to do. We have to stop being snobs and saying, "Our product is so unique and since you can't get it anywhere else, people are just going to have to deal with long lines at the restrooms and rude personnel and knee-chewing. It's just the price of Broadway." We have stop saying that. Otherwise, people may choose to experience something else.

October 16, 2007

What the Fuerzabruta?

When I went to see <u>Fuerzabruta</u> (the new guerrilla-style Cirque du Soleil from the creators of De La Guarda) on Sunday night, I couldn't help but think how many lawyers, insurance agents, accountants and yes, producers, probably told them that there was no way to do some of the things they wanted to do.

Kudos to the creative team for not listening.

And kudos to those lawyers, insurance agents, accountants and yes, producers, for figuring out solutions to new problems.

Because by doing things that seem impractical, irrational, and dangerous, they created something worth talking about.

And that's the best insurance policy a show can have.

October 18, 2007

The Marketing of Marketing

I hate *marketing.* I love *sales.*

A great marketer is a great salesman: someone who produces quantifiable and trackable results, and then uses those results to create growth . . . and then does that over and over and over.

But no one likes the word salesman anymore. It conjures up too many images of used cars and door-to-door encyclopedia hawkers.

So, someone actually marketed the word sales . . . and it became marketing.

And that person must have been really lazy.

Look at the two words . . . which one makes you feel that you have to produce hard data, and which one is more vague and ambiguous in terms of your goals?

Be a salesman. Hawking encyclopedias is hard work and it's not for the faint of heart. But it's a lot more rewarding and you'll learn a hawk of a lot more in the process.

October 19, 2007

Your roots are showing.

I'm in the process of looking for composers for a few musicals I have in development.

You know what I've discovered?

When the root word of Musical is MUSIC . . . it's a big freekin' decision!

Music is why people see musicals. Simple as that. It's what makes them unique.

And how many celebrity lyricists do you know? How many celebrity book writers do you know?

Even when shows fail, good music can still live on your iPod long after the investors have claimed the losses on their tax returns (*Parade*, anyone?). Thousands of people know the words to "Meadowlark" from *The Baker's Wife*, but I don't ever hear people humming the dialogue from Act II, scene iii. (And how many of you even knew it was from *The Baker's Wife*?)

Yep, it's a big one. So I'm going to take my time and make sure I get my roots just right. Because these roots show all the time. Even when your dye job costs $10 million dollars.

You know what else?

The root word of Play is . . . PLAY. Hmmmmm

October 20, 2007

Cooler than the other side of the pillow.

BroadwaySpace got mentioned on the Ning Blog today.

Theatre is such an insulated and archaic industry with its own set of economics and politics that it's a real honor when companies outside of it take notice. Thanks, Ning!

Oh, and I just love the fact that the CEO joined BroadwaySpace. She has 110,000 networks on Ning. And she took time to join up, fill out a profile, and message me back and forth. Cool.

October 21, 2007

Speak up, Louise!

I was honored to be asked to speak on a panel on 'Guerrilla Tactics in Theater Publicity' at The Center of Communication this coming Thursday, October 25th at 6:30 PM.

Click here for all of the details.

Should be a fun panel . . . not that I am a guerrilla publicity guy or anything.

Although, I do wonder what the Back Street Boys did with that rubber chicken I FedExed them when they didn't show up for the Altar Boyz Boy Band Battle. And that 'Virgins Get In Free' promotion for the opening night of My First Time truly was a service for the chaste.

The most fun part of the panel is that it's going to be moderated by Michael Reidel, the infamous Perez Hilton of Broadway.

Michael and I go way back. He hammered Bernadette Peters in *Gypsy* when I was the Associate General Manager. It eventually closed, and I'm sure his pen had something to do with it.

You'd think I'd be mad, but I've forgiven him. After all, if *Gypsy* had never closed, I'd probably still be managing shows instead of producing them.

See you at The Center!

October 22, 2007

We're one pitch away from a Strikeout.

A lot of people have been asking me whether or not I think the Local 1/Broadway League contract negotiation will result in a strike.

My answer is simply . . . no. There will be no Local 1 strike.

In fact, I'll bet $100 on it. Any takers? I'll pay 10:1.

Why am I so confident? Because of a man named Mr. Trocchio, my high school history teacher who taught me that to determine the course of the future, you must look at the events of the past (ok, every history teacher teaches that . . . but Mr. Trocchio sticks out in my mind because he used to grade our papers while eating pasta and once I had spaghetti sauce on my ten-pager about the Treaty of Versailles).

Anyway . . . when you look at the history of modern labor negotiations in the theater, you will see that there have been only two strikes on Broadway since 1975.

That data alone would be enough to give even odds that there will be no strike.

Here's why I'm giving 10:1:

BOTH of those strikes in the last 32 years have been by the SAME union . . . Local 802. The musicians.

And, in fact, Local 1 has never struck Broadway.

The League and all of the other unions it negotiates with, from the Actors to the Ushers, have always been able to resolve their issues without a walkout. Always. No matter how contentious those negotiations can get.

A major contract negotiation is like the Fourth of July. Both are on the calendar. And both have lots and lots of fireworks.

But that doesn't mean Broadway is going to blow its hand off.

(Although, I have to be honest. As the producer of three Off-Broadway shows that would have a lot less competition if there was a Broadway strike, there's a part of me that's secretly hoping for one.)

What Mr. Trocchio would really be interested in, besides a plate of ravioli, is why the musicians walk out more than anyone else? What is it about those negotiations that don't go as well?

This is something we should all start looking at now, or I may be betting the other way when their negotiations come up next.

Until then, watch my Red Sox win the series if you're looking for strikes.

Oh, and if there are any Federal Agents reading this blog, please know that the above referenced bet was made in jest. This is not an online gambling site and we have no way of taking money, even though if someone was interested in taking that bet, they could email me using the address to the left of this blog. Happy Strike Watch!

October 23, 2007

Be stupid, Stupid.

Last May, I bought the domain name <u>BestMusical.com</u> and put together a website that I hoped would spread like my favorite <u>"Laughing Baby"</u> video on YouTube.

At the height of the campaign, Best Musical got a whopping 182 unique visitors in one day, and now it struggles to break double digits, averaging about 6 visitors a day. 2 of those are me, checking to make sure the site still works.

BestMusical.com is arguably the biggest failure of my publicity-stunting life.

So, of course, I had to obsess about its failure so that I didn't repeat it in the future (see Mr. Trocchio's lesson from yesterday).

At first I didn't understand why it wasn't working. I thought it was so clever and so cool. It cracked up everyone in my office.

And then, "The Laughing Baby" gave me the answer.

Let's look at all of the <u>'Top Favorites'</u> of all time on YouTube: the aforementioned "Laughing Baby", a one man "Evolution of Dance", four guys doing Talking Heads-style choreography on treadmills, and something called "The Potter Puppet Pals".

All of these videos have something in common. They are just plain stupid.

And yet the "Evolution of Dance" has been seen almost 62 MILLION times.

All of a sudden, they are not so stupid. 62 million is more than 20% of the <u>entire population</u> of the US. They are appealing to the majority, and what's wrong with that?

Simple and stupid funny is what people want. People <u>falling</u> down, <u>anchorwomen</u> making mistakes, etc. If you're too hip and too clever, you alienate most everyone, which is the antithesis of the viral campaign.

Virals are about as many impressions as possible, so you better be a lot more like the Laughing Baby than BestMusical.com.

Think for a moment about the types of emails you send to your friends.

Anyone want to buy a domain name?

October 24, 2007

Television 2.0.

CBS canceled Hugh Jackman's musical television series, <u>Viva Laughlin</u>, today. After only two outings. Ouch.

But that's not what's interesting to me (I mean, did anyone think the show would work? It reeked of mid-season cancellation).

What interested me was what was taking its time slot: *The Amazing Race.*

Hold on a second. I'm not going where you think I'm going.

Everyone knocks Reality Television. But why? Everyone loves Web 2.0., don't they?

Reality television is the ultimate form of <u>User Generated Content</u> . . . just on television instead of the web. It's TV 2.0.

One could argue that the birth of Reality TV in the US (with <u>Survivor</u> in 2000) is what spawned the User Generated Content movement which began in 2005.

American Idol is Users singing and Users voting. Like EBay, the show just provides the opportunity and the platform for the two sets of Users to meet each other and interact. And then it gets out of the way. It's television social networking.

So don't knock Reality TV. There's a connection between these two forms of media and entertainment.   If you love one, you gotta love the other.

Now how does theatre, the eternal late-adopter, fit into this UGC movement?

We have a lot to learn from the audience that would rather watch *The Amazing Race* over a multi-million dollar slickly-produced show like *Viva.*

October 25, 2007

I'm gonna say it . . .

. . . cuz I know you're all thinking it.

Sondheim is the Shakespeare of the American Musical Theater.

(Wait for it. Wait for it.)

Like Bill's, Sondheim's material is so incredibly rich. It demands attention. It needs to be studied by anyone who wants to pursue a career in the theater. It needs to be read, listened to, and dissected so we can debate and learn from every little detail. It's that brilliant.

(Here it comes.)

But like Shakespeare's, it's not that exciting to watch.

Ok, ok, before you call me a heathen, I know that most of you think the same thing, so don't even start.

I've got the attendance and recoupment records for all of Sondheim's prior productions to back me up.

Brilliance doesn't always work on Broadway.

October 26, 2007

Be kind to the animals.

A friend of mine was telling a story today and he used Cats as a reference. And, on cue, most of the group snickered.

What's so funny about Cats?

I'm going to spare you an essay on whether or not Cats is a good musical. That's not my point.

My point is that whether you like it or not, Cats is a classic of American Musical Theater.

Here's why:

A classic is something that stands the test of time.

Cats ran for 7485 performances. Almost 18 years.

If modern musical theater began around the turn of the century (some say it started with <u>The Black Crook</u>, others say Show Boat, so I'm picking a mid point), that means that Cats had a run on Broadway equivalent to almost 20% of the medium's life.

Imagine a book (other than the bible) staying on the NY Times Bestseller list for 18 years!

And just because it closed on Broadway doesn't mean that its life is over.

On the contrary, 18 years is just the beginning. Like Show Boat, Cats will continue to purr around the world in regional productions and high schools for many more than 9 lives.

So instead of kicking the kitties, let's figure out <u>what makes people want to see them</u> now . . . and forever.

October 27, 2007

<u>What the #&$@ is my job, anyway?</u>

I've been lucky enough to speak on a number of panels lately, and one of the most common questions I get is, "What does a producer actually do?"

It usually takes me about fifteen minutes to explain how a producer's job may vary from raising money to selling merchandise to giving notes to a director to explaining to a hair dresser that the star of the show doesn't want her in her dressing room because her feet smell. (True story)

And after that fifteen minute lecture, my other panelists are usually ready to gag me because I've taken so much of their time.

So, I decided I needed to distill my definition down to one succinct sentence. So here goes:

A <u>commercial producer's</u> job is to get as many people to see his or her show as possible.

That task can be accomplished through raising money to get the show up, through giving notes to the authors in order to make it a better show that people want to see, through marketing and advertising, and yes through buying some odor eaters so that star's nasal passages don't swell and cause her to miss another show.

But everything you do is in order for it to be seen by as many people as possible.

Because if lots and lots and lots of people see it . . . the investors should be happy because they are *hopefully* making money, and the authors should be happy because their voice is being heard.

Future fellow panelists, you can leave the gags at home now. Although, maybe that's not a smart idea. I've got some other things to say.

Speaking of panels, I've been asked to be a part of a very exciting panel at the Word of Mouth Marketing Association conference in Las Vegas on 11/15. It's the largest conference on word of mouth marketing, so it should be a lot of fun. And right after my panel, there's a keynote address by Andy Sernovitz who wrote "Word of Mouth Marketing: How Smart Companies Get People Talking". I'm an Andy fan. He's smart. Oh, and he mentions *Altar Boyz* in his book. :-)

October 29, 2007

<u>**Is "Vanity" a sin?**</u>

I got into a discussion about "Vanity Projects" today.

I've thought about this term before, because I'm sure some people have called my shows VPs. I do wear a lot of hats on my shows at times, depending on the scope and size of the project, and, to be honest, how much is in the budget (I work cheap when I'm negotiating with myself) and who else is available.

But what really is a Vanity Project?

A Vanity Project is a term used to describe shows that don't work, AFTER they don't work. It's the entertainment industry's version of Monday morning quarterbacking.

Has anyone ever called *Rocky* a Vanity Project? Sly wrote and starred in the first one (winning an Oscar), and wrote, starred and directed the rest of the series (except for *Rocky V*, where he let the original director get behind the camera again).

How about *Star Wars*? Written and Directed by Mr. Lucas.

Hedwig? No.

Rent? Nope.

In The Heights? Don't think so.

In My Life? (alarm goes off) Most people in Shubert Alley would say yes.

Collaboration is why I love the theatre. But that doesn't mean that wearing a few hats is a bad thing, as long as you deliver.

So no, Vanity is not a sin.

But sucking definitely is.

October 30, 2007

<u>Starry, Starry Night!</u>

Below is a list of the longest running shows in Broadway history:

1. The Phantom of the Opera
2. Cats
3. Les Miserables
4. A Chorus Line
5. Oh! Calcutta!
6. Beauty and the Beast
7. Rent
8. Chicago
9. Miss Saigon
10. The Lion King

What do 9 of these 10 shows have in common?

Not one of them opened with a Star.

Make the show the Star. That's the key to a long runner. In a new show, stars are nothing but expensive insurance policies for those who lack the confidence in their own material. Stars make us lazy. And they ask for crazy things like special luxury wallpaper (true story).

And once you go Star, you can never go back. Save the Stars for the revivals (like the 1 out of the 10 above) because they need them.

Now, look back at that list . . . how many musical theater Stars were born from the shows above? I count at least as many as there are shows on that list.

Make Stars, don't count on them.

NOVEMBER 2007

November 1, 2007

My Favorite Food is Stake.

During last night's performance of my favorite improv troupe, The Nuclear Family (they improvise a complete musical at each performance and they've never failed to have me doubled over in laughter), one of the cast members reminded me of one of the most important elements of all forms of entertainment.

In the middle of a scene, the actor noticed that the drama and conflict had slipped out of the improvised story line, so he feigned a phone called to a Starbucks and asked if he could order up a "double whipped low fat *high stakes* latte."

I told you they were funny.

Any successful drama, whether on television, film or on the stage, requires high stakes.
This is especially true for musical theater, which is a heightened form of expression by nature.

So if you're writing a musical you better have some porterhouse-sized, rare and juicy stakes to go along with it.

Wait, there's more.

As I type this, *Grey's Anatomy* is on in the background (It's on just for the noise. I'm not really watching it, really . . . but . . . . is this George and Izzie thing gonna last?).
Television understands the need for high stakes. So much so that it continually repeats the same types of shows.

There are three common types of prime time serials: legal dramas, medical dramas, and police dramas. *Hill Street Blues, St. Elsewhere, LA Law, Perry Mason, Matlock, NYPD Blue, Columbo, The Practice, ER*, and yes *Grey's*. And I could go on and on. Why the repetition?
Because life or death, the highest and juiciest stake of all, is built into the stories of each one of those types of professions. Writing one of these dramas is like buying a car and getting the power windows, the GPS and the seat/butt warmers for no additional price. The high stakes are included.

So either Hollywood is really, really smart to keep wading in the same pool of subject matter because it has this necessary component . . . or Hollywood is really, really lazy because it refuses to look for and *create* high stakes elsewhere.

You know what else is interesting?

Police, legal and medical dramas, those successful prime time serials . . . do *not* work on the musical stage.

By the way, the best stake of all is <u>here.</u>

November 2, 2007

Is there a Doctor in the theater?

From the American Heritage Dictionary:

re-vive
v. *tr.*
1. To bring back to life or consciousness; resuscitate.

For example, "The Doctors *revived* the comatose man."

So that means if you're reviving something, you have to consider that man, woman or musical . . . dead.

And bringing someone, something or some show back from the dead takes an awful lot. You can't just revive anything by using <u>"The Secret"</u> or because you liked the show when you saw it 20 years ago.

To have a successful revival on Broadway, you need the following:

1. A major revisionist thinking, or a decidedly new take on the material.
2. A major star (and not one that we've all seen 20 times in other shows . . . give us someone new)

And if you really want a smash revival . . . give us <u>both</u>

November 3, 2007

8 shows a what?

Does anyone know where the 8 show a week model came from?

Is it arbitrary? Is it based on The Beatles song? Was there any business analysis done on the actual demand for theatrical performances at the time?

My gut says that someone just picked it. It somehow made sense at that moment, which was probably at least 50 years ago.

And thus, all of our agreements with labor unions, with landlords, etc., were based on this archaic idea that the demand for all shows, regardless of their cast or their subject matter, is the same.

So *Mamma Mia* does eight shows a week and so does *Macbeth*.

That's like Barnes and Noble stocking the same number of copies of the latest installment of *Harry Potter* as a Hungarian cookbook.

Smarter industries have more of a throttle on demand. There are more flights by an airline during the holidays (and the prices go up). There are less waiters and cooks on staff at a restaurant during a Tuesday lunch hour.

Wouldn't it be great to find a way to break this model? For so many shows (especially Off-Broadway), there isn't the demand for 8 shows, but since we have to pay for them, we all do them. And, we end up chasing our advertising tails, by spending huge bucks trying to fill the additional shows, when we could save money if we had fewer shows to fill.

And the fewer shows would be better sold, creating a harder to get ticket, which would actually increase demand as well as increase the experience for that audience (an audience of 500 is never as good as an audience of 1000).

I can hear the naysayers now: "Ken, but there are people that want to see a show on Tuesday night, so you should capture whatever you can." Are you really telling me that if 2 people wanted to come to see *Altar Boyz* on a Tuesday, that they wouldn't come on a Thursday if the Tuesday wasn't available?

Two of my shows do less than 8 shows a week. It's a challenge to make it work with the venues, my staffs, etc. but I'm very lucky to have wonderful forward-thinking partners that make it possible.

Yep, it's definitely a challenge. But I'd have a much greater challenge if they weren't running at all.

November 6, 2007

<u>**Houston, we have a distribution problem.**</u>

Broadway is in the heart of Times Square in New York City . . . and nowhere else.

And, no matter how much I want to get a petition going to move it to sunny southern California, it doesn't look like it's going anywhere soon.

Broadway isn't like Tide detergent, available in every grocery store around the country. It's not like the latest Avril Lavigne album available in every Virgin Megastore and on iTunes on the computer you're working on right now. It's not like *American Gangster,* which will play in movie theaters in New York City and in Nashville, and in every city around the country and around the world at the same time.

Unless you're one of the lucky shows with <u>15 companies worldwide</u>, you've got only one distribution channel . . . right here in New York City.

If your distribution channels are limited, then obviously you can't market your show in the same way.

In this Sunday's Arts & Leisure section of the New York Times, there was a full page ad for *The Little Mermaid* on Broadway.

And, of course, just a few pages away, there were full page advertisements for films like *American Gangster.*

Which one is a better value?

A New York Times reader in New Mexico can't see *Mermaid*, but most likely he can see *Gangster.*

Yet both full page ads cost about the same amount of money. Doesn't seem fair does it? *Mermaid's* potential customers are severely diminished because of its one distribution channel.

Billboards pose the same problem.

There is a giant <u>*Young Frankenstein*</u> billboard in Times Square. There is also a billboard for *Target.*

The impression that the Target billboard makes on the tourist can be converted the following week when the tourist is back home. Or when the tourist is visiting another city two weeks later.

The impression that the *Young Frankenstein* billboard makes can only be converted within 5 blocks of that billboard. Once he or she goes back home, the impression becomes so much less valuable.

90% of shows can't afford the same sort of subtle branding that most other products can afford. Our advertising has to be a much stronger call to action.

So what do we do? Use your advertising to sell, not just brand (that is, until you have 15 companies worldwide and can split the advertising costs among them).

Or more significantly, perhaps we should stop throwing money at giant media companies like the NY Times who refuse to recognize that we are different than Tide, Avril Lavigne and *American Gangster*, and therefore should have appropriate pricing scales.

When it comes to advertising, pay for *your* potential. Don't pay for someone else's.

And yes, Avril Lavigne is on my iPhone.

November 7, 2007

Size does matter . . .

But not in the way you think.

General Managers and Producers are always trying to figure out how to make shows work economically.

The old trick is that if it's not working in a specific theater . . . put it in a bigger one! Your Gross Potential goes up, and therefore when you show an investor a recoupment schedule based on percentages, the show looks more viable.

70% of 2000 seats is a lot better than 70% of 1000 seats, right?

But here's the rub.

Just because you put the show in a bigger theater, that doesn't mean that more people are going to go. Duh, right?

Here's what I like to think of when I choose a theater.

Yes, economics are important, without a doubt. And I'd look at the average # of people coming to see Broadway or Off-Broadway shows on a nightly basis to determine what is appropriate.

But just as important is the feel and the energy inside the theater.

I like my theaters to feel like a soda can that is shaken up - so filled with energy and excitement that it could burst!

And then, when you open the doors at the end of the show and let your audience out, it's like opening up that shaken soda can . . . and all those people go spilling into the streets and all over everything else, gushing about what they just saw, because they can't help it.

Those are the people that are going to sell tickets for you.

And a smaller more energized theater also means a harder to get ticket, less seats to fill so less advertising expenses, lower theater expenses and an overall better experience for the audience.

So get people excited with something smaller.

November 8, 2007

Size does matter . . . Part II

It's not the size of the office that defines a Company.

It's the passion of the people inside it.

November 9, 2007

Not everyone should play poker.

Anyone that has played a lot of poker knows that if you get a player that sits down at the table that doesn't know how to play very well, it can really affect your game.

Oh, you'd think you could just take all of their money pretty easily, but it's not that simple.

Bad players make stupid bets not based on odds, drive up the pots, read the cards wrong, and play on emotion. And they can even win a big pot every once in awhile making them think they know how to play.

And sometimes, they can draw you in to playing their style of the game.

And when they pull you in, you end up making bad bets and the next thing you know, you're heading for the buffet, as they are buying tickets to the latest Cirque show with your money.

Or they just mess up the game for everyone else that's trying to play.

This happens all too often in the theater, a business where sometimes a big checkbook is all you need. Most recently, I watched a high profile show whose fate had been sealed some time ago start doing random media buys, including full page ads in papers, etc. And then this week, they sent out an offer for free tickets to every single one of their performances . . . to a list of people that usually paid for tickets (guess which list is going to be hard to retrain that they have to pay for theater now - thanks for ruining that hand for the rest of the players, guys!)

And after all that . . . this week, they announced their closing.

When you see big ads, and lots of questionable media, it's easy to start to think you need to do the same thing. But don't get sucked in, just because someone raises the bet.

Good poker players sit back behind sunglasses and play the numbers, calculating pot odds, determining when to raise and when to fold based on data first and then gut, while watching others flail around.

Oh, and knowing when to fold and close a show and limit your losses to your investors is one of the hardest lessons to learn, but one of the most important.

November 10, 2007

I owe a lot of people a lot of money.

The stagehands are going on strike tomorrow morning, which means I lost my bet.

But, as an Off-Broadway producer of three shows that will be up and running throughout the strike, I am happy to pay up. :-)

I'll comment more on the strike and why I was wrong later. Right now I've got a few things to do to make sure people know that Off-Broadway is open for business!

November 12, 2007

Strike Thought of the Day: What's wrong with a little therapy?

Here's something to consider as all of you contemplate which "side" you're on in regards to the current Broadway Stagehands strike.

The mayor of New York City offered to provide both the League and Stagehands with a mediator as well as neutral territory to help bring this strike to a quicker resolution. You might recall that his help was instrumental in ending the Local 802 strike in 2003.

Local 1 continues to refuse his offer of assistance.

The League has welcomed his help.

Hmmmm . . .

Why would the Stagehands not welcome an objective party to help bring these two organizations closer together which would put people back to work faster and satisfy thousands of theatergoers sooner?

Could it be that they are afraid that an objective and impartial mediator would take a look at their demands and current work rules and advise them that what they are striking for is not fair in the current economic climate on Broadway and in the United States?

If this contract negotiation were like a marriage going through a troubled time, then Local 1 would be the stubborn husband who refuses to go to therapy. What's wrong with talking to someone, Local 1? It's just a therapist. They don't bite. Although, if you have cheated on your partner, then you may end up sweating a bit . . .

This marriage needs help. Divorce isn't an option. Both parties have kids to think about. And those kids really, really want to see *The Little Mermaid.*

November 13, 2007

A picture is worth so much more than a thousand words.

I bet you thought this post was about the strike, didn't you?

Why wouldn't you? The first thing you looked at was the picture, right?

And who could blame you for looking at the picture first. Pictures are pretty. They have color. They tell a story very, very quickly and with little effort required.

But this post is not about the strike.

See, I was looking through my previous posts and I noticed that they had one thing in common: no pictures.

I have committed the cardinal sin of maintaining a web site and for this I am very, very sorry.

So, the community service that the blog gods are forcing me to do is to share the following with you:

All of the websites that I have managed and maintained have had one thing in common. The most popular page on all of the websites was the photo gallery. Always. Without fail. Photos are what visitors to websites want.

So if you have a website for your show or your product (even if it's a MySpace page), make sure you have more pictures than you can take. *And update them constantly.*

More pictures mean more visitors staying on your site for more time.

Who could ask for anything more when marketing on the web?

November 18, 2007

Ouch! I've been branded!

I just returned from speaking at the Word of Mouth Marketing Association conference in Las Vegas. My panel was on *branding.* There I was, seated next to some giant Brands like Southwest Airlines and Doubletree Hotels (I have to say I did love hearing my shows and Southwest Airlines mentioned in the same sentence. I made a joke that our advertising budget on *My First Time* is probably about the same amount as one business class airline ticket).

The speaker from Doubletree told the story about the infamous PowerPoint presentation prepared by two very unhappy Doubletree customers that appeared on the internet in 2001. I call it the "Complaint Heard 'Round the World" and for me it represents the beginning of the new era of customer/user reviews and the use of the internet as a word of mouth weapon for your consumers.

The Doubletree representative said that this complaint was meant to "inflict pain" on Doubletree.

And that's when I realized something about branding.

In the media world, I think we've forgotten where the term "branding" comes from. It comes from cattle. When ranchers don't want to lose their cattle, they take a red hot iron and burn their "tag" into their skin.

In the cave man days of advertising, this is exactly what the big companies did. They spent millions on major advertising buys (TV, print, etc.) and since there was no competition, these big buys were the equivalent of a red hot iron used on the consumer. The consumer had no choice, especially when faced with an iron the size of Proctor and Gamble's, etc. And without even knowing it, all of a sudden they had a P&G brand on their butt.

But times have changed. There are more choices now. And customers have their own branding irons: blogs, user reviews, creative PowerPoint presentations, etc. And they're a bit PO'ed. Wouldn't you be?

So what do you do as someone with customers who are ready to brand back?

Be prepared to take it.

The best companies recognize that power is shifting. They recognize that in this consumer driven market, their ass is sticking up in the air waiting for a customer to burn their "tag" into them.   And online, those tags are permanent. They never go away.

And when you're that exposed, the only way to really <u>CYA</u> (cover your ass) is by being responsible to your customers.

The great thing is, not only will you win with your customers and make them even more loyal, but they'll probably go out and burn the butt of one of your competitors.

November 19, 2007

<u>Different is nice, but it sure isn't pretty . . .</u>

Musical Theater and Straight Plays are different.

I'm not just talking about the fact that one has chorus girls and sequins and higher price tickets.

There is an inherent difference in the expectations of the audiences that creators of musicals need to recognize.

Need an example?

At the end of *Romeo & Juliet,* what happens? They both die. Tragedy. Sadness. Love itself dies with them.

Now, let's look at the musical adaptation of *Romeo & Juliet, West Side Story,* arguably the greatest musical ever written because of its seamless integration of music, book and dance.

What happens at the end of *West Side Story*? Only ONE of them dies. Ah ha! Already you're starting to see the difference.

But wait for it . . . wait for it . . . *West Side* isn't over yet.

After Maria's feisty "How many bullets are left" speech, the Jets start to carry off Tony's dead body. But, like Jesus carrying the cross, they falter. Who comes running to their aid? A Shark! That's right; the two warring gangs come together right before your eyes. And a ray of sunshine is cast on what was a very dark tragedy. Suddenly, there is *hope* that the future will be better.

Doesn't sound like *R&J,* does it?

Musical theater audiences don't mind tragedy. In fact, they love a little drama. But you can't leave them with a tragic aftertaste. No matter how dark your tale, it's important to leave them with the idea that things could get better. That the sun will come out . . . you know when.

Want another great example of this? Look at the ending of the original London production of *Miss Saigon.* Then look at what they did when they came to Broadway. It's a subtle change that demonstrates exactly what I'm talking about.

Email me if you figure it out.

November 20, 2007

It's hard for me to enjoy theater.

The problem is that when you work in an industry and then you're asked to sit back and give yourself over to a product from that same industry, it's hard to stop your mind from spinning and wondering, "how much did that cost" or "why did they cast that actress" or "what did they do in terms of marketing to actually get me to buy a ticket?" Or, sometimes, like when watching *Dance of the Vampires,* you just wonder . . . "Why?"

It's not just theater. It's every business. I mean, if you run a cheese factory, and all that you think about all day and all night are the differences between provolone and Swiss, it's not going to be easy to keep your curds in check if a friend offers you a grilled brie sandwich. (Ok, I'll admit, that sentence was the cheesiest thing I've ever written. :-) Ok. I'll stop now.)

So that's why it's hard for me to enjoy theater.

And that's also how I know when I'm witnessing something truly spectacular, because if a show can get me to STOP asking questions, then it's something truly remarkable. And that's how I felt last week when I saw <u>KA</u>.

Cirque has done this to me once before, when I saw <u>O</u>. They do things on stage and with stages that most people could never even dream about. I'm convinced that the production budget for their shows includes a line item for hallucinogens. You just wouldn't believe the stuff they do if I told you, so you just have to see it. And, in true "remarkable" style, there is only one place to see it . . . Las Vegas. It's an amazing example of a <u>Purple Cow</u>.

I'll admit that whenever I see one of their shows, I'm a little envious of the amazing things they do on stage. And then I remember . . .

Theater in Las Vegas isn't the primary revenue stream. It doesn't have to make artistic sense OR financial sense, because it's there just to draw other people to gamble everything they've earned at their cheese factory.

That doesn't work for Broadway. We're not feeding another revenue stream (unless maybe you are Disney). We are the revenue stream.

So no hallucinogens for you when you are planning your next show.

But definitely go see what they've been smoking in Vegas.

Oh yeah, and at KA, they let me have <u>popcorn and coke</u> at my seat.

November 21, 2007

<u>**I love turkey!**</u>

Q: What's better than celebrating Thanksgiving with a big, juicy, turkey?

A: Celebrating with three of them!

Here are my favorites:

The Capeman: Proof that just because one of the world's best songwriters and a Nobel Prize winner for literature get together, doesn't mean they'll make a great musical. (It did have some great tunes, and despite the fact that the CD was recorded (and features Marc Anthony), Paul Simon has refused to release it. (I have an advance copy, but don't tell anyone.))

The Goodbye Girl: Proof that just because you have one of America's most prolific comedic playwrights, the composer of one of the greatest musicals of all time, a Tony Award winning lyricist, a movie star and a theater star, doesn't mean you'll have a show that achieves even close to the same success as the movie on which it is based.

Lestat: Proof that just because you have a movie company with almost an unlimited budget as a producer, one of the world's greatest popular music artists as a composer, and source material enjoyed by millions and millions of people, doesn't mean that your musical won't suck (pun intended). Oh yeah, and by the way, vampire musicals just don't work on stage. Duh.

So what's to learn from having eaten all this turkey, laced with so much tryptophan, it put so many of us to sleep?

Two things:

1 - Musicals are a collaborative art form. Creating a musical is not writing a novel, where you sit in a room by yourself at your keyboard and crank it out page by page. Creating a musical is not painting a picture, where you sit in front of a canvas and use your own set of brushes and colors to complete your vision. Creating a great musical can't be done with just one person. It needs a composer, a lyricist, a book writer, a producer, actors, designers, an orchestrator, musicians, and so on and so on. And every single one of those people needs to be delivering 110%. That's one of the reasons the failure rate for musicals is so high. Put something that requires perfection for not one party but *several* into an incredibly restrictive financial model, and all of a sudden that 80% failure rate makes sense.

2 - Applying converse logic to the above list says that if extremely well recognized, experienced and lauded artists can produce flops, then unrecognized and inexperienced artists can produce great shows. So don't think that just because you haven't won an award or sold a million records that you can't create a great show.

Because if they can suck, then you can succeed.

November 23, 2007

<u>**Why I was wrong.**</u>

Ok, I was <u>wrong</u> about the strike. I admit it. Now the fun part is trying to understand why.

I didn't think there would be a Broadway stagehands strike because of the history of the two organizations at the crux of this confrontation.

What I failed to take into account is how the makeup of those organizations, especially The Broadway League, has changed over the past several years.

We forget that the theater industry is a young one. The modern theater is less than one hundred years old. The golden age of musicals ended less than 50 years ago, and some of the individuals that played such a crucial role in the birth of the business are still active players in the industry. But to quote a <u>turkey</u> from last year, the times are a changin' . . . and I'm seeing a whole generation of these incredible leaders start to play less and less of a role in the day to day operations of the theater, as a new group of producers comes into their own. It's the theater industry's version of the "baby boomer" phenomenon.

The last three major negotiations have been more contentious than their previous years. Local 1 (strike), Local 802 (strike), AEA (no strike, but it resulted in a major restructuring of the touring market). This is not a coincidence. This is a result of these baby boomers getting in there and shaking things up. Which is exactly what's needed.

And what else is different about these three negotiations?

They are all post 9/11.

We live in a new theatrical economy now. The way we live changed significantly that day, and therefore the way we do business has to change with it. Whether we like it or not.

November 26, 2007

<u>**As the strikes comes closer to a resolution, I'm getting more riled up.**</u>

I've tried to remain calm during all of this and I've tried to look at both sides of this destructive dispute since I have friends on both sides of the table. But now I'm irritated.

Here's a paragraph from yesterday's New York Times with a quote from Bruce Cohen, the spokesperson for Local 1:

"They want all this great flexibility after a performance," Mr. Cohen said. "They want us to work one hour, two hours, three hours after a performance. We want to go home and make our train. We live in the suburbs, and we want to make the last train out of Penn Station, and they don't seem to recognize that."

Mr. Cohen . . . are you really saying that the League should take into consideration where a person CHOOSES to live when negotiating a collective contract? And are you really making a sweeping generalization suggesting that all of your members live in the suburbs (I know a few that live on the Upper West Side that might disagree with you). You want to make your train??? What the . . .

Can you imagine what the Local would say if the Producers had said that they needed to make their train to their house in the suburbs?

If a person wants to live in the city, outside the city, or in a box in Sri Lanka, that is his or her choice, and to state that the contract governing his employ should recognize his CHOICE is just absurd.

What's next . . . is Mr. Cohen going to a make gross generalization suggesting that Local 1 members choose to drive SUVs and therefore require more money for gas? Or that they choose high protein diets so they need more money to pay for steaks? Or that Local 1 members like collecting Faberge eggs? All of these are absurd fabrications on my part . . . yet all are lifestyle choices that have nothing to do with an employer's obligation to an employee.

If I don't want to commute to work, then I must move closer to work. If I want a more suburban lifestyle, then I have to commute to work. If I want to raise pigs in my spare time, then I have to wake up early and pay for slop. Or . . . I can change jobs to fit the lifestyle that I want. I have that choice. Simple.

You know what makes me more upset (And Local 1 members should be just as upset)? The fact that Mr. Cohen is a spokesperson. He's a press rep. He should be a lot smarter than this.

November 27, 2007

This blog is about . . . exactly what you think it's about.

For those of you who have seen my <u>iPhone commercial</u> (it still blows my mind to even type those words), you've heard my description of my latest show, _My First Time_. "It's about . . . exactly what you think it's about."

A <u>friend</u> of mine was mocking me with a spot-on impersonation the other day and the more he repeated those words, the more I realized something:

My First Time <u>is</u> about what you think it's about. And that has made my job as a <u>salesman</u> (aka marketer) that much easier.

Let's look at my other shows:

The Awesome 80s Prom. Well, that's about exactly what you think it's about too. A Prom. In the 80s. And it is awesome (full disclosure - I am related to the producer therefore I may be biased).

Altar Boyz. Hmmmm. Not as easy. Is it really about altar boys? And is it really about what our current society thinks of when they think of altar boys? Nope. And guess what our biggest problem with marketing _Altar Boyz_ has been? Convincing people that it was _not_ about what they thought it was about. Oops.

Your title is the name of your product. It's your first crack at marketing. Word of mouth is always going to include the name of your product, so that word of mouth is spread a lot easier when the title helps to explain exactly what your product is.

Sales/marketing to people who have never heard about your show is initially about education. You have to educate them that your show is an option. And then you have to educate them as to what your show is about. It certainly helps when your title helps do that for you.

Because like it or not, people do judge a book by its title.

November 28, 2007

Oops. He did it again.

Here is a quote from the Local 1 press release yesterday stating that talks for the Broadway stagehands strike have stalled once again:

"I'm going home to get some sleep, shut off my phones and not check e-mails for the next few hours." - Bruce Cohen, spokesperson for Local 1.

Wow. Good to know that during this crisis, while thousands of people, Local 1 members included, are staying awake at night wondering when their next paycheck is coming, Mr. Cohen isn't available to take their calls or anyone else's. I guess if the League wanted to settle and put everyone back to work, and get the shows open for the thousands of disappointed tourists, Mr. Cohen would be unavailable.

And, remember, Mr. Cohen WROTE this release. He wanted everyone to know that he was taking a nap.

Being a leader means being available; whether you're running a company, a country, or a canasta competition. Being a leader means that people depend on you. And when people depend on you for their checks or their confidence, you have a responsibility.

There are a lot of perks that come with being a leader (including getting paid during strikes while everyone else is out of work, I'm sure), and if you have to sacrifice some sleep during moments of great crisis, then so be it.

DECEMBER 2007

December 03, 2007

You Can't Build A Beach House In The Middle of Times Square.

It's just not possible.

There's no salt water. No sand. No surf. Nothing.

I was in Las Vegas a couple of weeks ago, a city with more live entertainment than most states! There are magic shows, topless shows, animal shows, impersonators, and even a few Broadway musicals. As I stared at the marquees for all these different types of shows it dawned on me how important it is to consider your location when deciding where to produce your show.

The elements necessary for a successful show in Las Vegas vary wildly from the elements necessary for a successful show in New York City. You don't see *Thunder From Down Under* here. You don't see people who make F-16s disappear or Elvis impersonators sitting down in Broadway theaters year after year, like they do in Las Vegas. And vice versa! How many Broadway shows have we now seen struggle to plant roots in the Vegas desert?

Why? Because they are different locations, with different elements that make up their landscape. And if you don't have the necessary elements to build a specific type of structure, you'd be foolish to try.

Broadway is a very specific place. And not every show can be built here. Sometimes, because it has a reputation for being the "pinnacle" of success for the theater industry, people make Broadway their ultimate goal, without analyzing the landscape. It becomes the default end of the journey . . . like the Olympics for amateur athletes.

But it doesn't have to be. There are a bunch of other options to Broadway. There's nothing wrong with Vegas, or a regional theater, or Europe, or a children's theater, in case you realize that your show might be more of a beach house than a skyscraper.

Because a show running somewhere else is better than a show *not* running on Broadway.

December 04, 2007

Give away tickets, sure, but don't paper.

Every smart company knows that with any product launch, you've got to give away some product to start the snowball of word of mouth marketing rolling down the hill.

What separates the great marketers from the mass marketers is who that product is given to.

Ten years ago, there were one or two "papering" *organizations* in the theater business that had a list of people who were interested in seeing theater that could be mobilized quickly to fill a house.

Now, there are at least four major papering *companies* that charge their members a service fee of a few dollars for getting these tickets. Shows, big and small, give these organizations free tickets, and then these companies profit from being able to get rid of them. And they're growing. One company recently sent me a direct mail offer to sign up. They are spending more media dollars than my shows.

The hope for the shows is that the members help spread the word of mouth and turn their friends into paying customers.

And maybe that happened ten years ago. But do you know what's really happening now?

Word of mouth is spreading about these companies and a way to get a $4 ticket to a show, rather than the show itself! How do I know this? Simple . . . the growth of the number of companies engaging in this activity proves the growth in the market. Where there are competitors, there is a market share to be had. And that's bad news for the theater. We're increasing the size of an audience looking for free or extremely discounted tickets.

On top of that . . . does anyone really think that this is the best way to spread word of mouth? These people that use these services are now trained to *expect* free tickets. There is no reciprocity factor any more. There is no feeling of "Wow, I got a free ticket to a show and can't wait to see it." And if you were one of these people and actually saw a great show, wouldn't one of the first things you said to a friend be "I saw a great show and I only paid $4!"

Giving away product is fine, but choose wisely. It may be easier to call a papering company to get rid of 100 tickets to a preview, but you'll be much better served seeking out corporations and hair dressers and banks and anywhere where they don't usually get this sort of offer (and you can pick specific geographic locations where you think your demographic may be hiding). These people will be super-excited to get the offer (and therefore more inclined to talk positively about the experience) and since they are hand picked by you, more inclined to enjoy your product. And, by avoiding these companies that profit off our paper, you'll be helping to prevent the disintegration of our paying audience.

Avoid papering companies like they are vampire musicals.

December 05, 2007

I don't borrow. I steal.

Yep, I steal from giant corporations all the time. And you should too.

Ok, as much as I'd like to build up some "street cred" with a bad boy reputation, let me explain what I mean.

Shows open and close so fast and have such limited budgets, that it's difficult for us to try and stay ahead of the marketing and technology curve. But that doesn't mean we can't benefit from those with the resources.

Watch what the Big Boys do. Sign up for the Banana Republic email newsletter and see what happens when your birthday rolls around. See how Amazon.com communicates with you and recommends item after item. See how Las Vegas hotels take care of their high rollers (their version of the premium ticket buyer).

Let companies with bigger budgets pay for your research. Learn from what they do well. And learn from their mistakes.

An example of something I just learned from one of the biggest American marketing machines tomorrow.

December 10, 2007

Sorry for the tease.

In my last blog, I said . . .

"An example of something I just learned from one of the biggest American marketing machines <u>tomorrow</u>."

And then . . . nothing.

I received thousands of emails from concerned readers all wondering if I had been kidnapped by Bruce Cohen's family or if I had caught the same illness that affected Michael Crawford when he signed on to do *Dance of The Vampires*.

I am happy to report that I am fine. (You can stop sending the thousand emails a day now, Mom.)

Here's what happened. I wrote the follow up to that blog that same night and thought I was really cool when I figured out how to automatically post it the next morning since I was going to be traveling all day.

And, as you know . . . it didn't work.

Sorry for that mishap. I'm re-writing the blog now and it will be up later. Hopefully this version will turn out better anyway. I had to rewrite my high school graduation address in 1990 when my Commodore 64 crashed, and that worked out OK.

Rewrites generally do.

So the next time that you lose a paper, an email, a version of a script, or a well constructed and almost award winning and publishable blog entry (ok, I'm exaggerating), take it as a reminder that the key to writing is rewriting.

Sure you can bang your head against the wall and take TypePad's name in vain . . . or you can just sit back down, stop bitching and make the next one even better.

Or you can use your situation as inspiration to write something brand spanking new.

Like I just did. Wait a minute. I didn't mean to do that. That wasn't my intention when I started this entry. Dang it!

The follow- up coming soon. And I mean it this time.

December 11, 2007

Print Ads Don't Smoke Anymore (aka Last Week's Blog Rewritten)

Check out this article from The NY Times about one of the largest media buyers in the world . . . a tobacco company. Here's the paragraph that most interested me:

"The R.J. Reynolds Tobacco Company disclosed this week that it would run no ads in 2008 in consumer magazines and newspapers for cigarette brands like Camel, Winston and Pall Mall.

Instead, Reynolds said it would concentrate its marketing in three areas that already make up the bulk of its marketing spending: stores, bars and nightclubs; Web sites; and direct mail."

What was fascinating to me was not that R.J. was pulling out of print. Everyone knows that print is dying faster than a two-pack-a-day smoker of brands like Camel, Winston and Pall Mall. What is interesting to me is where they are putting their money.

(Here's where you and I can learn from watching how the big boys play with their big boy budgets.)

What do stores, bars, nightclubs, and websites have in common? You can buy cigarettes there. The tobacco companies are putting their money closer to their point of purchase. They realize that a nicotine craving might be intensified by the right ad and their conversion rates will be higher if cigarettes and a guy willing to take your money are only a few steps (or clicks) away from that ad. Makes sense, doesn't it?

Why would they advertise in a magazine, where they can't control where their ad is going to be seen? Magazines are read on planes, trains and in bathrooms. The odds of getting a consumer to purchase a pack of Pall Malls while on the potty are nil. If you expect your ad to stay in the consumer's mind until they are at a point of purchase, it either has to be that much stronger (bigger), or it has to be seen much more frequently. It makes more sense to not take that risk, and find a way to get to where the consumer is more likely to make a purchase.

Tobacco companies are smart. With all that we know about how bad cigarettes are for our bodies, people still do it, which means they are doing something disgustingly right. So what is it?

For starters, they realize that mass marketing is on its way out. Strategic and targeted marketing is here. They are finding out where their customers are, and where they are most likely to purchase their product. It's like modern day warfare. Their campaigns are becoming a bunch of smart missiles instead of blanket bombs.

Where are your audiences hiding?

December 12, 2007

Putting What Broadway Bears Into A Box.

When you sit down and prepare to budget a show, what's the first thing you do?

Figure out how much the theater is going to cost? Figure out how much the creative fees are going to be? Or how much you're going to spend on hair styling bills for a star that submits a receipt for reimbursement every time she steps outside? (true story)

It makes sense to start off with this stuff. But I recommend that before you work on your own show . . . work on everyone else's first.

For example, I've got a bee in my you-know-what about reviving a certain Broadway musical. So I'm looking at all the other revivals of the last 20+ years first.

And by looking at their numbers, I can create the beginnings of a budgetary box that I can fit my show into based on hard empirical data on *what the market can bear.*

What's the first thing I looked for in this search? Length of run. Here, exclusive to you, oh faithful blog reader, are the results of numbers crunched by me and my assistant Nicole, thanks to raw data provided by the Broadway League.

The following is the average length of runs of productions on Broadway since 1984 (note: some of the productions included in these calculations may still be running)

New Musical	52.67 weeks
Revival of a Musical	51.59 weeks
New Play	24.40 weeks
Revival of a Play	15.65 weeks

Interesting stuff, huh? Now, if I know that an average revival only runs 51.59 weeks, I know I better figure out how to recoup the investment in that short period of time.

But Nicole and I are not done yet. The next figure that will help me build my budgetary box? Average price of a ticket. For a revival. Of a musical.

Stay tuned.

December 13, 2007

Bears vs. Bares. Part II

This just in . . .

Crunching more numbers provided by The Guru of Statistics at the <u>Broadway League</u>, Neal Freeman, the average paid admission to a *revival of a musical* in the 07-08 Broadway Season is . . . . drum roll please . . .

On second thought . . . let's play a game.

Pick one:

A. $73.76
B. $53.51
C. $61.01
D. $69.61

The answer will be revealed at the end of this post (no cheating).

But the answer isn't as important as what you do with it.

Now that I know what the market is bearing in terms of ticket price, AND what kind of <u>shelf-life</u> I can expect, I can start to build a proper budget that is based on reality, not fantasy.

As my shrink once told me . . . it's ok to fantasize, as long as you know you're going to be ok if the fantasy doesn't come true. For example, I will be ok if Winona Ryder doesn't go to my high school prom with me (that was my fantasy in 1990, but you get the point).

Well, if a budget based in fantasy (with higher than average ticket prices and higher than average attendance figures) doesn't come true, your investors are NOT going to be ok. They're going to have lost a lot of money. And you'll lose investors. Which means you'll produce less shows. Which means the world will not be a better place.

D. $69.61

And if you're curious, the average paid admission to a revival of a play is $55.67.

When you think about it, what the market bears, is similar to what the market *bares*. By looking at the hard numbers, you're looking at the industry naked. No Versace or Marc Jacobs dressing it up. Just cold flesh.

Unfortunately, it's not always good naked. Happy Holidays!

December 15, 2007

My Mission Statement and Yours.

Exceed expectations.

When you exceed people's expectations, you become exceptional by definition.

And people, whether that's your audience, your husband, your boss, etc. will have no choice but to talk about you and respect you.

In fact, exceeding expectations is the best way to prevent people from becoming your ex-audience, ex-husband, or ex-boss.

December 17, 2007

News flash: Numbers can talk!

In addition to using the numbers we crunched last week to create a budget that increases your odds of success, here's another simple use:

One of the hardest things for producers to do is to say "No." Who wants to say no when a director, a designer, your child, or anybody asks for something? Believe it or not, we would love to be able to say "Yes" to everything. Unfortunately, it's our job to say no when the request doesn't assist us with our #1 responsibility.

So, whenever possible, I let my numbers say no for me.

There's no arguing with numbers. While artistic tastes may vary, numbers are not ambiguous. They are indisputable (as long as they are from reputable sources and triple verified). I find this most helpful during negotiations. And the great thing is, it's not a negotiating trick or tactic. It's not a game. It's just the truth.

For example, with my Backed-In Budget (my name for designing a budget based on what the market is bearing), we know the average length of a run for a Broadway revival. So use it. When an agent asks for something that doesn't fit in the model, say, "Did you know that since 1984, the average run of a musical revival was only 51.59 weeks" and so on, using the statistics for average attendance and ticket price and so on. Most likely, the model for your production will be higher than the average, so you'll be able to tell the agent that you're already above and beyond what the market is bearing, so there is no way to justify additional expenses.

Here's what I predict will be the response, if you've done your homework:

Silence.

Because there is no response to the right set of numbers.

Want a practical example? When I was negotiating contracts for *Altar Boyz* and an agent or someone asked for something that didn't fit in the model, my response was, "If you can tell me the name of an Off-Broadway book musical that recouped its investment in the last 10 years, I'll give you double what you want."

Silence.

There's a bet I knew I wouldn't lose.

Again, it wasn't a tactic or me trying to bully anyone. It was the unfortunate truth. To make it up to the people who were making sacrifices for the show we bonused them with a portion of profits post-recoupment. We kept costs down trying to get us to this seemingly impossible feat, and if we got there, everyone would win . . . and most likely they will earn more than they wanted in the first place.

And we'll get to recoupment. I'm going to make damn sure that no other Producer can use that same question in a future negotiation. Sorry, guys. :-)

Even if you think you're a great negotiator, always let the figures talk first *and* last. Because numbers are the best negotiators.

December 19, 2007

The Funniest Advertising on Broadway!

I was walking through Shubert Alley yesterday, and this caught me eye and made me chuckle:

Can we really expect a consumer to believe either of these things? Especially when they are *right next to each other?*

Self-proclamations are fine. I use them . . . judiciously. It shows confidence. It's just believing in yourself, which every self-help book preaches, so why shouldn't your business use the same principles?

NBA players have to believe they are all as good as Michael Jordan when they step on the court. Models have to believe they are the "hottest" when they walk down the runway. So why shouldn't shows believe it and shout it... when appropriate.

You have to be careful where and when you use such a proclamation. If you do it and it doesn't make sense to the consumer ("My blog is the best blog on the web!"), or when it's in a cluttered environment (like the one above), you actually risk having the consumer discredit you and your product.

You know what the kicker of the above is? Both shows are handled by the same advertising agency . . . which is arguably "The Best Advertising Agency on Broadway!"

More on the issue of agencies tomorrow.

December 20, 2007

Be Careful! Your Competition Is In The Same Room!

There are 3 advertising agencies that handle the bulk of Broadway business.

3.

In the 2005-2006, Broadway season, there were 39 new productions on Broadway. There were also 32 continuing productions from the previous season.

71 shows. Handled by 3 agencies.

Divided equally (which they are not), means that each agency handled an average of 23.67 shows. In reality, 2 of those agencies handled the majority of the shows.

To demonstrate a huge practical problem associated with these numbers, let's look at the four nominees for Best Musical in 2007: *Curtains*, *Grey Gardens*, *Mary Poppins* and *Spring Awakening*.

All FOUR of these musicals were represented by the same advertising agency.

That means that Tony campaigns, sales figures, etc. were all discussed, strategized and planned in the same house.

So when you're doing your next show, you should understand that your meetings will probably be held in the same conference room as your direct competition.

Can you imagine if Microsoft and Apple were handled by the same advertising agency? *And shared a conference room?* Or Coke and Pepsi? Or even small hometown grocery stores?

It's not even smart business to consider these facts before making your choice of your agency, it's just common sense. I'm not insinuating that anything unethical is happening at any of these agencies, but with millions and millions of dollars on the line, why would you take the chance of all that information under one roof? Even the most ethical and honest employee would have to be subconsciously influenced with the knowledge of what one show's competitors are doing, wouldn't you think?

In other industries, companies refuse to allow their advertising agencies to rep competitors. Duh.

I know what people will say: "Ken, the reason there is so much overlapping is because there isn't enough consistent work to go around to keep these agencies running."

I disagree. 23.67 shows is a lot of commission. And besides, I've seen the sizes of each of their offices. And conversely, I've seen the sizes of all of the Producers' offices in this city. The agencies don't need to take on this much work.

But this isn't their fault. They are just growing their business. We're the ones ignoring the reality and allowing these practices to continue.

The other argument is that there aren't enough qualified advertising agencies in business. This may be true.

Anyone out there want to hang a shingle?

Or better, maybe producers should start doing advertising in-house.

December 21, 2007

Life Is Like A Snow Globe!

Special thanks to my friends at Travelzoo for the most inspired Christmas card of the year . . . and for giving me a new analogy to use (I love analogies. Ask my staff how many times they've heard me say, "Off-Broadway is like a rowboat . . . ")

The simile is simple. Life (and business) is like a snow globe. Sure, a snow globe is pretty to look at when sitting on your desk, but you only get the full potential from it when you *shake it up*.

I'm going out to buy a snow globe today so I can be reminded of this every single day.

Back to my "Off-Broadway is like a rowboat" analogy. $100 to anyone who can finish my thought. Employees of Davenport Theatrical are not eligible (nice try, guys).

December 24, 2007

New Businesses Are Like Children . . .

Children grow very quickly in the first few years of life.

And then, eventually, that growth slows down.

New businesses (and new shows) . . . are the same.

It's easy to get them to grow during the first few years (or months if you're talking about a show). The hard part is to continue that growth, long after puberty is over.

Because otherwise, they just get old and die.

December 25, 2007

Christmas Card Clutter

Mailboxes are worse than the entertainment pages of the New York Times this time of year.

With all of the Christmas cards that everyone receives, how do you compete for the receiver's attention? Is your card really going to make an impression? And in today's green-times, is it really worth a slice of a Sequoia to send a card in such a cluttered environment?

Don't get me wrong, I'm very grateful for the time people take to remember me, but sending Christmas cards is like taking out an ABC in the New York Times. People just keep doing it without realizing it isn't as effective as it may have been.

OK, I'll try and take my Scrooge hat off now and be a bit more constructive. Let's say you feel compelled to send cards to your clients, friends or family. Here are a few quick ideas on how to get your cards through the CCC (Christmas Card Clutter):

1. Be First

Make sure your card arrives before everyone else's. The day after Thanksgiving. Or, if you really want to make an impression? *Send it in July.*

2. Be Last

Embrace your procrastination and use it to your advantage. Send your card right after people are clearing off their mantles so it arrives in their mailbox in January, at the same time as their December credit card bills.

3. Make It Personal

Speaks for itself. Photos, letters (yes, even form letters), etc. Cards usually wrap up a year, so take a moment to remind the recipient about a very positive experience you shared at some point during the year.

4. Make It Your Own With a Custom Design

Send fewer letters and make a bigger impression for the same money with a custom design that says what is unique about your company. If you're a vendor, send a card that has your company's name or logo on the FRONT of the card. Think about how cards are displayed on desks or mantles. It's never with the signature on the outside. With the right design, Christmas cards can be mini-billboards.

Can't afford a designer and don't know how to work Photoshop? Do it old school and make your cards like a 2nd grader. They'll stand out big time.

5. Put Something In The Card

Include a coupon. 10% off the client's first service in the New Year. A coupon for a free hug. Whatever. But something that adds value to the card (and can be tracked).

6. Don't Send a Card

Send something else. Again, spend a little more money on less people and make it count. And make it something that doesn't get tossed out after the New Year, but that will sit on a desk, constantly reminding that person of you.

Or send a one dollar bill in a plain white envelope and with a post-it note attached that says, "We have trouble picking out cards for our diverse client list. Here's a dollar. Feel free to buy a card that suits you best. Or buy a hot dog."

I realize that people are shaking their head at me right now because I'm breaking down a time-honored tradition of spreading joy into a marketing strategy. Shake away, but here's the thing: *everything we do in life is a form of marketing.* If you get a new hair cut or buy a new suit, you're redesigning your brand's image. If you send text messages or mass emails to friends, you're engaging in direct response. Christmas cards are just another form of marketing in our own lives.

And my point is that if you're going to do it (like any form of advertising), do it effectively.

Personally, I'd rather my vendors and casual acquaintances save the paper and the postage and make a $1 donation to a favorite <u>charity</u>.

Do you have any ideas on how to break through the CCC? Or have you received any great CCs that got your attention? Email me and I'll post the <u>best</u>.

December 26, 2007

<u>Booya! Elaine Got Called Out!</u>

Someone finally stood up to Elaine Stritch and her expense antics. Read about it in The Post <u>here</u>.

I laughed out loud when I read this today, because it brought back a lot of memories. As the former Associate Company Manager for the Broadway production of Livent's *Show Boat*, I can tell you that a lot of these exact same bills crossed my desk every week. If Elaine went outside of the *hotel room* where she <u>lived</u>, we got charged for hair, limo, massages, the works.

My favorite Elaine memory was the day I got a letter from her with a receipt for close to $200 from Orso, at least *six months after she left the show*. There was a note attached. "Dear Steve," (she called me Steve, don't ask me why), "<u>Garth</u> and I were supposed to have dinner this week, but he canceled his trip. So . . . he told me to have dinner on him. Here's the bill."

The real funny part? We were instructed to pay it. Maybe that's one of the reasons the company that produced some of the <u>grandest productions of its time</u> went bankrupt.

You gotta love Elaine. Talented and ballsy.

Maybe she should give up acting and produce, with mad skills like that. I'd like to see what she would do if someone submitted hair bills to her.

And good for Michael Riedel of The Post (and of <u>Theater Talk</u>) for slipping this tidbit to Page 6 on the other side of his office.

December 27, 2007

<u>**Trivia Time: Who Has Produced the Most Broadway Shows In The Last 20 Years?**</u>

Cameron Macintosh? Disney? The Weisslers?

Nope.

<u>The Roundabout.</u>

They've produced more Broadway shows than anyone. More in one SEASON than most producers produce over two decades.

And they are a non-profit. Coincidence? Or evidence that a different economic model is what is needed to be a prolific producer.

<u>Off-Broadway Shows Are Like Rowboats . . .</u>

Ok, it's time to announce the answer to the Off-Broadway <u>rowboat riddle</u>!

Unfortunately there were no winners to my $100 challenge. A couple came close, but here's a longer version of what I was going for.

The analogy actually starts like this:

Broadway shows are like giant steamships, kind of like the Titanic. They are so big, so cumbersome and require so much energy to get going, that once you actually get them in the water . . . there's not much you can do to veer them from their destination.

They are either going to hit the iceberg, or they won't.

Off-Broadway shows are more like rowboats. You can turn them a lot quicker and with a lot less effort. One quick row of an oar and you're headed in a new direction.

Unfortunately, they also sink a lot faster. (In fact, 89% of all commercial Off-Broadway shows close within 6 months).

Here are a couple of my favorite entries from some of the readers out there:

- "Off-Broadway is like a rowboat. You only get somewhere after working hard to move yourself."

- "Off-Broadway is like a rowboat. The more people you have rowing in the same direction, the faster and farther you go."

Thanks, guys. And for being a runner up, I'm giving both of you iTunes gift cards! Keep your eye on your inbox.

And I suggest you get this song with your first purchase.

December 28, 2007

Long Runners on Broadway vs. Long Runners Off-Broadway

The top three longest running Broadway shows according to Playbill.com are:

Phantom of the Opera	8279 performances and counting.
Cats	7485 performances
Les Misérables	6680 performances

The top three longest running Off-Broadway shows are:

The Fantasticks	17,162 performances
Perfect Crime	8,421 performances and counting.
Blue Man Group: Tubes	8,406 performances and counting.

Hmmm. Interesting. The #3 long runner Off-Broadway has performed more shows than the #1 marathoner on Broadway.

Let's keep going and look at the top ten long runners.

The combined number of performances for the top ten long runners on Broadway is 57,764 performances with four shows still going.

The combined number of performances for the top ten long runners Off-Broadway is *approximately* 65,145 performances with six shows still going.

I say "approximately" because if you'll notice in that Playbill article, the data from the Off-Broadway shows is almost a year older than the Broadway shows. Oh, and they stopped counting *Forbidden Broadway* in 1987. Um, that's right, 1987. 2 years BEFORE *The Awesome 80s Prom* even takes place. Oh, and they also decided not to include *Tony 'n Tina's* since 2004. So I made some educated assumptions to get to the total.

What's the takeaway here?

Surprise, surprise, it's good news for Off-Broadway!

Off-Broadway hits have a greater stamina than Broadway hits. Once you break on through to the other side (penetrate the tourist market), you'll just run and run and run, and not even *The Phantom of the Opera* will catch up. That's right, I'm betting another $100 that both *Perfect Crime* and *Blue Man Group* run longer than The Masked Man. And that no Broadway show ever catches *The Fantasticks*.

Oh, and you know what else these numbers teach us?

That the Off-Broadway community has got to come together more to aggregate their data. How can we say what we are . . . without knowing what we are? More on a specific example of this problem in the Off-Broadway community tomorrow.

More Breaking News about Elaine's Hair!

My apologies to one of my faithful readers who emailed me about my <u>post</u> congratulating Theater Talk for standing up to Elaine Stritch's demand for payment of her hair expenses.

It turns out that Theater Talk isn't the only one who refused to pay for Elaine's hair.

Here's the scoop:

In 2002, Elaine appeared at <u>The Drama League Awards</u>. She requested payment of her hair bill in advance. They refused.

So, WDED? (What did Elaine do?)

She protested the "frugality" of the show by showing up in curlers!

Pictures below provided by my anonymous tipster:

December 29, 2007

What's Grosser than Gross?

Not knowing what your industry's grosses are.

At the first meeting of the <u>Off-Broadway Brainstormers</u>, founded by the Executive Director of <u>New World Stages</u>, Beverley D. Mac Keen (who is one of the most foreword thinkers I know), a proposal was made by now president of the <u>League of Off-Broadway Theatres and Producers</u>, George Forbes, to collect grosses from all currently running Off-Broadway shows, in an effort to truly understand our own economic impact.

It was one of those very simple proposals that made perfect sense. How can we formulate budgets, contemplate theater sizes, etc. without knowing what our market <u>bears</u>. Right?

Well, believe it or not, this idea met (and still meets) with resistance from some of my fellow producers.

The League and The Brainstormers came up with a great policy to address some very valid concerns:

- We made agreements with the ticketing companies so grosses would be sent directly to the League so no additional work would be required on behalf of the production.

- The grosses would be sent to one person at the League, and only three high-ranking individuals would have access to the show's individual data, and would sign confidentiality agreements never to share the information.

- No show's individual grosses would ever be released to any party.

- The aggregated data would also never be released unless a committee at the League approved of its use.

Despite all of these efforts to keep the data confidential and to install safeguards so that it was only used for the good of the industry, many producers still refused to allow their grosses to be reported.

Most simply say that they don't want their grosses getting out to their competition. I kind of understand this, but, uhhhh, remember the confidentiality agreements and the fact that only 3 people can access the data??? And that we're not releasing an individual show's data, but only looking at the combined results?

Oh, and this is my favorite part . . . do these producers remember that these numbers are sent to unions every week? ATPAM has a sliding scale compensation that is based on gross so they have to send them the numbers. Most likely their show has an SSDC director on a royalty pool, which means that union is getting their information (and the director and the director's agent, and his assistant, etc.). If there was "competition", wouldn't the unions be the competition more than The League? Add the <u>advertising agencies</u> (which we already know leak like the Titanic), box office personnel, managers, etc. to the list of people that already get grosses, and you've got more people who know your business than a public company!

I mean, really, are three more people who sign confidentiality agreements and work for the League going to all of a sudden open up your show to attention from the National Enquirer? (If only!)

Sorry, but no one, other than the people trying to figure out how to solve the Off-Broadway problem, cares that much.

Sharing your grosses publicly (like Broadway shows do in Variety) is up for debate, and I'm not sure where I stand on that just yet, but sharing numbers in a private, protected environment for study and analysis is not only smart, it's essential. And just like your mom told you, it's just plain selfish not to share.

What are people afraid of? That we might see some low numbers? Guess what, with all the Off-Broadway shows that come and go, I think we have a clue that you're not doing so well.

And besides, we learn from the bad ones. It's just like learning to ride a bike. You learn more when you fall off than you do when you don't.

So why do some of these very smart people choose not to opt-in to this program? Look, I'm a control freak. As an Off-Broadway producer, I'm not in control very often. I think that most producers are just like me. And they are refusing to release their numbers (even though they are released other ways), because it is one of the few things that they can control.

If any Producers out there are struggling with this issue, let me know. I see a therapist once a week to help me get over it and would be happy to give you a recommendation. The industry will be better off as a result.

P.S. What do you think of Broadway shows publicly sharing numbers in Variety? I've turned my comments on, so comment away if you'd like (yes, even you Mom).

December 30, 2007

You Know You're A Brand When . . .

. . . Parking Lot Attendants do your marketing for you.

Look at this piece of "outdoor advertising" I found at a lot on 49th St.

If I was Larry Page or Sergey Brin (the lucky-brilliant-ducks that came up with Google), I would take the above as a sign (pun intended) that I had satisfied my mission statement.

December 31, 2007

Broadway Stagehands Talk Back

I recently discovered a website (thanks to another tip from one of my loyal readers) that allows Broadway stagehands to voice their opinions about issues facing them. It's called a "member's website" . . . a kind of social networking for stagehands.

It's another example that proves that online water coolers are the future of the proliferation of ideas.

Check it out at www.BroadwayLocalOne.com and click on the "Stagehands Talk Back" section to read all about their thoughts on the Broadway Strike, the WGA strike, their leaders, the producers, and much, much more.

I read it for hours.

JANUARY 2008

January 02, 2008

Christmas Card Clutter - The Sequel

Well, wouldn't you know it. Days after I posted my Grinch-like "Christmas Card Clutter" blog, I got one last holiday card. And this one made my heart "grow three sizes".

It was from Andy Sernovitz, author of _Word of Mouth Marketing_ (in which he mentions one of our _Altar Boyz_ e-marketing tactics).

I met Andy at the Word of Mouth Marketing Association conference back in October when I spoke on a "brands" panel. And today I got his holiday card. And, as you would expect, it was a masterfully remarkable card.

First of all, it wasn't a holiday card. It didn't talk about Christmas. Second, it came after Christmas. Third, he put something in it. And here's where Andy is brilliant.

It was a luggage tag . . . and it already had my address in it. How? Well, Andy took my business card when we met. And like a magician asking for a handkerchief, he did something with that business card that I wasn't expecting at all. He laminated it and sent it to me weeks later. So simple, yet personal, sticky and surprising.

Did it work? You bet. It got him this blog post to say the least.

Surprise your customers. Surprise your audience members, your business partners, your boyfriends, your wanna-be business partners, your mom, etc. You'll put a smile on their face.

And smiles are the stickiest advertising of all.

January 03, 2008

Playbill.com, Dressing Rooms & "The Nibble"

I was interviewed this week for a column on Playbill.com about how dressing rooms are distributed on Broadway.

At the end of the article I talk about "extras" that agents often try to get tossed into contracts: couches, microwaves, TVs, VCRs, humidifiers, expensive wallpaper, plants, refrigerators, shag carpeting, air purifiers, bottled water. I've even seen a few "dressing room designers" in my day.

The problem with these requests is two-fold:

1 - They cost money. Duh.

I'm a big fan of spending money on things that the audience is going to see. Wouldn't it suck to have to tell your set designer that he can't have that extra drop, knowing that you just spent $20k on a dressing room that is empty most of the day? (The funny thing is, the great and dedicated actors would probably rather you spend the money on the show . . . it's the agent that gets in the way. I often say that to the agent . . . "Sure, your client can have a new tiled bathroom, but when we can't give her the dress she wants in Act II, you can tell her why.")

2 - The bigger problem I have with these "extra" requests is that they are often a prime example of the negotiating tactic that I call "the nibble".

The biggest issue with any deal is money, right? So that is usually done first. Haggling about money can last for days, weeks, even months, depending on how complicated you want to get. Just when you're done, and you are patting yourself on the back because you came in on budget, the agent says, "there are just a few more things."

Did you feel that?

Nibble.

Like a fish on your leg when you're standing in a lake.

"We need a private dressing room with a couch, paint, microwave, TV (with cable), a phone installed . . . "

Nibble.

"Oh, and car service, weekly massage, makeup reimbursement ... "

Nibble, nibble.

I call it the nibble because the requests are usually relatively small, in terms of the big picture. They are too small to jeopardize the whole deal, and psychologically, you're most likely in a place where you just want to finish it so you end up saying yes. They are only little things, right? Piranhas wouldn't kill you with one bite. It would be whole bunch of little ones.

To protect yourself from being eaten alive, make a point of asking the agent or the lawyer (ewww) *up front* for all of the client's requests. It doesn't mean you have to grant them. And it doesn't mean you won't, either. In some cases, you're going to have to provide the custom cabinetry, the dog-walker, and the green M&Ms. But you need to know in advance, before you settle on a salary, so you can determine what you can truly afford.

So get all the details out on the table so you can call the agent on it if they try and nibble at you later. And don't be afraid to say no if you can get away with it. Do you think someone would turn down a job over a microwave?

They may seem like little things. But remember, a bunch of little things add up to one big one.

January 05, 2008

100% of Zero is Zero.

Speaking of <u>publishing statistics</u> , one of the most gossiped about stats around Broadway water coolers is percentage attendance.

"Did you see Variety? Moose Murders only did 30% capacity!"
But this number actually does very little to diagnose the fiscal health of a show. It just counts bodies in the house (including comps). Even Moose Murders could get up to 100% if it really wanted to.

My favorite number in Variety? Average Ticket Price. This is where you can really see the market's demand for a show. If the ticket price is close to the full price, you know you're in good shape.

And then look at the percentage. Get a high average ticket price and a high percentage attendance, and you should be feeling pretty high yourself.

January 07, 2008

Get Lost!

I got lost over the weekend while driving through Columbus, Ohio (I was scouting for a documentary that I'm producing and directing, but more on that later).

While I was trying to figure out how an interstate that ran East and West could all of sudden run East and South, I realized two things:

1. I'm buying a GPS.

2. Getting lost is OK.

Sure, I was an hour late and lost my voice screaming at the Lord of the Highways, but I still made it to my destination.

Whenever you're lost, you always end up getting to your destination eventually, don't you? You never just pull over and say, "That's it. I'm done. I'm going to sit in my rental car until the scavengers pick over my bones." No, you stop, regroup, pick up a McDonald's fountain Coke, ask for directions, get mad, listen to music, get mad again, call friends for help, and then finally, you make it.

Remember this the next time you're writing or producing a project and are frustrated that you're not reaching your deadline on time.

It's OK to be late . . . The Lord of the Highways knows it took us 4 years to get *Altar Boyz* right and we took many a wrong turn along the way (remind me to tell you about the time that Abraham's name was Leonard and Luke was addicted to Vicodin).

Sure we would have liked to have gotten there a lot faster, but making sure you get there is the most important part.

Just ask these guys how happy they were that they didn't turn around and go home at some point during their 7 year trip.

January 08, 2008

The Definition of a Jukebox Musical

Wikipedia is wrong.

According to everyone's favorite online encyclopedia, "A jukebox musical is a stage or film musical that uses previously released popular songs as its musical score."

I disagree. And I'd bet another $100 that Hal Prince would too. Would you want to tell him that *LoveMusik* was a jukebox musical?

Here's my definition:

"A jukebox musical is an original stage musical not based on a film that uses previously released popular songs that have no direct relation to the story as its musical score."

Ok, so I'm no Webster's. Let me explain with examples:

Mamma Mia = Jukebox Musical (An original story about a girl searching for her father using Abba music)

All Shook Up = Jukebox Musical (Shakespeare's Twelfth Night using Elvis tunes)

Jersey Boys = NOT a Jukebox Musical (Four Seasons music telling the Four Seasons story)

See what I mean? *Jersey Boys* just doesn't feel like a Jukebox musical.

Times They Are a Changin'? Yes. *Movin' Out*? Yes. *Good Vibrations*? Put another dime in the jukebox, baby.

Lennon? No.

Lennon is dependent upon that music. It couldn't be done with *The Carpenters* catalog. *Mamma Mia* (with a different title), on the other hand, could have been attempted with Lawrence Welk music. Sure, it would have sucked, but that's not the point. Same thing with *LoveMusik*. These are **Bio Musicals**, not jukebox musicals.

Xanadu, Saturday Night Fever . . . not Jukebox musicals. They are musical adaptations of movies that already had the music integrated.

Here's what's crazy . . . both Wiki's definition and my definition make shows like *Crazy For You* and *Forever Plaid*, jukebox musicals.

Maybe we should add something to the definition that states it only applies to shows after 2001 (the year when *Mamma Mia* hit Broadway).

Any other definitions out there?

January 09, 2008

Your High Rollers.

The "Golden Rule" in casinos doesn't have anything to do with being nice to your neighbor. Their most important axiom is the ol' Pareto Principle, or the 80-20 rule.

The casinos know that as much as they love when John and Suzy from Tulsa come for the weekend and lose $150 in the slots and buy the $7.99 buffet, John and Suzy aren't paying for the Picassos in their lobbies and the shows in their theatres.

What's paying for the luxury that keeps John and Suzy coming, are the <u>Whales</u>.

Don't think High Rollers are exclusive to that one glittering city in the desert (or an Indian reservation near)? High Rollers are in every industry, including the theatre.

High Rollers are your premium ticket buyers. High Rollers are your subscribers. In the Off-Broadway world, High Rollers are your full price buyers.

Even though they may not represent 80% of our revenue, these people, who are willing to spend top-dollar plus, are people we need to pay attention to and respect. More High Rollers means a higher profit margin. So how do you get more of them?

Think about what Vegas does to take care of their High Rollers.

Now what do you do to take care of yours? Do you greet them? Do you give them free stuff? Would you make a dinner reservation for them?

Watch your whales. High Rollers keep the money "rolling on in."

($10 iTunes gift certificate to the first person who posts a comment with the name of the musical that lyric is from. No googleating - my <u>sniglet</u> that means cheating using Google).

January 10, 2008

<u>**Entertainment Industry Expo**</u>

Conventions have always sounded boring to me. It's the word. Convention. Blech. Or Expo. Eww-o.

They just don't sound fun.

But they are. Whenever you get several thousand people who are all passionate about Star Trek, weddings, or whatever, in the same room, this really cool energy is created that is anything by convention-al.

<u>The Entertainment Industry Expo</u> is one of those conventions.

Stop by on the 27th of January. It's fun. And free!

Oh, and if you're there at 10:00 AM, you'll get to hear me spout a few Kenisms on the panel of producers they've put together.

January 12, 2008

The Answer is . . .

The lyric I quoted in my post earlier this week was from *Evita*.

Congrats to Mary for picking up the iTunes gift certificate.

A follow-up . . .

Evita closed on Broadway over 24 years ago . . . and has yet to be revived. Seems odd, considering that it was written by the most "successful" composer of the modern Broadway Theater and that it was responsible for solidifying star status for its two leads.

So why hasn't it been revived?

And, if it was revived right now, would it have the money rollin' on in?

One reason it hasn't been revived is that it was done pretty damn definitively the first time around, and no one has figured out a better way to tell that story . . . never mind finding someone worthy of standing on the Casa Rosada.

And we all know how important both of those things are.

Your thoughts on why it hasn't come back and 142 Sondheim shows have? Did we really need *Into The Woods* again? Wouldn't you all rather see *Evita* than another production of *Gypsy* (even if the original Eva is starring)?

January 13, 2008

Ah, the Double Standard of Entertainment

A debate of ethic proportions has emerged amongst Broadway producers recently.

The question . . . would you hire this man?

The entertainment industry has always had a "we'll hire you no matter what" attitude towards anyone with box office potential when it has come to drug use, DUIs, and even domestic violence.

Does this crime warrant more concern? Less?

Will there be protests at the theater? What if there are underage cast members in the show?

If we continue to hire individuals with bad track records, never mind criminal records, are we just teaching them that they are not accountable for their actions?

And are we teaching future artists that they don't have to be accountable as well? Or is the only thing we are accountable for the actual accounting.

Is it strange that companies across the world have drug tests for the simplest of tasks, yet there is no drug testing for Broadway employees, whether they are lifting fellow dancers above their heads or whether they are lifting heavy scenery above a dancer's head?

And do we not have drug testing because we all know that a huge majority of actors, etc., would fail?

I don't have an answer to whether or not I'd hire Mr. Barbour, but I do know this:

I've been trying to get this guy to do a musical for a long time. God help me if it ever happens. What would you do?

January 14, 2008

Last Minute Panel Alert: Today!

For any of you in midtown Manhattan today, there is a panel in (gulp) an hour and 20 minutes at New World Stages (340 W. 50th St.) on "The Business of Producing".

This panel is part of a series of discussions for the Off-Broadway community sponsored by The League of Off-Broadway Theatres and Producers. I'm not speaking, but I'll be listening . . . intently. :-)

Speakers include Terry Byrne (Westside Theatre), Nancy Gibbs (321 Management), Susan Mindell (Levine, Plotkin & Menin, LLP), Jonathan Pollard (*I Love You, You're Perfect* . . . Producer), William Russo (Playwrights Horizon) and it will be moderated by Carol Fishman (Aruba Productions).

If you can go, try to send an RSVP email to info@offbroadway.org beforehand. If not, try and crash it. I'm sure you'll get in. I promise more notice on the next one.

January 15, 2008

Stats Courtesy of Business Week

Network TV Ad Spending in 2006	16 billion
Network TV Ad Spending in 2007	15.5 billion
Internet Ad Spending in 2006	4.1 billion
Internet Ad Spending in 2007	5.2 billion

Duh.

But watch out, with this kind of growth on the 'net, we could be looking at a lot of clutter pretty soon (how many email discounts for Broadway shows do you get in your inbox every morning?).

The best Broadway Producers I've ever worked with are always exploiting the current trends and, at the same time, also figuring out how to take advantage of the next uncluttered space.

January 17, 2008

I Went To Church At An Airport.

When I travel, I like to take the first flight out in the morning. Less chance of being delayed, and I usually sleep better than I did when I saw *In My Life*.

Recently my first flight out had me at Chicago's Midway airport too early for me to head to my hotel. So, I bought a Wi-Fi connection, got a bagel, and set up an office. Then, I heard an announcement:

"Catholic mass will be celebrated in the chapel at 8:30. All are welcome. The service will last 30 minutes."

30 minutes! As someone who was raised Catholic (hence *Altar Boyz*), I've lived through homilies that were 30 minutes alone! And here's a chance to relieve some Catholic guilt and say that I've been to mass, with only a 30 minute investment? Done and done.

There is no question that the modern audience, for church or for entertainment, loves a short show. Don't your ears perk up when you hear that a show you are about to see is a short one? Don't you cringe when you hear that *August: Osage County* is 3.5 hours long, despite the great reviews and word of mouth?

Why is a quote like "90 minutes of Heavenly Hilarity" better than one without the time reference? (Tip: if you ever get a quote that says your show is 90 minutes, use it like a toothbrush - 3 times a day). Is it because attending the theater is a chore? Just like church? Is it because the theater isn't a <u>comfortable experience</u> so we don't want to be trapped?

Is it because everything in our world is shorter and faster (we've gone from letters to faxes to emails to text messages), and that this advancement and fast-paced lifestyle is bleeding over into entertainment? (First sitcoms, then 2 minute YouTube videos, and next, micro-clips on our mobile phones?)

Or (and I worry about this one), is it because audiences aren't enjoying a majority of the theater they see, so they want to know that if they don't like it, at least they will be back on their couch in time to watch *Will and Grace* in syndication on the CW?

I don't know the answer, but I do know that when I try to get people to see my shows, it's a lot easier after I tell them they are ALL less than 90 minutes.

From a totally commercial perspective, it's something to think about when creating your shows. It's easier to sell short.
I mean, don't you all enjoy my blogs more when they are shorter???

January 18, 2008

The 3 Fs
I like to make up dorky abbreviations and acronyms to help keep me on track with a goal.
For example:

<u>EAI</u> - "Easily Actionable Item" A short term task that is easy to accomplish that helps demonstrate forward motion to an organization (just ask the <u>Off-Broadway Brainstormers</u> about this one!)

And here's my latest!

I am in the midst of looking for new projects, so I came up with a three stage structure to define the steps a producer needs to take when developing a new project. Rather than naming it "A Producer's Three Stage Structure" and sound like an MBA candidate writing a (boring) paper, I called it "The 3 Fs". And since I'm not an MBA candidate and no one is forced to read my papers, I'm posting it here for your grade instead.

THE 3 Fs

1. FIND IT

Transferring a show from a regional theatre? Optioning a friend's play? Writing it yourself? This stage is all about locating the property that you believe deserves and demands to be seen. Think of this stage like adopting a child. (And you wouldn't rush that, would you?)

2. FLESH IT OUT

It's your job to assist in the development of the property so that it can grow stronger. The definition of development changes for each show. Some pieces may need help with the script. Some may need a new director that you can find. Some may need a place to rehearse. Some may need cash. Figure out what your show needs and get it. Even if whatever it needs is not your strength. Either find someone who can deliver what the show needs, or *learn how yourself.* Your kid is going through puberty.

3. (Bring it to) FRUITION

This is the practical part of producing: booking the theater, hiring the GM (or doing it yourself), preparing your marketing campaign, and getting that show to opening night. Your kid is 18 now. And without you, he or she would sit at home playing Wii, smoking doobies and not go to college. Don't let that happen.

There they are: The Three Fs. Say them with me five times fast. Find it, flesh it out, fruition. Find it, flesh it out, fruition. Find it . . . ok, you get the idea.

Grade me on them if you'd like. Or better, come up with your own better way of putting up a show.

Because the truth is, no matter what road you take, or what letter you use in your "Three Stage Structure", how you get your show to the stage is not as important as simply getting there.

(Oh and by the way, your kid may still flunk out of school and end up in prison even if you follow the 3Fs perfectly. But hey, producing shows is not like living in China. You can always have another kid. And don't ever let anyone tell you that you shouldn't.)

January 19, 2008

And Now A Few Words From Rocco!

If you haven't read <u>Freakonomics</u>, you should. It's a great lesson in out-of-the-box thinking combined with hard data analysis.

The boys from Freakonomics have a blog on NYTimes.com, and this week, they asked Broadway Producer and Theater Owner, <u>Rocco Landesman</u>, a few questions.

Some of the questions posed by the Freaks are a bit too simplistic, but it's always interesting and educational to hear someone like Rocco speak about the biz.

Read it <u>here</u>.

January 20, 2008

Don't Quit!

Don't worry, this isn't an <u>inspirational post</u> about making sure you get to the finish line of whatever you're working on (In fact, sometimes it's important NOT to get to the Finish line).

This is a post to get you to go see *Don't Quit Your Night Job*, an improv/sketch comedy/musical/cavalcade of stars that takes place once a month. It's face-hurtin' funny, stars some great <u>talent</u>, and the proceeds go to charity.

Yes, go to laugh your a$$ off and see some Broadway stars making fun of themselves, but also go for this reason:

Last year, a commercial run of *Don't Quit* tried to make it Off-Broadway. It didn't work. I think it could have. Do you? How could you have made it work?

Oh and big props to the creators for not letting the failure of a commercial run stop them from doing what they love to do and what they do so well. It would have been easy to "quit" after that, and most people would have. They deserve some credit for keeping on, keeping on.

Oh crap, here I go, turning this into an inspirational post again. Dang it!

The 4th F!

In my post about the 3Fs, I forgot an F!

And it's an important one.

The fourth F is . . .

F*** it.

Great producers know when to give up. Great producers know when to close a show, when to stop throwing good development money after bad, and when to move on to something else.

It's tough, because as artists we get very emotionally attached to our projects/children. But like investing in the stock market, you have to know when to sell a loser. It actually takes more courage to close a show than to open one.

We will all have to do it at some point in our careers. So embrace your inner swearin' sailor and say F*** it.

January 21, 2008

A Few of My Favorite Things . . . To Read!

I've gotten a few emails from readers asking if I have recommendations of books to read for people getting into Producing.

And, surprise, surprise, I do!

Here's my "Must Read" list, in no particular order. As I've mentioned before, I'm a big believer in the pot-luck kind of Producer. Don't specialize in one thing. Learn a bit of everything, and develop your own style. It's kind of like acting. Don't learn one "Method". Study Strasberg, Adler, Meisner, etc. and then *make your own method.*

The books recommended below, in no particular order, cover a wide variety of areas from marketing to writing to contracts. Enjoy!

1. Purple Cow by Seth Godin

My favorite blog. My favorite book. Learn how to sell *and* how to develop product in today's competitive market.

2. Influence by Robert B. Cialdini

Remember how I hate marketing? This is all about the science of selling. Brilliant. And scary. Wait until you read about how commercial airline disasters increase after highly publicized suicides.

3. Producing Theatre by Donald C. Farber

A chestnut. A bit outdated, but a good resource to have on your shelf when you need a refresher in the mechanics of a royalty pool, or how profits are distributed after recoupment.

4. The Writer's Journey by Christopher Vogler

Don't think there's a blueprint for story telling? Think again. Using Joseph Cambell's Hero theory, Vogler shows you how modern story telling is very similar to ancient myths . . . and why it has to be. Often used for screenplays, I think it's even more suited for structuring musicals (since musicals, like myths, are heightened forms of reality).

5. The Tipping Point by Malcom Gladwell

A new chestnut. And probably the most important book on what spreads ideas (word of mouth - our most important tool) ever written. Ever.

6. The Long Tail by Chris Anderson

Why concentrating on niche marketing and "doing it yourself" is the way to go in the age of the internet.

7. Made to Stick by Chip & Dan Heath

After you read the other marketing books, read this one. Fun, more specific, and the cover is cool.

8. Freakonomics by Steven D. Levitt & Stephen J. Dubner

A reminder that studying data is the way to solve almost all of our problems; from cheating teachers to the drug epidemic. It makes solving a Broadway budget problem look like opening a lemonade stand.

9. The Bible, The Secret, Anthony Robbins Awaken the Giant Within, Fortune Cookies, etc.

You need incredible amounts of faith and confidence to do what we do. Get it wherever you can.

10. (Insert your favorite here). Got one that helps you? Comments are open, so feel free to share! We could all use something else to read while waiting for the 1 train during rush hour.

January 22, 2008

Are The Two Cardinal Rules Of Producing Right?

<u>Max Bialystock:</u> The two cardinal rules of producing. One: Never put your own money in the show.

<u>Leo Bloom:</u> And two?

<u>Max Bialystock:</u> [*yelling*] Never put your own money in the show!

- - - - -

This line, obviously from *The Producers*, got one of the biggest laughs on opening night, when the audience was filled with actual Bialystocks and Frankels and Weinsteins, oh my!

But is it true?

Sure, Producers understand that the chances for actually recouping your investment in a Broadway or Off-Broadway show are like winning the lottery... on your birthday . . . while pigs are flying (by <u>Foy</u>).

But is it a sin to open up your own wallet?

The answer is no.

You might be able to avoid putting your own money in the show, but you better be willing to. Because if you're not willing to put your money where your mouth is, then you're not passionate enough to produce. And maybe you should look at the project a little closer.

I always put a little something in all of my shows, for two reasons:

1. I wouldn't want an investor of mine in any show that I didn't believe in myself.

2. It helps when you're raising money to be able to say to a potential investor, "I already wrote my check."

How would you feel if a producer was giving you the hard sell to invest in their show and then they told you that they didn't invest a penny? Insider activity is a very commonly watched stat when playing the stock market, so shouldn't we watch it when investing in shows?

By the way, for those looking for the response to an investor asking if you invested, and you haven't, it's this: "I had so much interest, I wanted to make room for as many investors as possible, so I backed out." A piece of advice: <u>only use this if it is true</u>. Don't treat your investors like they are one-time investors. Treat them like they are with you for your lifetime . . . and they will be. Even if you produce *Springtime for Hitler*.

January 23, 2008

<u>Double or Nothing!</u>

You all remember my infamous <u>bet</u> from last fall when I incorrectly predicted that the Producers and the Stagehands "would be friends".

Well, let's get ready to rumble! Or not.

The Actors' Equity Production (Broadway) Contract expires at the end of June. While emotions are still high from the fall fireworks, there will be no strike.

Why not? I don't see an issue that could escalate to that kind of action. Even if there isn't an agreement right away on raises, the hiring of aliens from overseas, etc., I'm sure talks will continue until they hammer out a deal. There may be a few threats (and expect Local 1 to express their unwavering support), but the marquees will stay lit.

Who wants a piece of this action? 2:1 odds in your favor.

One issue both sides should discuss? Health insurance. There will no doubt be an increase to the already high weekly cost of a producer's required weekly contribution to the co-administered League-Equity health fund - currently $153/week or $612/month or $7,956/year *per actor*!

It would be cheaper for the Producer to purchase their own insurance just like any other new company, and cover each actor from day 1 of employment, rather than make the actor <u>qualify</u> for insurance (the current plan requires that an actor work for 12 weeks to earn only 6 months of coverage, and 20 weeks for a full year).

Actors would get their insurance faster and producers would save money.

I realize that this idea is in exact opposition to the idea of union provided benefits.

But sometimes, when you're lost, you have to think about turning around and going the opposite direction to get you back on track again.

January 24, 2008

Show Boat Wasn't Slow Boat.

Here's some interesting trivia:

Edna Ferber's novel, *Show Boat*, was first published in 1926.

The musical version of *Show Boat* opened on Broadway in December, 1927.

Ahhh, come again? From the published novel to a fully produced musical in how long? When was the last time this happened in the modern theater?

It hasn't. Books go to movie companies first now. I can't tell you how many times I've tried to option a book and found that the rights have been wrapped up with the movie deal, or that the agent is afraid to release the stage rights because they are "holding out" for a film option.

This is another reason for the recent surge in the adaptation of movies into musicals. The movie companies are *sitting* on all the cards, sometimes not even wanting to play the game.

Another interesting tidbit . . . while doing some research on *Show Boat*, I was reminded that there were a few <u>songs</u> that were not written specifically for it, but were popular tunes interpolated into the score.

Does that mean it's a <u>jukebox musical</u>? ;-)

January 25, 2008

Three, Three, Three Posts in One!

Three quickies for you:

- A reminder that I'll be at the <u>Entertainment Industry Expo</u> this Sunday. If you go, please make sure you say hello. And no tough questions. It is Sunday morning. ;-) Here's the Playbill article about the <u>panel</u>.

- I found this great <u>article</u> about investing in the theater online. It's from 2001, but it's a very realistic analysis of the pros and cons of rolling the dice on Broadway.

- You heard it here first. 20at20, the Off-Broadway promotion from The Off-Broadway Brainstormers that gets you $20 tickets, 20 minutes before curtain for more than 20 Off-Broadway shows (including mine), returns at the end of February. It hasn't been officially announced yet, but since I'm the head of the committee, I thought I'd leak it to you first. Shhhh . . .

This qualifies as a short blog.

January 26, 2008

It Happens To The Stock Market And It Happens To Broadway.

We had our own version of a "market correction" 2 days ago when *Color Purple* announced that it is closing.

Although everyone knew that *Purple* was showing signs of weakness post-Fantasia, the announcement (leaving the Broadway Theater empty during the spring) was a bit of a shock, just like the Dow dropping a few hundred points in one day.

I should have predicted this one. I picked up on a sign that we were due for a correction a few weeks ago when Variety reported that Broadway grossed 15 million on 30 shows.

But what did it gross during the same week last year? 17 million. On 28 shows.

2 more million. 2 LESS shows. With last year's prices.

Something had to give. And it was Oprah.

While the closing of *Purple* is unfortunate, let's hope that it helps stabilize the street and sends us (and the Dow) back up.

This brings up an interesting point. Too often we worry about watching our grosses from week to week. We celebrate being "up from last week", or lament being down. For those of you who have never seen a box office statement, look at this . . . you'll see that the weekly comparison is part of the automatic reporting.

What's the problem with obsessing over week to week comparisons? Too many factors that affect sales change from week to week: holidays, Super Bowls, weather, etc. What we really should study is the gross changes from year to year.

Unfortunately, since the average run of a new musical on Broadway is only 52.67 weeks, most people don't bother to look at yearly trends.

Here's a graph of three years of data for one my shows. Look at how closely the weeks line up from year to year. Cool, huh?

Your sales trends emerge naturally. When you discover them, that's when you can really put your producing skills to work. Discounts (or cutting discounts during busier weeks), expense cutting, etc.

When I look at a graph like this, I think of the low points like enemy targets, and my initiatives are my missiles. By analyzing the trends over several years, I've isolated my targets. And when you isolate your targets, your missiles are much more effective.

Don't have a show that has run years? Graph overall Broadway/Off-Broadway trends from year to year. It is better than nothing.

(Anyone have any ideas what the giant spike is on that graph?)

January 27, 2008

Piggybacking Featured In The New York Times

As you know, I'm not a believer in the archaic 8 show a week model, especially for Off-Broadway shows. The New York Times did a story on the current trend of sharing spaces Off-Broadway to relieve some of this burden and I was fortunate enough to be interviewed for the article.

The Times calls sharing spaces piggy-backing. My press agent calls it bunk beds.

I call it *Blind Windows*.

That's a reference to the fictional screenplay in *Sunset Boulevard*. In *Blind Windows*, two people share the same apartment. One works during the day, one during the night and they never meet . . . even though they share the same bed.

You know what's better than being quoted in this article? The two pictures of my shows!

January 28, 2008

Sniff, Sniff. I Smell Press.

Anyone else out there think this is a faux story with the sole intention of getting press and getting mentioned on blogs like this (note - you have to register to read the article)? It smells funny to me.

If it is real, I guess the funny smell is just the lawyer for the plaintiff.

If it isn't real, the Bald and the Blue have done it again.

Remember, these are the boys that held a funeral for the 80s.

These are also the ear-less wonders who put out a velvet rope and stantions and stood guard at a door that looked like it could lead to the hottest club in town . . . but actually went to nowhere.

Brilliant. Why? Because each "stunt" (I hate that word) was so in the style of the show, that they didn't seem like stunts.

Having Maria from *The Sound of Music* stand guard at a fake nightclub in Soho wouldn't make sense. Asking the cast of *August: Osage County* to hold a funeral for the 80s?   Stunty McStunterson.

But having the *Altar Boyz* challenge the Backstreet Boys to a boy band battle and then sending them a rubber chicken when they don't show up? Or having a promotion where virgins got in free to the first performance of a show about virginity? I took classes at the Blue School of Press (when you graduate, you get a mention on *Extra*).

My favorite press event of all time isn't even mine. The producers of *Matt and Ben* started a rumor that Matt Damon and Ben Affleck were suing them. They got two major press hits: first when the story broke and then, when it was debunked. But they didn't stop. They posted "documents" and "voice mails" on their website that backed up their story. Yes! The event and show fit together - like a B-rate star and the revival of *Chicago*.

When you look at creative ways to get press for your shows (and you should) look at the show you're promoting first. Don't just come up with the kookiest idea known to man. Come up with an idea that makes so much sense for your show, it would be kooky NOT to do it.

That's the difference between a stunt and an event.

(The Backstreet Boys never responded, by the way. And then Kevin Richardson left the group and did *Chicago*. Coincidence?)

January 29, 2008

"How Do I Get The Stage Rights To A Book/Movie/Play, etc.?"

When I was a Company Manager, I used to tell my assistants that if we ever got the same question from more than two company members, we hadn't done our job. If more than two people asked what time our flight was to the next city, or asked us to explain their paychecks to them, then we hadn't anticipated the needs of our company or communicated information that was important to them fast enough.

I believe this is a great way to measure your success as a manager. No questions? Nice job.

Using that definition of my job as a blogger, I have failed you.

I have been asked a few times recently how to go about obtaining the rights to a book or movie or play, etc. in order to turn that property into a Broadway show.

The good news? It's easy to ask for the rights. The bad news? It's harder to get an answer.

Sometimes it's hard just figuring out where to start. Here are a few tips, classified by the type of property you are going after.

- BOOK
    - Find the Publisher of the book (look at the first few inside pages) and call them. Most publishing companies will have entire departments dedicated to rights. I find that I get the quickest answers on the availability of rights from publishers (probably because disposition of rights is such a large source of their revenue). If they can't give you a straight answer, they should be able to tell you the agent for the author and you can contact the agent directly. They may ask for something in writing (see below).
- MOVIE
    - The first question is to find out if the movie is an original or if it was based on earlier work. If it was based on a book or short story or a note jotted on a napkin, go after the original author first before approaching the movie company. Odds are that you are going to have to go to the movie company anyway, but you're much more likely to get a response (and

a positive one) from the person who has the most invested in the project (the original author), rather than someone in the legal department of a billion dollar conglomerate. You can get the original author on your side, find out more info about what rights the movie company actually owns, and develop a strategy from there.

- o If it's an original screenplay, then you are definitely going to have to approach the movie company. You can also approach the author of the screenplay at the same time, using the same theory as the above, but if the script was written for MGM, then expect MGM to hold most of the cards. Movie companies get a ton of rights requests (for clips, etc.) so they will always want something in writing. Call the company and find out to whom to send the request. Send it, and then follow up with a phone call. Then wait and wait. And keep following up. I once got a response, months later, via the mail. I mean, they couldn't just send an email?

- PLAY

  - o Theater writers always own their material, as opposed to screenwriters who have to sell their soul to the mighty movie companies. Therefore, seek out the author directly, through the Dramatists Guild (if they are a member) or their agent, or by visiting <u>Angus</u>.

- OTHER MEDIUMS

  - o All of the above principles can be applied to other mediums as well, from optioning websites to television shows to clothing lines. Most people have agents or lawyers or production companies that you can track down through Google. If at all possible, get to the person, not the agent.

Another related question I get is "Should I have a lawyer make this inquiry for me?" Lawyers can make you seem more "serious" or "official", especially if you lack credits. Lawyers can also get you a speedier response if you hire a firm that does business with these agents or movie companies all the time. The downside is that lawyers cost bucks. Beaucoup de bucks. So, I often advise people on limited budgets to make the request yourself first (do yourself a favor and make up some good looking fax stationery with a logo and a production company name). If you don't get a response, you can always go the lawyer route later.

This process is really easier than it seems. The key is just to start. Summon up some Oliver-like courage and just ask for what you want. Always thought your favorite book would make a great movie? Musical? Greeting card? Ask. It literally can take as little as 15 minutes to get the request off. Just by asking the question, you've started the ball rolling down the hill of getting your show done.

If they aren't available, you can move on to the next project, and stop saying, "_The Alienist_ would make such a good film!" (I just found out that Scott Rudin has been sitting on the rights. Scott, if you are reading (or if your assistant is reading this for you), I'll take those rights - name your price.)

And, you can keep asking for them. I sent one request per year for five years before I got the rights to _Somewhere In Time_. Put a reminder in your Outlook to ask every year at the same time. Don't give up until you get the rights or they take out a restraining order against you.

And then form a dummy corporation under another name and ask again.

January 30, 2008

I Have To Pee.

And I know exactly where I want to "go".

For the past two years, Charmin has set up public restrooms in the middle of Times Square for anyone and everyone to use.

For those of you who have seen the restrooms, but have never gone inside, you missed out on a true marketing trifecta.

Let's count the many reasons why this is one of the most genius non-stunts I have seen:

- They made restrooms remarkable.

    - Can you think of any other subject that is more delicate than the human elimination system? Well, Charmin celebrated it. They had cheerleaders. They had music. They cleaned each stall after each use. And my personal favorite? They had the softest carpet you've ever felt.

- They were guaranteed people's "business" (I'll stop with the puns now).

- o Restrooms are a necessary commodity. We all have to eat.
     And we all have to go. There will always be a market for
     restrooms at one of the busiest intersections in the world.

- They had no competition.

  - o Before the Charmin restrooms, there were no public
       restrooms in Times Square. They were the only supplier,
       and we're practically drowning in demand! It's like putting a
       water fountain in the middle of the Sahara.

- They incorporated trackable direct response.

  - o They gave away coupons, which will help drive sales and
       provide some sense of a R.O.I. Music to any marketer's
       ears.

- They surveyed.

  - o On your way out, they asked everyone where they were from
       and whether or not they preferred soft or strong. They
       learned about their customers, and then for fun they
       published the results on their website.

Why is this a trifecta? Because it contains the three Rs: It feels *Required*.
You get quantifiable *Results*. And it is soooo very *Remarkable*.

They'll even get a bonus R: *Return* customers. I know I'll be back next year.
How many bathrooms get repeaters? (If that sounded like a pun, it wasn't
meant to be. It was an accident. Hehe.)

FEBRUARY 2008

February 01, 2008

Get Your Audiences To Sing Along.

I'm in Ohio this week, shooting a documentary on one of the top unsigned <u>bands</u> in the country.

We've been in the recording studio all week, as the band finishes up their 8th independent album. This is the one we all hope will get them the big record deal and have them playing the "enormo-domes" across the country.

As the record producer was playing back one of their future hits yesterday, something happened to me.

I started singing along.

It was like being hypnotized. My mouth just opened, and out came the words and the tune, like I was on karaoke auto-pilot.

I didn't even realize it, until the record producer stopped the playback. And I kept singing. (Look out, Daughtry)

Why did I all of a sudden think I was an uber-cool American Idol winner?

The art *involved* me. What was created by five guys and their electric guitars and gravelly voices sucked me into the actual experience.

And what started as an observational or non-participatory art form became an interactive one.

This should be the goal of all artists. Because the fun begins when the fourth wall disappears.

I'm not saying that every show should be like *Jersey Boys* or *Mamma Mia* where the audience IS actually singing and dancing along (although it has to be noted that both of these shows are monster *international* hits). And all shows don't have to be like *The Awesome 80s Prom* where you can dance with the Captain of The Football Team.

But all shows do have to pick you up and transport you right into the heart of the experience, somehow making you believe that you are Daughtry.

Our job is not to put up fourth walls. Our job is to tear them down.

February 02, 2008

Producer Of Young Frankenstein Make Boo-Boo.

After getting a few public <u>spankings</u> from co-producer Mel Brooks last week, Robert Sillerman <u>admitted</u> that the monster-sized ticket price of $450 was a mistake.

He cited the critical backlash (Brantley mentioned the $450 in the 2nd paragraph of his <u>review</u>) as well as public perception that all tickets were $450 as a few of the repercussions of his poor judgment.

I could have told him that was going to happen.

These were the same problems that *The Producers* faced when they announced their sky-high prices seven years ago, which begs the question . . . how could he make this mistake?

In 1990, my <u>high school</u> baseball team was playing its biggest rival, Pingree (eww). We were down by one run in the 9th inning. One of my best friends, Jim O'Connor, was on third base. During some kind of distraction, Jim tried to steal home. It took us all by surprise, but there he was, tearing towards home plate, trying to tie up the game.

He got thrown out in an ultra close call. We lost.

My coach got frustrated, looked at Jimmy questionably, and then said to his assistant, "Why the &#$^ did he do that?" The assistant spit out a sunflower seed and said, "If he would have made it, he would have been a hero."

Jimmy was a great athlete. He knew baseball and he knew his skills. He surveyed the scene, and made a decision . . . which unfortunately for us, turned out to be the wrong one.

Robert Sillerman was almost a hero too. Can you imagine how much faster the show would have recouped with those $450 tickets if *YF* had been received as well as *The Producers*?

But Sillerman got called out at home.

So what? It happens all the time. People make mistakes. Robert Sillerman is an incredible <u>businessman</u>, and even incredible businessmen who run multi-billion dollar companies make mistakes.

And so will you. You'll make a lot of them. You'll produce a bad show, you'll hire the wrong person, and yes, you'll price something incorrectly.

This business is not about not making mistakes. You just have to to make sure you make more right decisions than wrong ones. Producing is cumulative. People don't judge you by one decision or one show. If they did, this guy would be in big trouble. Look at how long his first show ran. Then look at the success of his last three.

As much as I disagreed with Sillerman charging $450/ticket, I've got to give him credit. He made a mistake but owned up to it (and Mel should spend more time writing better shows than pointing his finger at others).

Who knows, when *Blazing Saddles* opens, he may want $1000/ticket.

Hopefully he'll hire me as a consultant before he does.

And hopefully I won't make a mistake.

February 04, 2008

"How Do I Find Investors for My Broadway or Off-Broadway Show?"

Unless you're a bazillionaire, you are all probably wondering just how in the hoo-ha you're going to find investors for your shows.

I'm going up to Columbia Univ. today to speak to a producing class on this same subject and, well, I can't tell them before I tell you . . . so here are a few of my strategies on getting people to show you the moola.

Strategy 1: Field of Dreams

Call me a can of Easy-Cheese if you want, but that creepy voice in the corn field was right: "If you build it, they will come."

Spend your time worrying about your product, not about how you're going to pay for it. There are plenty of people in the world that enjoy investing in shows (even in bad ones). Think like a high-tech company (another high-risk business). Put your time and whatever money you do have in R&D.

If you create something remarkable and Purple-Cow like, you'll find people throwing money at you. At the same time you'll be more passionate about your product, which makes it that much easier to sell to investors. Passion is contagious.

Strategy 2: Cub Scouts

When I was a kid, I sold chocolate bars to raise money for my Cub Scout troupe. I also sold Cutco, stationery products, and I even set up a candy shop at my father's office after he taught me the wonders of wholesale (I called it *Kenneth's Kandy Shop.* I thought the "K" for Candy was the Koolest.).

No matter what I was selling, I always started the same way . . . with my family. Then my friends, my neighbors, my father's secretary, etc.

Getting investors is no different than hawking scissors that cut a penny in half. Start with the people you know. And then, ask them if they know people who would be interested in your product.

The people that are closest to you are going to be most inclined to give you money, because they are going to invest in YOU, regardless of what you're selling. Do you think my Mom really needed the scissors that cut a penny in half?

When I was pitching a show (hard) to my very first and biggest investor he cut me off and said, "Ken, I'm giving you the money, but not because I believe the show is going to make a fortune or even return its investment. I don't invest in projects. I invest in people."

True that.

Strategy 3: Where The Wild Things aka Rich People Are

There is a big difference between bazillionaires and people with disposable income. There are more people with disposable income out there than you think. Lots of folks do well enough to spend money on nice vacations, a second home, a nice car, and even theater tickets! GASP!

Your job? Find them. Go to charity benefits. Go to Wall Street bars. Go to art openings. As my dad tells me all the time, "You have to show face." You'll find people will be interested in what you are doing. And getting a few thousand out of these folks is not as hard as you think. Most people in the middle class to upper middle class have some extra investment money that they'd rather not invest in a boring blue-chip. I often tell these people that investing in the entertainment industry is just an extension of the diversification of their portfolio.

These are my three principle strategies of raising money, but there are thousands more. Just like anything else, you have to find out what works for you.

However you get them, this next part is crucial . . .

Take care of them. I'm not saying you have to produce record breaking hit after recording breaking hit (although that helps). You do have to *communicate* with them. Send them t-shirts., introduce them to the actors, send them something unique at Christmas (but, please, anything but a <u>card</u>), etc. Why? Because people, like cigarettes, travel in packs. People that invest in the theater know people that invest in the theatre, who know people that will invest in whatever you are doing.

One of my biggest investors was introduced to me by one of my smallest investors two years after we met. How did I meet him? He walked up to me at one of my shows and said, "This is cool. How can I get involved?"

The lesson? Produce stuff that people think is cool, and then . . . well, you remember how I said your first investors will most likely *be* your family? Your last investors have to be treated *like* family, so they'll stay with you . . . through thick and <u>thin</u>.

February 05, 2008

One of My Favorite Quotes

The recent announcement of the <u>closing</u> of *Rent* made me think of one of my favorite quotes.

When Jonathan Larson's sister accepted the Tony Award on his behalf, she said: "It took Johnnie 15 years of really hard work to become an overnight sensation."

Very few people in this business, or in this world, "make-it" without a whole lot of work. It may look like people just "arrive", but it rarely happens that way.

So don't waste time wondering how someone got lucky enough to have written or have produced *Rent*. Just keep working and working hard, and you'll be discovered as well. It just may take 15 years. But when you love what you do, and Jonathan did, who cares how long it takes.

And then, when it does happen (and it will), it'll feel even better.

February 06, 2008

Why Announce Recouping One Show When You Can Announce Three!

Yesterday was the most Super Tuesday ever. We announced the recoupment of all three of my shows: *Altar Boyz, The Awesome 80s Prom* and *My First Time.*

Read the article in the New York Times here, and the Playbill article here.

Ok, truth time. *Altar Boyz* and *My First Time* did both recoup at the end of 2007 and at the same time. However, *The Awesome 80s Prom* recouped a year or so ago.

Why did I wait to announce it?

Certainly I was itching to get it out there that I had returned the investment of my first show out of the box. But press releases can't be about ego. They have to be about press. The goal of each release is to get as many media members as possible to write about it, which increases the possibility that more people will read it, which increases the possibility that more people will buy tickets, and so on and so on.

I didn't release it last year because I knew no one would have written about it (a fact confirmed by one of the reporters who interviewed me about all three recouping). And even if someone did, it wouldn't have gotten a lot of attention from readers. It just wasn't exciting enough.

But put it back to back with two other releases announcing the recoupment of shows from the same producer, emailed to the media within seconds of each other? All of a sudden it feels more exciting, doesn't it?

Be objective about the news you have and don't talk unless you know people are listening. Eli Manning wouldn't throw a pass that he knew didn't have a prayer of being caught. He'd wait, scramble in the pocket (almost getting sacked), and *then* throw it when he knew there was at least a possibility of completion.

So wait until you have open receivers.

(I have to wonder if that is the first ever football/theater analogy in the history of the blogosphere. My step-dad would be very proud, even though he's from Massachusetts and probably still sitting in his Patriots jersey and sobbing.)

Oh, the other reason I announced three shows recouping at once? I wanted to stick it to these bitterinas who last year said that "Commercial Off-Broadway is Dead". Hopefully this will prove that it's not dead. It's just sick. And it has been for a long time.

So here's the question: if someone you loved was very ill and possibly dying, would you just keep giving them the same boring 'ol medicine year after year? No, you'd try everything: experimental drugs, holistic medicine, and even The Secret. Off-Broadway isn't dead. It just needs new medicine.

And as a Producer, you are the pharmaceutical company.

February 07, 2008

<u>**"Tawk amongst yourselves. I'll give you a topic."**</u>

Here's a quickie <u>Coffee Talk</u> question for you:

Why is it that in popular music the singer of the song is referred to as the author of the song?

For example, why is it on *American Idol* (not that I'm watching it or anything) you hear contestants say, "I'm going to sing 'Oops, I Did It Again' by Britney Spears."

You never hear someone say, "I'm going to sing 'Oops, I Did It Again' by <u>Max Martin</u>.

Can you imagine if it was that way in the theatre?

"Hi , Simon, Randy and Paula. I'm going to sing 'This Is The Moment' by Robert Cuccioli."

Something tells me that Frank Wildhorn, who has been on both sides of this discussion ('Where Do Broken Hearts Go' by Whitney Houston) might have a problem with this.

Or what about, "Hi snotty British guy, big guy no one knows, and ex-80s star on too much prescription medication. I'm going to sing "Pretty Women" by Johnny Depp and Alan Rickman."

Sacrilege to our <u>Shakespeare</u>!

Our Authors get more respect here. Because they deserve it.

And frankly, Max Martin deserves it too. With all due respect to those battling mental craziness and psycho-pseudo managers (and also on too much prescription medication), he is more talented than the "artist" he helped create.

Ooooh, here is another question! Why are the performers called artists and the scribes called writers? Aren't the writers artists too?

There you go. As Ms. Myers would say . . . "Discuss."

Oh, and why are Simon's teeth so white? Every time he smiles I feel like that girl in Poltergeist and I want to start walking towards them! (Ok, I am watching - but this is my first season!)

February 08, 2008

He's just not that into you.

When I recommended <u>books</u>, I forgot one: the famous <u>dating manual</u> for "20-plus career women". The theory behind the book is simple. Someone doesn't call? He's just not that into you. Someone keeps telling you they are busy? Just not that into you. Someone dating 17 other people of different sexes? JNTIU. This is an important lesson for 20-plus producers as well.

Want an investor to come to a reading and they aren't responding to your postcards, emails and phone calls? Want an actor to do your show and they blow off the audition? Want the rights to a book and the agent never calls you back? Sorry, but they are all just not that interested.

So what do you do? Do you give up? That sounds very anti-Ken, right?

You don't have to give up, but you do have to invest your time and emotion wisely. Why spend hours going after the same investor who isn't responding when you can use the time to find others that might. Why want an actor who disrespects your project by blowing off the audition? Do you think his attitude will get better when you are in rehearsals? Why start a negotiation with an agent if they've already made you feel like a call from them is a call from above? They'll get you to give away the store without even trying.

There will always be other investors, other actors, other projects, and yes other men (and women) that WILL be into you.

I know, you think that this investor, actor or project is "the one", right? Fine. You can still be open to a relationship with them, as long as you're OK if that relationship never materializes. And most importantly, don't let the fantasy of a future relationship slow you down.

For example: I have the rights to *Somewhere In Time*. What you don't know is that they were denied to me the first time I asked. After some post-rejection healing, I let go and pursued other things. But once a year, in January, I sent the author a "Happy New Year" fax with an update on what I was doing. It took five minutes to write, once a year. No commitment and no expectations.

Four years later, and with a few shows under my belt, he called me.

When I answered the phone, I felt like a fourteen year old girl who had been asked to the Prom . . . by Zac Efron.

Finally, he was into me. And it took me moving on for it to happen.

February 09, 2008

Numbers are hot.

So here's a few to spice up your weekend:

Let's look at Tony Award nominees and winners of the two big categories, Best Musical and Best Play, and their corresponding reviews in the New York Times over the last 11 seasons (since 1997).

BEST MUSICAL NOMINEES		BEST PLAY NOMINEES	
Positive Reviews	40%	Positive Reviews	68%
Mixed Reviews	30%	Mixed Reviews	16%
Negative Reviews	30%	Negative Reviews	16%

BEST MUSICAL WINNERS		BEST PLAY WINNERS	
Positive Reviews	64%	Positive Reviews	82%
Mixed Reviews	18%	Mixed Reviews	18%
Negative Reviews	18%	Negative Reviews	0%

What does all this mean? Does the New York Times favor plays? Are Tony voters voting with The Times or because of The Times? Do reviews not matter for musicals looking to be nominated for a trophy, or is it just that the lower numbers of new musicals means easier nominations?

What does it mean?

That's for you to decide.

Any accountant, comptroller or high school kid with a pirated copy of Excel can deliver you a set of good looking numbers.

It's a Producer's job to figure out what they mean. And when you do, it's not hot. It's beau-tastic.

(Oh, and in case you are wondering (and you should be, because data is only as good as its source), we used the Variety Pro/Con/Mixed meter to determine the status of the reviews.)

February 10, 2008

Favorite Quotes: Volume II

"If they don't let you in the front door, go down the chimney." - James L. Nederlander

Persistence is the key to making it in any industry. But Jimmy Jr. is right. You can't just keep pounding on the door waiting for someone to open it. Even if they did finally open it, can you imagine how annoyed they would be?

There's always another way in. Find it.

February 11, 2008

The Lean Forward Factor

I saw *Farnsworth* on Saturday; a good play made into an even better one because of a little Kenism I like to call, 'The Lean Forward Factor.'

Like most things that are a significant part of our adult lives, good or bad, the Lean Forward Factor is something I learned as a kid.

One of my first experiences with the LFF was when I saw the original *Texas Chainsaw Massacre*. I was already scared to see it, but then, right when the movie started, a simple text teaser crawled across the screen explaining that what we were about to see was based on a true story. Gulp! An actual Leatherface? Holy crap. What did I do besides almost pee in my PJs? I *leaned forward*. All of a sudden I was really scared . . . and really <u>involved</u>.

My other childhood LFF experience that would forever change my view of entertainment? *The Littles*. *The Littles* were a series of kids' books about people living in the walls. They had mice tails and were so small they used sewing spools for tables and were always afraid the cat was going to eat them.

When I got to the end of one of the books, I noticed a note from the author buried on the last page. It said that only he and the illustrator knew the true whereabouts of The Littles, and he had been sworn to secrecy. Actual little people living in the walls? What did I do? I *leaned forward*. And I wouldn't let my cat inside the house for 3 days.

Both of these are classic examples of LFF. By using a tease of truth, the authors got me much more involved.

Your audience will always be more affected by your work if they think it could affect them personally, or in the case of *Farnsworth*, if it already has affected them personally (it's hard not to ahh, when you hear how NBC was formed, or laugh when a character makes a comment about how no one would dirty their living room with an ugly television set).

True crime novels, movies like *JFK*, musicals like *Ragtime*, reality television, Shakespeare and even Santa Claus all use LFF to help draw you in and heighten your experience.

How do you use it?

(Ironically, both *Chainsaw* and *The Littles* weren't even being honest . . . but did it matter? I still get freaked out by Leatherface. And I don't have a cat.)

February 12, 2008

A Risky Business Tom Cruise would be proud of.

You've heard me talk about the importance of a title.

You've heard me talk about how today's audience enjoys shorter entertainment.

And then along comes a play that is almost 3.5 hours long, has no stars, has a title no one can understand or pronounce . . . and will probably be the most profitable non-star driven play of the last several years and win the Pulitzer.

Look at it on paper, and producing *August* looks like a very risky venture. Props to Producer Jeffrey Richards for taking the chance. Inside sources tell me that he agreed to do it after a read and a recommendation. He probably could have waited to see the regional production, but instead, he just jumped on board.

He read it. He liked it. And he also knew it had inherent marketing problems.

But, to quote one of my favorite 80s movies, *Risky Business* . . .

"Sometimes you just gotta say . . . "What the f***." "What the f***" gives you freedom. Freedom brings opportunity. Opportunity makes your future."

Does the success of *August* mean that my previous blogs were wrong? No. Would August be easier to sell under a different title? Yes. Would it be easier to sell if it was shorter? Yes.

Maybe it would have made even *more* money.

But does recouping 200% compared to 175% really matter when you have to make that much of a compromise?

This is the challenge of the commercial producer: what's the right mixture of art and commerce? Obviously Jeffrey believed without a doubt that his product was so good that it didn't need the perfect canned marketing strategy. He believed it could survive a bad title and a length that makes *Les Miz* look like a *Family Guy* episode.

He was right. Remarkable product always proves the smartest marketers wrong. That's why it's the first <u>P</u>.

If he didn't believe that it was a home run, maybe he would have begged for a different title or a shorter length to prevent those overtime bills. After all, there is a big difference between 75% recouped and 100% recouped, right?

But nope, he believed in the product and in the marketplace for that product.

So here's the question:

If *August: Osage County* landed on your desk instead of Mr. Richards', would you have produced it?

February 13, 2008

<u>Favorite Quotes: Volume III</u>

"There are potentially more talented writers and directors than I working in shoe stores and Burger Kings across the nation; the difference is I was willing to put in the nine years of effort and they weren't."
     - 3 time Academy Award nominee, <u>Frank Darabont</u>

This blog should be categorized under REALLY favorite quotes, because the quote is such a good one.

How many people do you know that say, "I've got this great idea," and nothing ever happens with it.

How many people do you know that criticize other's people's work, always saying how they could do better . . . but they never do.

I bet you know lots of people like this. I bet, at times, you're even one of them.

I know I am.

It's hard not to be one of those people, because it's so much easier to sit back, watch an episode of *American Idol*, and let someone else do the hard (and scary) stuff.

So what's the secret to becoming more like Frank?

Sorry, no over-priced pharmaceutical can help. No Tony Robbins-style self help book is gonna do it either.

You just have to keep promises to yourself. You keep them to your boss, right? You keep them to your husband or wife, right? Why, because you "have to"? Why not keep them to yourself for the same reason.

The next time you say you're going to do something, shut off the *American Idol and* start. There's always TiVo. You can always watch it later. When you finish.

Ironically, *Idol* started as just an idea once. A pretty simple one, actually. And I'd bet a bunch of other people in shoe stores and Burger Kings had the same one (Ooooooh, I bet they are bitter now!).

I'd keep writing now, but I have to go. I promised a good buddy of mine that I'd do something for him.

To read the article that Frank wrote that contained the above quote, click <u>here</u>.

February 14, 2008

I'm gonna have people start calling me Kenneth . . .

Only so there's the slight chance they'll confuse me with this Kenneth . . .

The story for Kenneth Cole started four years ago when savvy designer Kenneth Cole had a bright idea. After lining up factories, and going to Europe to design a collection of shoes, his idea was to borrow a 40 ft truck and park it in midtown Manhattan during the weekend of the big Shoe Show and sell out the back of the trailer. At the time, a shoe company had two options. One was get a room at the Hilton and become 1 of about 1100 shoes companies selling their goods. Kenneth Cole did not feel like it provided the identity or image he felt necessary for a new company, plus it cost a lot more money than he had to spend. The other way was to do what big companies were doing and get a fancy showroom in the Midtown Manhattan area not too far from the Hilton. This was even more expensive. So the idea of selling out of a truck made sense to him.

He called a friend in the trucking business and asked to borrow one of his trucks to park in Midtown Manhattan. He said sure, but good luck getting permission. Kenneth Cole then went to the Mayor's office and asked how one gets permission to park a 40 foot trailer truck in Midtown Manhattan. The Major said one doesn't. The only people the city gives parking permits to are production companies shooting full length motion pictures and utility companies like Con Ed or AT&T. So that day all the company letterhead was changed from Kenneth Cole, Inc. to Kenneth Cole Productions, Inc. and the next day they applied for a permit to shoot a full length film entitled "The Birth of a Shoe Company."

With Kenneth Cole Productions painted on the side of the truck, they parked at 1370 6th Avenue, across from the New York Hilton, the day of shoe show. They opened for business with a fully furnished 40 ft trailer, a director, models as actresses, and two of New York's finest, compliments of Mayor Koch, as our doormen. Kenneth Cole sold 40 thousand pairs of shoes in two and a half days (the entire available production) and we were off and running.

Ever since then, the company has grown from a shoe company to a global multi line entity making not just shoes, but also handbags, apparel and accessories. Kenneth Cole product can be seen worn by celebrities such as Jessica Alba, Carrie Underwood, Charlize Theron, and much, much more. (www.designerathletic.com)

Wow. Now that's how you kick off a company, Kenny.

And doesn't it just make you want to kick yourself? Because the idea seems so simple, so obvious, so right for a fashion company.

It's the kind of idea that just makes *cents*.

For more on Ken's story, read here.

Oh and here's a question . . . how many people do you think laughed at Ken when he told them about this idea?

You know what I think? Explorers and pioneers, no matter what industry you're in, whether it's shoes or show business, are like comedians.

When people laugh at you . . . you're on to something.

February 15, 2008

Why investing in the theater is better than investing in the stock market.

Whenever you are selling anything . . . from tickets, to why a star should sign on to your show, to a vacuum, you have to remember that you're never selling IN a vacuum.

There is always something that your "consumer" could buy instead. They could always get tickets to another show (or, God forbid, a movie). The star could always sign on to another show (or, God forbid, a movie). And they could always get a Swiffer (or, God forbid, they could just leave their apartment a mess and *go* to the movies.)

You not only have to sell why your product is worth whatever price they are paying, you also have to sell why your product is better than the other products that are out there.

For example, when raising money, one of the common questions that I always have to be ready for (and one that you should be ready for when you start raising money) is, "Why should I throw money into such a high risk venture when I could throw it in the stock market instead?"

Hmmm, good question, right? Actually it's a great question.

There are of course a bunch of reasons why someone would invest in the theater as opposed to the market: opening night tickets, high risk but big upside potential, house seats, billing, potential tax write off, or just because they believe in you.

But most of those are indirect comparisons. When you're selling stuff, you need to find direct comparisons between the competition, like . . .

Yes, investing in the market is safer, without a doubt. And you should encourage your investors to do so, to create the most diversified portfolio possible.

But when you buy a stock, you not only have to know when to buy . . . you also have to know when to sell. Stocks go up, but they also come down. You could invest in a blue chip a year ago that everyone was recommending and a year later it could post almost a 10 billion dollar loss. And no matter how much your stock went up over the last year, if you didn't get out in time, you lose. You may have made a smart decision a year ago, but if you're not an expert market watcher, then you could end up with a tax write-off anyway.

Here's the thing about shows . . . once they get over that humungo hurdle and actually recoup, they never go the other direction. Once you've got a winner, you've got a winner, and your gains only increase. Sure, the gains may be small, or they may slow down when the Broadway show closes and when your show is only being done in high schools, but you never have to worry about selling. Returns diminish, but never reverse (barring some sort of extreme circumstance like litigation).

When you buy a stock, you have to be smart twice. When you buy Broadway, the pressure is on only once.

Ok, that's not true. You also have to figure out what to wear to the opening night party. (And there's another reason why people invest in the theater instead of the market - you don't see Citigroup throwing parties for investors when they buy 100 shares, do you?)

Would the traders at Goldman Sachs punch holes in the above theory and find direct comparisons of their own to prove why investing in the market is better than a musical? Probably.

That's just as much their job as it is yours. Then again, they were also recommending Citigroup last year.

So don't sell in a vacuum (insert your own Davenport-style "sucking" reference here).

February 17, 2008

It's not the size of your lever.

A little Pumbaa told me an interesting tid-bit recently:

During the first week of performances of the national tour of *The Lion King* in each city, the local ABC affiliate does a half-hour television special on the arrival of the show, featuring interviews with cast members, a behind the scenes look at the costumes and scenery, etc. It's a half-hour commercial that doesn't look like a commercial, because it "teaches" the audience about the show in a news format.

How come everyone doesn't do this?

Well, maybe it's because not every Producer owns a television network.

Yep, in case you didn't know, Disney owns ABC.

Ahh, the wonderful world of leverage.

Don't get depressed because you think you'll never have a list of subsidiaries longer than the lines at Space Mountain.

There are all sorts of levers out there of various shapes and sizes: restaurants, limo companies, charities, dentists, etc. Anywhere that has a consumer base similar to yours.

Your job, find a partner that can benefit from promoting you and vice-versa.

You'll find it much more economical, and the promotion will actually mean more to the consumer, because it's comes from a vendor that already has their trust (like a news station).

So until you own a television network, find a way to exploit the levers that you do have or go out and find a few.

Because leverage is supercalifragilisticexpialidocious.

February 18, 2008

I've got the mouse on my mind.

I was looking at a bunch of different Broadway budgets recently and I wanted to compare the budgeted breakevens with what the market was currently <u>bearing</u>.

I wanted to see what shows were grossing over $700k, even in the tourist-free winter months, so I flipped open my Variety and here's what I found:

Broadway Grosses w/e 02/10/2008

Wicked	$1,310,705
Jersey Boys	$1,127,362
The Lion King	$962,925
The Little Mermaid	$889,942
Mary Poppins	$731,687

What's interesting about this?

The mouse has 3 of the 5 shows above $700k.

And this list looks very similar if you look at the week before. And the week before that. AND the week before that.

Leverage works. So well, in fact, that it's a little scary.

You know what else is interesting?

Of these five musical behemoths, only 2 got good reviews from the New York Times.

February 19, 2008

I'm not the only bloggin' Producer.

For a few weeks, *Chicago* Producer and stunt-caster extraordinaire Barry Weissler was blogging on Yahoo Broadway. Unfortunately, they seemed to have removed it (let's start a rumor that Barry insisted that it be taken down, shall we?).

It was pretty neat - Barry talked about how he started off doing children's theater with Robert De Niro, he talked about his relationship with Ben Brantley and more.

Barry is one of the best. During the decade of corporate producing on Broadway (the mid/late 90s), Barry and Fran were one of the only Mom & Pop organizations consistently doing it, and making money. What they've done with *Chicago* is nothing short of a producing miracle.

So how do they do it? And what can we learn from it?

If you look at their resume, only four of the nineteen shows they are credited with producing weren't revivals. One of those four shows was a jukebox musical, and another was *Falsettos*, which was the juxtaposition of two previously existing works, which leaves only two original pieces.

The Weisslers have chosen to mitigate their risk by making sure they start with material already accepted by the public and build an exciting production around it.

Look at their first few shows . . . you can't start with a better playwright than Bill himself.

Not the most adventuresome model, but it sure has gotten them one killer apartment (Yahoo didn't take down the best part of the blog: the video).

February 20, 2008

Favorite Quotes: Volume IV

"Ambition wins over genius 99 percent of the time. Sooner or later, the other guy is going to have to eat, drink, go to the bathroom, get laid, or take a vacation, and that's when I catch him."
                    - Jay Leno

Jay doesn't think he's that smart. Ironic, because I think it takes a genius to say what he did and to do what he has done.

Does what he says work? Well, when both he and Letterman went back to work *without* writers, he came out on top. In fact, when the ratings came out, NBC Late Night Programming Chief Rick Ludwin said, "The audience made the decision of which of the two hosts they wanted to watch . . . They made the decision 13 years ago."

Boo-ya!

I get called a workaholic a lot. I hate that word, because I don't think it's work when you love what you do. But hey, if Jay is a workaholic, then by all means folks, slur away, because that's some nice company and maybe Jay can take me for a ride in one of his 180 cars at the workaholic convention.

Want to read more about Leno's work ethic and how much he loves what he does . . . so much in fact that he acknowledges that it was ok that he trumped Letterman and got paid less? Click here.

February 21, 2008

This just in . . . theater tickets are expensive.

Ok, you knew that already.

But here's something you may not have known . . . They've *always* been expensive.

Hal Prince once gave a speech where he confirmed my theory that people have been complaining about theater prices since *The Black Crook* opened.

Yet one of the most common complaints I still hear at meetings regarding the problems of Broadway and the theater in general is that tickets are too expensive and if we could only fix that, the theater would be restored to its past glory!

Sorry, not gonna happen.

As Hal insinuated, it's time we acknowledge that theater tickets are expensive and get over it, because it's not gonna change.

Theater tickets are a high priced commodity. They are a luxury good. But are they *too* expensive?

Let's compare Broadway theater tickets to other live entertainment options:

- A recent scan of the web found me a pair of Bon Jovi tickets for a top price of $129.50 in *Wisconsin* (something tells me people in Milwaukee may earn less than people in New York City so $129.50 might feel like a heck of a lot more to them).

- The Yankees offer a bunch of different ticket options, including SEVEN price levels at $100 or higher (up to $400).

- Top price for Ka in Las Vegas? $169.50.

- Disney World? $71.

Our ticket prices are not out of line. They are even cheap by some comparisons (something tells me those $400 Yankees tickets will go faster than premiums to *A Catered Affair*). And most Producers (as they should) have a small allocation of much lower priced seats to offer those who can't afford the high priced options (lotteries, rush, etc.)

People will pay the $125, $250 or sometimes even $500 for the right ticket to the right show, which demonstrates that people are not price resistant.

They are *value* resistant.

We need to stop worrying about how to decrease prices and start worrying about how to increase value.

Your customers *will* pay top dollar plus for an experience that they believe is worth it. Your job is to make the value of your ticket seem even higher than the price your customer is paying so it seems like they got a bargain.

Oh and to all the people that say we need to cut the price of the ticket to save the American theater, I point to all of the shows that have discounted tickets down to the $20s and $30s to "save their show" only to still see them close (there is no value in a crappy show).

And, vice-versa, every time I've raised prices on a Broadway or Off-Broadway show, attendance never drops.

The day of the $1,000 theater ticket will be here some day, and as depressing as that sounds, don't worry. It'll still be less than what a lot of people pay for tickets to the Super Bowl or The Kentucky Derby.

February 22, 2008

<u>Guess where I am?</u>

Which hotel do you think I was in when I took this <u>picture</u> of the guest services aka concierge counter?

Ok, it's not a hotel.

So which casino do you think I was in?

Sorry, wrong again.

I wasn't at a hotel or a casino.

I was at a movie theater.

Once again, we got <u>beat</u>.

Wouldn't it be great if theaters had concierges? (I would actually argue that the theater-going crowd is probably more likely to expect and utilize such services.)

A theater concierge could get a limo for you, a dinner reservation, or . . . wait for it . . . build up enough trust with the client in order to recommend and sell tickets to other shows in the same complex or theater chain! :-)

They could do everything that a traditional concierge could do, and through commissions, tips, etc., could probably pay for itself with little or no financial strain on the venue. At the same time, the venue would create a trusting relationship with their audience that would turn into loyalty and additional business (and a great mailing list). At the very least it would create a remarkable experience that would get talked about.

Then again, maybe they wouldn't do anything except let people know where the bathrooms are. But that's enough for me. Hotels, casinos, and other luxury service providers are there to take care of their customers not just when they need them, but IF they need them. And we should be too.

It's this type of <u>value</u> that keeps people coming back *and* paying the big bucks.

Let's not get beat by the movies again, Ok? They only charge $11.75. That's when we really start to look bad.

February 23, 2008

This just in . . . theater tickets are cheap. :-)

I wanted to remind everyone that starting this Monday, February 25th and through Sunday, March 9th, The Off-Broadway Brainstormers are sponsoring the 3rd "20at20" campaign.

During <u>20at20</u>, you can see over 20 of the best Off-Broadway shows (including my three) for only $20.

The only catch is that the tickets are only available 20 minutes before curtain.

I bet some of you might be surprised to hear that I'm the chairman of this committee after my "theater tickets are expensive" post.

20at20 is a perfect example of the type of program that demonstrates that there are lower entry points for seeing theater that make it accessible to all, despite our "rep" for high prices.

But frankly, Off-Broadway shows can't survive on $20 tickets. So why else would we do it?

The challenge and ultimate success of programs like this is not selling the $20 tickets. That should be easy.

The challenge and **goal** is to take the thousands of $20 ticket buyers over the next two weeks, and convert them to higher price ticket buyers throughout the rest of the year that will increase the overall growth of our industry.

20at20 is the Off-Broadway version of a pharmaceutical company giving a doctor samples of a new cholesterol drug, or a soft-drink company giving away beverages on the street, or Gillette sending me a Mach 3 razor (with only 1 blade) for free.

It's what Captain Andy does in *Show Boat*. He gives away just a "sample" of his show on the street and then watches the audience file in. Not too much and not too little.

How do you sample?

Oh, and take these 2 weeks to see an Off-Broadway show, even if it's not one of mine. Visit www.20at20.com to get the full list of shows and additional information on the program.

And while you're there, sign up to get email updates on the program and other offers . . . and to see just how we try to convert *you* to a higher price ticket throughout the year. ;-)

P.S. I've been shaving with a Gillette razor ever since that box with the Mach 3 arrived at my door 7 years ago.

February 24, 2008

My favorite game is "I'm The Producer!" Wanna play?

Back when I watched football more regularly, they had a feature called *You Make The Call*! They showed a play from an actual game and then you got to play referee, deciding things like if Joe Montana's pass was intentional grounding or not (can you tell how long it's been since I've watched football regularly?).

After a commercial, they'd reveal what the correct call was.

(Note to the all those NFL executives reading this blog - bring this feature back. The surge of interest in reality television and interactive entertainment makes it a natural for today's audiences.)

I like to play this game with Producing! Ready? Here's the "play" . . .

There has been a tremendous amount of excitement and buzz around the latest revival of The Scottish Play at BAM. Of course, talks to moving Mac-You-Know-What to Broadway have been heard all over Joe Allen's.

This production seems to have the two things that are necessary for a revival: a star and a new interpretation. And this one has a bonus - a "you must see this performance" review from Ben Brantley!

So, here's where the game begins:

You're the Producer. You get a call from Mr. Schoenfeld of the Shuberts who says, "Kid, I put my grudge with that bald British guy from Star Trek behind me. I'm giving you the theater with my name on it. But I need to know if you want it right now or I'm going to give it to the touring company of *Dora The Explorer*, ok? That little Dora and her monkey make me laugh. Plus that show grosses more in merchandise per week than *Journey's End* grossed during its entire run. The catch is that Dora wants the theater for a year, so you have to guarantee me a year. Do you want it, or does my theater turn into Crocodile Lake?"

Gulp. What do you do?

The first thing you do is ask Mr. Schoenfeld for some time to make a decision. Business is not your final Calculus exam. Business *is* an open book test. You need some time to take a look at research. If anyone ever tells me that I have to make a decision right there on the spot, I walk away. Period.

Mr. Schoenfeld gives you fifteen minutes.

Better, but no time to make a budget.   And considering he does have another offer, you can't begrudge him wanting to move quickly.

So what would your plan be? Take the theater and just see what happens?

Oh no, you're too smart for that. Let's look at the last twenty years of *commercial* theater productions of Shakespeare.

Show	Year	Star	Performances
Julius Caesar	2005	Denzel Washington	112
Macbeth	2000	Kelsey Grammer	21
A Midsummer's . . .	1996	None	78
The Tempest	1995	Patrick Stewart	95
Hamlet	1995	Ralph Fiennes	110
Merchant of Venice	1989	Dustin Hoffman	103
Macbeth	1988	Christopher Plummer	85

(Not as many as you thought for 20 years, right? I was surprised too.)

Ok, what have we learned? (Besides the obvious fact that formatting tables in blogging software blows?)

- Commercial Shakespeare productions have slowed in the last decade.
- If you're gonna do Shakespeare, have a star.
- Macbeth is a popular title to revive.

- Average length of run is 86.29 performances or 10.79 weeks (8 shows/week)

And there's your answer. While certainly the length of the runs of the majority of these shows were based on the star's availability (and the lack of it), there is no data to suggest that you could sustain a long run of a commercial Shakespearean production (if you had more time, you'd analyze all of the grosses of these productions, especially the trends at the end of the runs).

You'd call Mr. S. back, and tell him that you can't take it for a year. You'd show him the data (numbers are the best negotiators) and tell him your plan is for a 12 week limited run with a hope of an extension, but that's it. He'd be overwhelmed by your market savvy and give you the theater. Then you'd call your GM and figure out how to recoup in 6-8 weeks.

Did we win the game? Did we make the right call?

Unfortunately, there's no referee with a rule book to tell us if we're right. But there is recoupment, and you just gave yourselves a lot better odds at getting there by doing even the quickest bit of research.

If you hadn't done your homework you might have done a standard play budget that recouped in 6 months to a year and you'd be wishing you were at the bottom of Crocodile Lake when your investors came looking for you.

Play this game often. Every time you hear buzz about a show, think about how you'd get it to the next level. Where you'd produce it. If you'd produce it. Then keep a list of these notes.

The fun is checking back in on those shows a year later to see how you did.

February 25, 2008

Another pricing post. Don't "cry" - this one is only $54!

I couldn't help but continue with my pricing motif when I saw the _Cry Baby_ marquis this weekend advertising "All Tickets for Previews Only $54!" (The show is set in 1954. Get it? 1954. $54.)

The hopeful Producers of _Hairspray II_ are betting that this reduced price (about the same as what the price _would have been_ at the TKTS booth) will pull in more of an audience during the ever important early weeks, when a show's expenses are high and grosses are low.

But will it work?

By slashing their prices across the board, they have eliminated the consumer's option for choice, which breaks my Kardinal Kenism:

<u>There is always someone who wants to fly first class.</u>

First class may seem out of reach for most of us, and a full price ticket might seem too expensive for an unproven show in previews for most of us as well, but data shows there is always someone who will buy it, no matter what the price is. They just want "the best." *Dance of the Vampires, Moose Murders, Carrie* . . . all of the biggest flops in history had full price ticket buyers during previews. Stupid ones, but still. My opinion? Just take the money.

The other problem with across the board pricing strategy is that your TKTS price is proportionally adjusted. So, the Producers of *Cry Baby* aren't only losing income from the potential $115 ticket buyer who is now paying $54, but they're also losing money from the people who would have paid $57.50 at the booth (50% of $115) who are now going to pay $27 (and remember - at the TKTS booth, you don't see the actual prices display . . . only 25%, 35% or 50% off, so the customer thinks they are all the same).

The Producers of *Baby* are smart people. They understand the above theory. But obviously they believe two things:

- They believe they are going to sell approximately 2x the number of tickets from this promotion than they would have sold using traditional pricing. Even if they sell the same, they will have double the butts in the seats. And more bodies = more word of mouth.

- The public discount will allow them to spend less on advertising so they can avoid certain email blasts, direct mail, etc. which reduces their overall expenses.

Time and Variety will tell how this theory works, but if I were playing my favorite game, I would have made a different call.

I would have priced it more traditionally, based on my first class rule above, and because I don't believe that the price is that remarkable of a call to action.

Then I would price the entire house for just the first preview at $19.54.

That's a price worth talking about. And it would have gotten the most people in to the see the show early, so they would hopefully stop talking about price.

And start talking about the show.

February 26, 2008

I Google so much I'm afraid I'll go blind.

The other day, I was doing some research of popular plays so I opened up Firefox and typed in "Best Plays."

Makes sense, right?

Well, here are the results. Only 6 of the 10 results on page 1 were about dramatic plays. The rest were about the best *sports* plays.

Remember, just because something makes perfect sense in your world, doesn't mean it makes sense in everyone else's.

February 27, 2008

Come on, everybody does it . . .

. . . And you know you do too.

When you're all alone, and no one is watching . . . you Google you.

And no matter what your parents may have told you, Googling yourself is a good thing.

This sort of behavior, also referred to as "ego-surfing," used to be reserved exclusively for the obsessive actor, who got cheap thrills from seeing their name pop up multiple times.

However, in the age of the online consumer review, when blogs are bling and user generated content is king, it's essential that you Google yourself. And your show, your theatre company, your product, or anything and everything that your audience or customers may talk about online.

It's the cheapest focus group you can find.

When you find bad things, and you will, try and look at them objectively. Yes, take into account the source, the language, etc. but see if there's anything to learn from the worst of the worst. And if you see several people saying the same thing . . . take heed. Maybe you can make an adjustment that can prevent future online outbursts.

Same with the good stuff! Don't just pat yourself on the back. Examine exactly what people enjoy. Notice a trend? Exploit it! Advertise it, incorporate into copy, etc. There's as much to learn from the good as from the bad.

And don't stop there.

You know what's great about the web? It's a two way super-highway.

If someone wrote about your show and didn't have a good time (seats were uncomfortable, show wasn't what they thought it was going to be), reach out to them. Apologize. Offer to somehow make it right. Get them tickets to another show. People who purge themselves online usually don't stop there. They do it with friends, family and so on. You can try and stop the vile word of mouth by just saying you're sorry, and seeing if there's something you can do. Just hearing from you may shock them speechless.

And if someone said something nice? Thank them! Positive affirmation is the best way to keep people doing what you want them to do. Drop them a personal note. You'd be amazed at the kudos you'll get for dropping a fan of your show an email that comes "directly from the producer." Cost to you? 30 seconds. And now they have another reason to talk about your show.

I like to do a few things when I find a good post or blog about one of my shows. I send an email as mentioned above, then I ask for their address so I can send them a gift (an autographed program, a sample CD, etc.). Not only have I given them some great positive reinforcement to continue doing their "good work" . . . but I've also gotten their actual address in case I want to market my next show to them

Think about someone talking about you online like a call to your customer service department. Don't be like a company that outsources its customer service to a foreign country. Surprise your customer. Pick up the phone, listen, and talk back . . . in English.

KEN'S TIP O' THE DAY: Google introduced an incredible service a few years ago that leaves the Googling to them. Rather than have to remember to search for yourself or your show every day, you can set up a Google alert on whatever keyword you want. Google will email you whenever that word appears on the web. I have one for all of my shows and some of my competitors. You should too. Set them up here.

February 28, 2008

<u>John Grisham is rich and famous.</u>

But that's not why he started writing.

<u>John Grisham</u> wrote his <u>first novel</u> with no dreams of making $9 million a year, or of selling 235 million copies of his books worldwide, or of having six baseball fields on his property.

John Grisham wrote his first novel why? So he could say he wrote a novel. That's all. He just wanted to be able to point to a stack of white paper on his desk and say, "Look! I wrote a novel." He ran across a subject that he felt needed to be written, so he wrote it, even though he had never written before.

He wrote it by getting up at 5 AM every morning for three years, while he was working 60 - 80 hours a week as a state representative.

"When he first started writing, Grisham says, he had 'these little rituals that were silly and brutal but very important. The alarm clock would go off at 5, and I'd jump in the shower. My office was 5 minutes away. And I had to be at my desk, at my office, with the first cup of coffee, a legal pad and write the first word at 5:30, five days a week.' His goal: to write a page every day." (CNN.com)

"Anybody can write a page a day. If you sit down and write a page a day, do you know what you'll have 365 days later? You'll have a novel!" (Kennesaw.edu)

When he finished that novel, two things happened:

1. He was rejected by 15 publishers.

2. He started writing *The Firm* the very next day. The movie rights sold before he even found a publisher, and he was on his way.

And now, after all of the success, he still squeezes out a novel a year.

Doing something, anything, to "be famous" or to "be rich" is fine, but it's not art. There are a zillion ways to <u>"be famous"</u> or <u>"be rich"</u>, and they're a lot easier than what we do.

Write, act, produce, design because you *have* to do it, and for no other reason. If you're diligent and harder on yourself than any boss could ever be, all the other stuff will come.

And when it does, you'll still want to keep doing it, just like John. Even if you have 12 baseball fields on your property.

If it doesn't come? Well, who cares? Something tells me John Grisham would still be getting up at 5 AM every morning to write, even if he never sold a single copy of his stack of white paper.

The only difference is by now he'd be able to say, "Look! I wrote 21 novels."

Anyone out there know what John Grisham and Hal Prince have in common? Free $25 iTunes gift card to the first "commenter" that comes up with what I'm looking for.

And hey, no "gheating". I know you guys so well.

February 29, 2008

Got a craving for Stew?

I saw *Passing Strange* on Wednesday night.

If you like <u>Stew</u>, and you want to see him in *concert*, then you will love this show.

You should also see this show if you think only commercial stuff that appeals to the masses gets produced on Broadway.

Because it's not true.

Non-commercial stuff gets produced all the time (and thank God we have "Patron of the Arts" Producers like the ones above the title on *Passing Strange* that are in a position to push our manila envelope).

The non-commercial stuff usually just doesn't run or recoup.

Not that there's anything wrong with that, as long as you and your investors know why you're doing what you're doing.

Establish expectations early. Then if you exceed them and actually return money, it'll be like finding a $20 bill in you pocket after doing the laundry.

There are zillions of reasons to produce shows that are exceptionally high risk and "non-commercial": commitment to the arts, possible Tony Awards, and so on.

My favorite reason for doing something that may not be the next *Mamma-Mia* is to develop and foster relationships with the creatives, something I urge all young Producers to do.

Produce the plays of the passionate people around you. Your peers are the playwrights of tomorrow, even if their plays of today may not be taking home Pulitzers. But what about the one they haven't even thought of yet?

And here's a wonderful fact about human nature: reciprocity works. Do something for someone today, and they'll be inclined to do something for you tomorrow, especially if you took a risk when no one else would . . . and lost.

My favorite example of this concept is the birth of one of the youngest producing houses on Broadway in the last few decades: The Araca Group.

One of Araca's first plays was called *Skyscraper.* Cost them $30k and they lost it.

However, It was also the first play by David Auburn.

When David Auburn was at the Fringe Festival being wowed by a small musical, guess who he called first, *before the show was even over!*

"David called me at intermission and said, 'You must come and see this show,'" Michael Rego recalled. So they did. Within months, they had secured the rights to *Urinetown* . . . " - New York Times

Careers begin, like life, with relationships. It's no coincidence that the *Altar Boyz* creative team consists of a guy I shared a room with in summer stock, a guy I shared a show with at the former Ford Center, and two guys I shared a tour with in 2000.

I got lucky. My first one paid off. The people behind *Passing Strange* most likely won't be so lucky.

But that's ok. They know why they're doing it. And since one of the lead Producers is the owner of the theater, they have a little more control over one of Broadway's biggest weekly expenses: rent.

Read the full story about the birth of Araca here. Click below to see my favorite example of producing a show for a relationship in the last decade here. But before you do . . . guess what the show was.

Click here as you think. Click here for the results

BREAKING NEWS: I wrote this blog last night, before Isherwood's rave in the Times this morning. It will be interesting to see if this review has an effect on the show's financial and commercial viability. Anyone want to take any bets?

MARCH 2008

March 03, 2008

How is John Grisham like Hal Prince? Winner announced!

Here's what I was looking for:

And Hal is so unlike anybody I know from my generation. The day
after he opens a show, he has a production meeting for the next one.
The day after I open a show, I'm ready for a rest home.
   - James Lapine

For both Hal and John, It's not about basking in the glory of their last success,
and it's not about wallowing in a failure (and they've had both).   It's about the
work. And doing more and more of it.

Knowing human nature as they do, they both set up this simple ritual to keep
them focused on the work.

What simple rituals can you establish to keep you focused on what you want
to accomplish?

Congratulations to Broadway Mouth, who'll soon find a $25 iTunes gift
certificate in his inbox.

A special shout out to Gonzalo Guitart for discovering the Schumacher
connection. Deep!

While I was researching this post, I found a great interview with Hal where he
discusses investor expectations, the subject of my last post.

Hal Prince did a number of incredibly daring and artistic productions in his day
that all . . . well . . . flopped.

Read about how he raised money for those shows here.

(FYI, this link goes to the middle of the interview. After you read this page,
start at the beginning. No one did it better than Hal.)

March 04, 2008

Me? Really? Are you sure?

Every other day I tell someone how I believe Broadway is 10 years behind every other industry out there. And that if we just tried to take some basic lessons from the traditional business world, perhaps we could smooth out some of our rough spots.

I have a tremendous amount of respect for the people that run the Microsoft's and the Apple's and even the Dick's Tire Barn's in this country.

So today, when that business world recognized me . . . well, you can imagine how honored I felt.

It feels strange to be on this list next to people who work for Google and Travelocity, but, honestly, it also feels pretty cool.

And maybe, just maybe, if we all started running our shows like they run companies like Google and Travelocity, people might actually consider Broadway an actual business.

Thanks to Crain's for the recognition. You've put the pressure on me now!

And a special shout-out to Miriam Souccar, who has the tough job of writing about the business of Broadway, which she does very, very well.

March 05, 2008

Why did he name it August: Osage County anyway?

I got a sneak peek at a script for *August* recently, and found something on the first page that I thought you should all see, since it follows up on our discussion on _August_ and on titles:

DEDICATION:

I could never come up with a title as brilliant as *August: Osage County*. Mr. Howard Starks, gentleman, teacher, poet, genius, mentor, friend, created that title for an extraordinary poem that is one of the inspirations for my play. I steal the title with deference, yet without apology - Howard, I'm sure, would have it no other way - and I dedicate this play to his memory.

So there it is . . . arguably one of the worst titles since *Flahooley* for one of the best plays of the last decade was the title of a poem that inspired the author.

This reminded me of the origin of another title . . .

When I was negotiating for the rights to *Somewhere In Time*, I discovered that the original title of the book was *Bid Time Return*, from a Shakespearean verse. I asked the author why he changed it when the book became a movie.

He looked at me like I had two heads and half a brain between them.

"That's a big change," I said, "why did you do it?"

"Simple. The movie company tested the title. It came back 100% negative. So we had to come up with something else."

The something else turned out to be *Somewhere In Time*, which was suggested by the wife of the Producer.

Should someone have tested *August* before it opened?

Is it appropriate for a Producer to meddle in such matters that are "artistic" in nature?

Should Broadway be as calculating and "cold" as Hollywood?

Should playwright deals mimic screenwriter deals to allow us greater control, even at a greater financial cost?

These are all questions that you'll have to answer as you develop your own style.

March 06, 2008

<u>Don't ask for it back.</u>

I get a lot of submissions. Scripts, CDs, headshots, etc. I take the time to go through every one.

Every once in awhile, someone asks me for their materials back if I send them a note saying their project is not for me.

Bad idea.

Sending materials to someone is like trying to plant a mine deep inside enemy territory. Yes, it's true, it might not blow up when you want. But let it lie dormant. You never know when it'll go off.

Example:

I got a demo of a musical about 10 years ago that I thought had potential. They never got the piece finished from what I remember.

Flash forward 10 years. I was digging through old CDs and bingo, there it was. I popped it in and remembered how much I enjoyed it. Then I looked at the composer's name, which I had forgotten.

Well, would you look at that! The composer was a guy that just so happened to be having a reading of a new musical a couple of weeks from now and his agent had just sent me an invite! I was originally going to skip it, but not anymore! All because of that old CD.

I also often pass scripts and CDs to my staff, director friends, other producers, etc. who may be looking for new material and may have different tastes as well. Just because it's not for me, doesn't mean it's not for somebody.

Truth? Yes, I do *recycle* some scripts as well. But take the chance. I know that CDs and binding are expensive, but it's an investment.

If you ask for it back? There's no chance it'll blow up.

March 10, 2008

Bloggin' From Britain (with a stop in Belgium)

I've been on a whirlwind of a trip for the last 2.5 days. But I got to see 3 show including *Billy Elliot*, <u>*Brief Encounter*</u>, and a Belgian dance piece starring an 80s pop star who played the electric violin.

While trying to fall asleep in my twin bed in my hotel room the size of a refrigerator magnet, I thought about some of the differences between theater on the West End and theater on Broadway.

Here are my top three:

1. HALF-PRICE TKTS BOOTHS ARE EVERYWHERE

In London, you can get half-price tickets to shows at a ton of small shops. There is no exclusive arrangement on who offers these tickets. There are countless brokers who have access to discounted tickets, which decrease the lines and probably moves more tickets.

There IS an "official" TKTS booth, just like ours (<u>see bottom picture</u>). However, when I walked by, it was closed . . . at 7 PM.

What if there were half-price ticket shops on every block here? Could the monopoly of the TKTS booth be broken if a scalper opened up a shop in Times Square and sold half-price tickets instead of premium tickets?

It could easily be done, especially with the recent change in the scalping laws. In fact, if you've visited the corner of 46th and Broadway recently, you've probably seen it happen already. At the right time of night you can catch scalpers selling half-price tickets to everything. They just don't have an office . . . yet.

Let's hope it doesn't happen here. The 50% ticket still feels a bit special to the consumer, and I think it's important for them to work for it a bit by standing in line (or searching online). Put half-price tickets everywhere, and the full price ticket's value decreases even more.

2. THERE'S NO PLAYBILL

Instead of a playbill, every show has a "souvenir programme" . . . that costs money. Over $10, in fact. And if you don't buy it, you don't get a cast list, or song list, etc.

Can you imagine that meeting . . . "How can we increase the souvenir programme sales. I've got it! Take away the free one!"

Would you take your Playbill away if you could? Not me. To me, it's one of the stickiest form of advertising there is. People collect these things. They leave them on their dining room tables. Some obsessive kids cut out the pictures and make collages with their covers and then frame them (uhhhh . . . TMI?)

Playbills and programs are the best kind of advertising there is . . . because they don't look like advertising. They provide information. If you could only get people to read your ads for as long as they read their playbills.

3. JUKEBOX MUSICALS ARE KING

Mamma Mia began here. *We Will Rock You* still rocks there, and will never even try to make it on Broadway. Musicals featuring the music of Take That, Madness, Blondie, and so on and so on. Why do they do well here, despite getting lambasted by the critics?

Here's my theory . . .

You know what's close to England? France. Spain. Germany. The Netherlands.

You know what's close to Broadway? Canada.

The West End Theater has to appeal to many more non-English speakers than we do. The West End is a train ride away from the rest of Europe. And the West End, like Broadway, is very much dependent upon the tourist. We have to cater to the weekend travelers from Ohio. And they have to cater to the weekend travelers from Frankfurt.

And we all know that the international language is sweet pop music.

Anyone else have any favorite reasons why we're different? Besides the fact that our currency has the value of a piece of pocket lint compared to theirs?

March 11, 2008

At this performance, the role of Ken will be played by . . .

Thanks to the flu and the lack of a power converter at the Belgium International Airport, I missed a couple of blog posts recently.

After those missed "performances", I started thinking about one of the huge problems we face in the live theater: absenteeism and the dreaded white slip of paper found in most Playbills known affectionately as *The Stuffer*.

I'm not here to debate whether or not today's performers have the work ethic of the Ethel Merman's of the past.

I'm here to talk about what we can do about it, because it's here, and it's the equivalent of a branding and an expense termite, eating away at us slowly from the inside, without us even realizing it.

How many of you have seen a show recently and had one of those stuffers fall out of your playbill? How did you feel about plunking down your $100+ then? The value dropped tremendously, didn't it?

Now, here's the problem . . . when was the last time you went to see a movie, and the star called out? Can you imagine going to see *There Will Be Blood* and hearing an announcement saying that the role usually played by Daniel Day Lewis was now going to be played by James O'Connor in his film debut?

Or what about going to see Bon Jovi at the Meadowlands, and hearing that Johnny Bonny was being replaced by Joey Veneziano from Hoboken.

Going to the theater has become even riskier than ever because of absenteeism. Not only could you not like the show, but odds are you're not even going to see the primary cast!

So what can we do to limit this problem?

Let's look at the rulebook and the requirements for replacements:

If a Broadway performer playing an identifiable role (either a principal or a featured ensemble role, as defined by Actors' Equity) misses a performance, the Producers are required to notify the audience in 2 out of 3 ways:

1. A sign in the lobby

2. An announcement right before the curtain goes up.

3. The aforementioned S-word.

#1 is a no brainer. Very simple. Gets the word out. Not too expensive.

#2 is a problem. Breaks the mood and disappoints an audience right before the show, kind of like getting to a theme park and being told the big roller coaster is broken right when you get in the gate. Have fun, kids! (Oh, and there's also this annoying Local 802 (musicians) rule that arbitrarily states that anytime you do a live announcement, whether it's about a cast change, or about cell phones, you are required to announce who is conducting the orchestra. Huh? Come on, guys. Really? Ego check anyone? I call this rule the Magnificent Maestro Rule, and it's just plain annoying. They've already got their own sign in the lobby.)

Then there's #3, which you're all very familiar with.

To accomplish the 2 out of 3 required by the rulebook, Producers normally opt for the sign and the stuffer, because they are the least intrusive from a branding point of view, although still damaging.

Here's the huge problem for Producers with stuffers: they aren't free.

Thousands of dollars a week can be spent making those slips of paper and paying the required usher fees to stuff them. Thousand of dollars that usually aren't budgeted for specifically. Hear the termites in the walls?

But forget about the money. The worst part about stuffers that affects *everyone*, no matter what side of the footlights you are on?

They eat away at the environment.

Lets say an average of 1 stuffer a night for the 40,000 plus seats on Broadway. 8 stuffers on 1 page. That's 5000 sheets of paper a night or 2,080,000 a year. 2 million plus. Holy trees, Batman.

So what's the compromise?

Actors' Equity isn't going to give up the stuffers without getting something back, even though they should, considering the impact on the environment. They'll just say "announce" (but we know that's a bigger branding problem).

My idea? Producers, you're paying out ridiculous amounts of cash in stuffer after stuffer, not to mention the hours it takes to order and manage those stuffers. Stop putting your money in paper. Put it in people.

Raise the salary increment required for understudies in exchange for a reduction of the requirement to 1 out of 3 instead of 2 out of 3. I bet that an ensemble member would rather have a few extra dollars every week than a stuffer for when they go on for a bit part anyway (the program does list that they understudy the role, so it's not like they aren't represented).

Actors make more money. Producers save money.

We all save trees.

March 12, 2008

There's the pitch, the swing . . . and it's a hit!

Looks like they've done it again.

Lead producers of *In The Heights*, Kevin McCollum and Jeffrey Seller, have another hit on their hands. Word of mouth is good, reviews were good, and I'd put my money down now that these two will have another trophy on Tony night.

But let's do more than pat them on the back. If we want to look at what makes hits, let's think like baseball players. If we want to be better batters, we'd analyze David Ortiz's swing and adopt some of the mechanics to our own.

So let's look at Kevin and Jeffrey's swing . . .

Since they burst on the scene with *Rent* in 1996 they have produced four new musicals on Broadway together:

- *Rent*
- *Avenue Q*
- *High Fidelity*
- *In The Heights*

If *In The Heights* holds, that's 3 out of 4 hits.   They're batting .750 in terms of hits, and could be batting .750 in terms of Tonys! Not a bad record for producing new musicals.

So what do these three hit musicals have in common?

1. Geography

First thing that struck me? *Rent, Q* and *In The Heights* are all about small geographic subcultures in New York City. Hmmmm. Funny, isn't? I hadn't thought about it either until yesterday. Lower East Side, a mythical last stop in an outer borough, and Washington Heights.

What does it mean? Well, I'm not sure this is the most important characteristic for us to focus on, but it is important. All of these communities have very distinct voices that we hadn't heard from before on Broadway. These shows taught us about the issues facing the youth of these three very distinct NYC communities.

Hmm, there's another one. All three of them have to do with young people, starting their lives. Huh.

2. Who Wrote Them Again?

This for me is the most important element. You probably never heard of the writers of these musicals before their shows opened.

That's because each one made their Broadway debut with these musicals.

3 hits. 3 Broadway debuts of a book writer, a composer and a lyricist.

K&J use new writers. New voices. They invest in people that have stories that they feel *must* be told. The writers' passion for their projects goes right on the page and then bleeds right onto the stage. You can feel it.

3. What's That Director's Name?

You know what I'm gonna say don't you. But you can't believe it either.

Yet, it's true.

3 hits. 3 brand spanking new Broadway directors all making their Broadway debuts . . . just like the writers!

$10 million dollar musicals on the shoulders of Broadway Babies.

This is an unbelievable trend. Hal Prince once told me that if I wanted a musical to happen, all that I needed to do was to hire a name director, and the money would come, and the show would happen. He was right.

But Kevin and Jeffrey are demonstrating that if you want a HIT new musical, a name is the last thing you might want.

They even proved their own theory with their one flop. That one was directed by a <u>veteran</u>.

4. <u>No Stars</u>.

See this previous <u>entry</u>.

5. <u>No Spectacle</u>

No chandeliers, no helicopters and no flying monkeys, dragons, green girls, etc.

6. <u>No Stars + No Spectacle < $15 Million Dollars</u>

All of their shows are economical. They don't try to produce the biggest musicals ever. Just the best that have budgets that can be recouped in a realistic time frame.

There's a lot to learn from studying the swing of these heavy hitters and future hall of famers, just like there's a lot to learn from all of the major leaguers. My advice to you is to watch them all and learn. Study the game tapes. Pick up some tips on what to do with your elbow. No two swings are alike, but there are powerful fundamentals that you've gotta get under your belt.

Then step up to the plate, because the only way to see if you've got game is to take a swing at a couple of pitches.

(Side note: Kevin produced another show in the last ten years without Jeffrey . . .*The Drowsy Chaperone*. Another recouped hit where *all* of these rules applied (except the NYC subculture thing).

March 13, 2008

"What does a press agent do?"

Here are a few answers to this reader's question:

- Sends out press releases about the show (i.e. opening night, cast changes, dreaded "final weeks", etc.)

- Extends invitations to all of the critics and coordinates their tickets (There is always a debate as to where to put "you-know-who" - which side of the house is best, who is sitting next to Him, etc.)

- Pitches feature stories on the show, the actors, the creators, to various publications and media outlets.

And there are a zillion other things that the good Press Agents do.

But all of those things can be summed up in this beautiful quote I heard today from one of my favorite marketers in the biz, Scott Moore. Scott was the key man behind building the *Chicago* marketing machine, and was also the first Company Manager I ever worked for on the first, non-reality show, revival of *Grease* (we bonded over Chicken McNuggets).

This afternoon, in a discussion about the development of art for a show, a debate emerged over just how much about a show could be depicted in a logo. Does that drawing of young Cosette really tell the story of Les Miz? What does that blue haired albino really say about the struggles of Tracy in *Hairspray*? (No one can argue that these are great logos.)

Scott believes that although we should try and get as much across as possible in the art, that we have to be realistic in how much we can expect that art to communicate.

Then he said, "I believe it's a press agent's responsibility to fill any holes left by the art." (I'm slightly paraphrasing, because I loved the statement so much that I was in quote-shock and forgot to write it down.)

There is only so much you can expect your logo to accomplish. Print advertising just juices word of mouth and reminds people of something that they heard about or read about in a word of mouth or editorial context (unless it's the announcement of a major star, etc.)

I think about it this way. All art is really black and white. The press agent is the one that gets the stories about the actors, the writers, why the show is relevant, etc.

The press agent puts the context . . . and the color . . . into the art.

March 14, 2008

Let's get ready to rumble, Marsha Norman and Frank Rich!

A healthy fight emerged about the power of critics in the modern theater on a NY Times blog a week or so ago.

In this corner, Marsha "Night Mother" Norman!

And in this corner, Frank "Butcher of Broadway" Rich!

(I'll refrain from telling you what color trunks they were wearing and what they were weighing in at.)

My feeling about critics today?

They're like aging mob bosses. They had huge amounts of power at one point, but that power and influence is waning. The FEDs have got them in their sights. And some of them are just acting crazy in order to get insanity defenses.

Even though their fedoras are fading, unfortunately, there will always be some people that these ex-Godfathers can extort.

My advice? If what you're fighting for is popular in your "neighborhood" then hold your ground. Stick. And don't let them scare you. Eventually they'll go off and bother somebody else.

Remember (especially when you get a bad review), there's a new newspaper every day. But be careful. There is a new Dapper Don in town.

Who is he? You.

The user is the Ben Brantley of tomorrow. Pay very special attention to your User Reviews.

March 15, 2008

Favorite Quotes: Volume V

"The future of our theater is in the names of people I do not know."
          - Michael David

Another favorite quote of mine that furthers this week's theme of the passionate newcomer.

And isn't it cool how Michael, who wears sneakers with everything and has a thing for McDonalds' Happy Meals, refers to the theater as *ours*.

He's saying that the theater is something that we all own. Something that we all have to take care of and be responsible for if it's going to prosper.

Something that is *ours* is something we have to take pride in.

You know what else is cool? After a few years of *Jersey Boys* success, no one even remembers that Michael produced *Good Vibrations* and *Dracula*.

March 16, 2008

It's a pretty award in theory, but in practice?

Can you feel it? Or more importantly, can you *see* it?

We're getting closer and closer to award season, and if you look closely, you can see the potential crop of nominees readying their stations for battle. A few have already starting taking out bigger-than-necessary ads and outdoor ads as they start to position themselves amongst the voters.

We'll talk more about awards and nominations as we get closer to T-Day, but yesterday I was inspired to do some digging after a conversation with a member of the board of the Drama Desk Awards, the only award that combines all New York Theatrical productions under one umbrella.

From their website:

"At the time of the Drama Desk's founding, the only major awards honoring New York theatre's creative men and women were the Antoinette Perry Awards, better known as "The Tonys." These awards only celebrate those productions produced in Broadway theatres, while ignoring the hundreds of stage productions presented each year Off-Broadway, Off-Off Broadway and in legitimate not-for-profit theatres. Since Drama Desk members cover not only Broadway productions, but all New York theatre productions, the organization decided in 1955 to create its own awards celebrating creative stage achievements wherever they were presented."

That's a beautiful sentiment, isn't it? They don't discriminate. Theater is Theatre, whether it's on Broadway or Off-Broadway, or whether it's spelled with an "er" or an "re".

It's a great theory. But does it work in practice?

As Jerry Lewis says every Labor Day, "Let's go to the tote board!"

The 'Best Musical' Drama Desk Award started during the 1974-1975 season. In the last 32 years, how many Off-Broadway musicals have won the Best Musical Award?

Zero.

Hmmmmmm . . .

Ok, prior to the Best Musical Award, the DDs gave an award for Best Overall Production.

How many Off-Broadway musicals won this award?

One. Kind of.

In the '62-63 season a musical called *The Coach with Six Insides* won but it was not the only winner. It shared the award with *The Boys From Syracuse*. (And you know it wasn't an exact tie - it's almost as if the board said, "We can't just give it to an Off-Broadway show . . . Broadway will be mad at us!")

So, in 53 years, there has only been one Off-Broadway show that has ever won the big prize. And it had to share.

Why? Is it because Off-Broadway shows move to Broadway before they are considered for the award? Is it because Off-Broadway shows that don't move aren't as good?

Or, is it because the Drama Desk voters are human like the rest of us, and they fall prey to the same mass marketing of the major shows. When it comes down to picking that winner, there is no doubt that the big Broadway shows are going to be more top of mind than any Off-Broadway show.

Let's look at the plays.

In the last 53 years, there have been 7 Off-Broadway plays that have received the Best Play award from the DDs. 14%. Still pretty low if you ask me.

So what should the Drama Desks do?

Well, because of the nature of our business, it's hard to give everyone a fair shot. If they really want to acknowledge everyone . . . if that is their mission statement . . . then they have to create separate awards for Off-Broadway and Off-Off-Broadway.

Awards are important for these productions. On *Altar Boyz*, we discovered in a survey that the fact that we won the Outer Critics Circle Award for Best Off-Broadway Musical was the strongest piece of info we had to convince someone to buy a ticket!

If the Drama Deskers don't want to separate the awards, then that's ok, too. It's their awards. But they should change their website, because whether they know it or not, the data demonstrates that they too are "ignoring the hundreds of stage productions presented each year Off-Broadway . . ."

Special thanks to my assistant, Michael Roderick, for the Drama Desk research.

March 17, 2008

<u>**Fire!**</u>

I was recently asked for advice on how to deal with someone on your team that is difficult, doesn't adhere to deadlines and creates tension in the workplace.

Do you have a heart-to-heart to inspire them? Do you pay them more money? Do you do some of the work yourself to take the pressure off?

No.

No.

No.

You fire them.

Actors, creative team members, marketing directors, etc. that are not delivering and causing you intense agita are like extra weight on a sailboat. They need to be tossed overboard.

As soon as you do, you'll feel that weight come off of *your* shoulders, and your boat will start picking up speed.

I've fired a number of people in my day, as a company manager, general manager and a producer. Stagehands, actors, management, web designers, and so on. Every time I've done it, without fail, it has benefited the show or my company.

We work in a small industry that's the equivalent of a high school cafeteria, where everyone knows everyone, and strong emotional ties are created. Sometimes it's hard to fire someone if they are a friend. But you have to.

Ending relationships is as important as starting ones, and terminating someone's employment is an essential part of every business, including ours.

Some termination tips:

- Decide you want to do it and don't look back. If you find yourself doubting, just think like a big business. WWMD? What would Microsoft do?

- Figure out your plan for the replacement (have someone or a strategy waiting in the wings).

- Do it quick and say goodbye. Don't let people work out their notice. Pay them to leave right then and there, even if that means giving them two weeks salary or a buyout to not show up. Take the financial hit and get them out of the building. Terminated employees are toxic.

- Get used to the feeling. If you are a great producer, this won't be the last time you fire someone.

March 18, 2008

Playbill.com takes a test. And passes just by taking it.

Playbill.com gets a lot of money for its email blasts. They charge shows like mine $6,200 to blast discount offers to its 325,000 members.

Each time they blast, they sell tickets. And every time they blast, they get unsubscribes. So, to blast when they are not getting paid is risky, because they lose some members, which could mean less tickets for the next client, which means it could be harder to justify the $6,200.

But this weekend, they sent a blast without getting paid, and without selling a thing.

They sent a survey.

They did it so they could get demographic info about their members, find out what they liked, what they didn't like, and so on. All information that they can use to make their members happier, and therefore grow their list, and then make even more money for their clients, justifying even higher costs.

I can't emphasize enough the importance of surveys and testing for every aspect of what we do. Like everything else in our internet-age, it's not that hard any more, so there is no excuse not to do it. Great companies like Survey Monkey make it ultra-easy and ultra-economical for you to send a survey asking for opinions on your artwork, your first act, your tag line, etc.

I got into a discussion with an industry pro who thought that testing wasn't worth it. I couldn't disagree more. Testing is part of every other part of our life, why shouldn't it be part of our business?

If you're sick, you take your temperature. But even if you're not sick, you still go in for a yearly physical.

If your car is making strange rattling noises, you take it to the shop. But even if it's running great, you take it in for an inspection and a tune-up.

If there is the possibility that you could do something better (and that should be all of us), then you must test. Props to Playbill for realizing that a short term loss (possible unsubscribes) could mean a long term gain.

Some testing tips:

- Who is taking your test is even more important than the test itself. Make sure it's an appropriate audience.

- If you test, you must be prepared to do something with the results, no matter what they say. If the SATs didn't count and you could just disregard them, they wouldn't be worth taking.

- Take tests yourself. Learn what to ask from what others are asking.

- Take the results and add them to your own instincts to make your final decisions. Colleges look at SATs yes, but they also look at personal essays. Testing is not the only tool in your box.

March 19, 2008

Will the internet and technology kill the theater?

There are a lot of doomsdayers out there.

As more and more options for entertainment become available to us on our computers, our cell phones, our cell phone/pda/waffle makers, etc., a lot of folks out there are predicting the end of Theater as we know it.

Not me.

I say, bring it on.

Bring on as many different forms of two dimensional entertainment as you silicon valley guys can dream up.

The more the market is flooded with 2D, the more rare the 3D experience becomes, which means the more valuable it is.

Scarcity increases value which then increases demand.

The more screens the consumer has to stare at all day and all night, the more opportunity there is for us to show them something much more exciting.

Something live.

They're gonna to be dying for it. So we just can't disappoint.

You up for the challenge?

March 20, 2008

Where is the profit in non-profit?

Have you ever visited the website CharityNavigator.org?

It's an incredible tool for those interested in making contributions to non-profit organizations. The site analyzes financial reports of charities giving the user the chance to see where his or her money is going.

You know what else it does?

It shows the salaries of the executives of each charity.

That's right. By accessing public records, this site gives you the chance to see how much the head honchos at organizations like Amnesty International, Mothers Against Drunk Driving and Feed The Children take home every year.

So what kind of numbers do you think would come up if you searched the site for, oh, I don't know, say some prominent "not-for-profit" theaters around the country?

Would you be shocked if I told you that execs of some of these theaters take home in excess of $300k?

How about $500k?

What if I told you that there were some that earned close to $700,000???

That's more than the guys who run The Red Cross, The American Cancer Society or The Partnership for a Drug Free America!

Don't believe me? Go on. Try it. If you're like me, you'll be typing in names of non-profits for hours (and maybe thinking about starting your own non-profit).

Let me make something clear. I don't mind when people make money. I don't begrudge someone being able to negotiate great deals for themselves. Good for them! Some of these Guys and Dolls have built these theaters up from plays in basements into major contributors to the modern theater. They deserve to be rewarded. Get your salary, guys. Go for it. If you can get your people to make donations to afford those payrolls, even if you're earning more than the guys at Oxfam, then you deserve it.

What I have trouble with, is that these not-for-profit theaters get better deals from vendors, some unions, actors, authors, etc. than their commercial producing counterparts, simply because of their "non-profit" status (someone did a helluva job marketing that "title"), no matter what folks at the tippy-top are being paid. Many own theaters in major cities all over the country and have the ability to get tax breaks and accept donations, and so on.

Commercial producers don't get these perks.

Yet, with 4 out of 5 Broadway shows failing to recoup their investment, and maybe 29 out of 30 Off-Broadway shows failing to recoup . . . the question is, aren't most commercial productions "non-profit" as well? As tough as non-profits have it (and it ain't easy, and I commend those that are so committed to mission statements that others, including myself, wouldn't touch), I believe the commercial producer has it tougher.

So perhaps all of the agents, vendors, etc. can stop looking at us commercial producers like the Scrooge McDucks of the theater world, especially when we lose 80% of the time.

Why don't you treat us the same way as those other guys that are taking home large *guaranteed* checks? Give us the same deals up front . . . and then, hit us harder when we recoup.

I'm happy to give you more money on the back than on the front. Just allow us to get there. You've already demonstrated that your clients, members, etc. can work for the lower amounts, so why not let us have access to those deals as well? And we'll even pay a higher premium on the back end just for our (ahem) "for-profit" status, since your peeps helped us get there.

Oh yeah, one more thing. As I've blogged about <u>before</u>, one of the questions I am asked most often is "Where can I find people who make enough bank that they may have some disposable income to put in a show?"

I think I just found a few.

March 21, 2008

Free tickets to Boom for this weekend.

Ben Brantley gave a bang-up review for Boom this morning, the new Off-Broadway play at Ars Nova.

And I've got some free tickets for this weekend, if any of you want to see it.

Here are the details.

Friday, March 21st (tonight) at 8 PM, Saturday, March 22nd at 8 PM

Ars Nova, 511 West 54th St.

To get your tickets, email rsvp@arsnovanyc.com. Tickets are very limited, but they'll accommodate at least 10 of you. First come, first Boomed.

I'm going tonight, so maybe I'll see you there. If you do, and I've never met you face to face, please say hello!   (I look like the guy in the upper left hand corner of this page.)

Oh, and props to Marketing Director, Rosey Strub, for finding talkers to give away tickets to without papering.

Stuck? See something else.

If you're like most writers, you probably visualize what you write.

You see the room that your characters are in. You see the color of your character's hair. You see the clothes they are wearing.

If you're like most writers, you probably get writer's block now and then too.

Then what do you do?

Here's one of my tricks for breaking the block:

See your characters in a totally different room. Change their hair color. Take off their clothes.

Writer's block is writer's rut. Just seeing the situation differently forces you to think differently.

And when you think differently, well, that's when the creativity comes, whether you're writing or budgeting or whatever.

March 22, 2008

Curtains closing. But what is missing?

Look at these three clippings announcing the final curtain of *Curtains*:

The New York Times   Broadway.com   Playbill.com

What is missing from each of these announcements?

Ok, you don't have to read them all, I'll tell you . . .

There's no indication of whether or not the show recouped or not. Which means . . . it didn't.

Sad.

This is what's wrong with the the *current* economics of our industry.

Here's a show that got some decent reviews, has stars (including one that won a Tony for his performance), ran more than a year, had decent word of mouth. It wasn't a great show, but it was fine.

I wouldn't expect stellar profits from a show like this, but I would expect to break-even, wouldn't you?

Maybe it will, eventually, through subsidiary rights and additional companies all over the world. But we should work hard at making our investors whole based on the Broadway experience alone (the more we give them back, the more they'll put it back in).

A great show (as determined by the audience) should produce great returns.

A decent show, should produce decent returns.

An ass show, should produce ass returns.

Or that's my goal anyway. I hope it's yours (except for the ass part).

March 23, 2008

If a tree falls in the woods . . .

You know how this cliché ends, so I'll spare you. But here's my version:

If a show is produced, and no one sees it, is it any good?

My answer? No.

A book needs a reader.

A steak needs someone to eat it (sorry, my vegan friends).

And a show needs someone to see it.

Recently, I questioned an author about whether he thought people would want to see what he had written. If he thought people would have an experience at his show that they could somehow relate to and that would move them.

The response went something like this . . .

"I don't know, and I don't really care. I didn't write this for them. This is *my* play and if people don't like it or don't get it, well that's too bad for them."

Too bad for him, actually, because I don't know anyone that would produce a play commercially without thinking about whether it's going to touch an audience.

Theater is like kindergarten. The first lesson we should learn, before ABCs and 123s, is sharing. If you don't share with your audience, you'll be like that kid who ate paste. No one is going to want to play with you. And your mouth will be stuck together and you won't have a voice anyway.

Writing without thinking about your audience is just selfish and stroking your own ego.

You can do it, and if that's what you want, then go for it. More power to you.

But don't come whining to me when you're the only one in the audience.

What is the sound of one playwright clapping

March 24, 2008

Your grandparents thought producing theater was risky too.

Here's a couple lines from an article I found online recently:

"Anyone who intends to produce a Broadway show needs his overhead examined . . . but even though fearless angels are easy to find, the risks are still great."

Not that interesting, is it. We all know this. Now what if I told you the article was from 1954!

Here's the full quote:

"Anyone who intends to produce a Broadway show needs his overhead examined. If he has a musical like *Wonderful Town*, he needs $225,000 to start with, has to pay out more than $44,000 a week and charge $7.20 top. If he is lucky enough to have such a rare hit as *Wonderful Town*, he can net more than $5,000 a week. But even though fearless angels are easy to find (178 contributed $300,000 to the forthcoming Shirley Booth musical, *By The Beautiful Sea*), the risks are still great."

Pretty clear, now, that it's from 1954, huh? $225k couldn't even pay for 25% of the stagehand cost alone for loading in a new musical!

But the inflation isn't what's interesting to me. What's interesting is that even in '54, producing theater was risky.

So all of us, including myself, need to stop complaining that we're playing a risky game. It's always been risky, and it always will be risky . . . and there's probably something in all of us that likes that risk. :-) So let's do what we can to reduce it, but at the same time embrace it, and use it to our advantage.

Producing theater is hard. So are relationships. So is raising a kid.

But the hard stuff in life is where you'll find the greatest rewards. Especially when you love it.

(The article goes on to talk about how Off-Broadway is booming, thanks to production costs as low as $10k. Let's hope history is about to repeat itself.)

Read the full article here.

March 25, 2008

I wanted to be a Goonie. Didn't you?

The Goonies was on TV in the wee hours last night.

I was 13 when I first saw it. When it was over, I started looking for buried treasure in my own backyard. Why not? I lived in an old and historical part of the country. If Sean Astin, Corey Haim and that red head that was also in *Lucas* could find some doubloons, surely I could too, right?

You all know this feeling, don't you? It's when you see *A Chorus Line* and you want to dance. When you see *American Idol* and you want to sing.

Your shows have to inspire people . . . to move them so much that they want to *do something*.

Do that, and then do you know what else they'll do?

They'll see your show over and over again.

That's right. You bet your Chunk I stayed up until 4 AM, watching Sloth save the day and One-Eyed Willy sail off into the sunset, even though I've seen it 30+ times before.

March 26, 2008

<u>Hit the street to find out how to sell.</u>

Guess what is happening in the <u>photo</u> to the right.

Give up? I'll tell you.

That's Janine and her daughter Ellen. They're from Ohio and they came in to New York last weekend. They're staying at the Milford Plaza and plan on seeing a musical and going to The Empire State Building.

That's Duane in the red sweatshirt. He's from the Bronx. He's an underground rapper who records his own music and then sells it on the street in midtown.

And that's Ellen, digging into her purse to buy this unknown artist's CD for $10, even though she's never heard of him before, and even though she *"doesn't really like rap."*

So what happened here? How the heck did Duane get a tourist to fork over cash in the middle of midtown, and how did he penetrate an alternative demographic?

There is nothing more powerful than the live pitch. It's why telemarketing, Tupperware parties and door-to-door sales still work. It's not as fast as the internet, but if you've got an unknown product and are trying to break through to a resistant demo, do you really think a banner ad is going to do it?

Duane believes in his product. And Janine and Ellen could feel that. And they aren't just buying a CD. They are buying Duane. Great sales people know how to make themselves a part of their product. That's not only how to convert one sale, but it's how to get a customer for life.

This is why who works at your box office and who is answering your phone line is so important. This is also why Broadway is at a significant disadvantage in its current model.

Box office ticket sellers are hired by the theater. Not by the Producer.

Imagine if you were the owner of a GAP. You rent a storefront on 5th avenue. You stock it with your product, you advertise, etc. And then your landlord sends in your sales team. Huh?

You don't get to screen them. You don't get to train them. They don't have to wear your product. You can't fire them. You don't even sign their checks, yet you have to reimburse the landlord for every penny of their salary and benefits.

You wouldn't stand for that, right? You'd find another storefront.

That's the way it works on Broadway. And because of the limited availability of "storefronts", we take it.

Same thing for the phones. As a producer, you have no control over Ticketmaster or Telecharge. And, as a producer, you also have no choice but to use them. They come packaged with your theater agreement. And yes, the theater owners get a kickback from the ticketing companies, and the Producer gets no financial benefit. In fact, Telecharge is owned by the Shubert Organization.

With the amount of money producers are risking on shows, we deserve to be able to choose the best sales team for us. Maybe we'd use Telecharge and maybe we'd hire a lot of the great Local 751 members out there. But we deserve that choice. Having a choice means competition. And competition is what makes businesses and industries stronger.

If I were choosing my sales team today, the first person I'd interview would be Duane.

March 27, 2008

Did I say inflation? I mean Enflation.

In Monday's post, the article I referred to mentioned a capitalization of *Wonderful Town* of $225,000 and a ticket price of $7.20 in 1954.

A reader turned me on to a site that could tell us what those numbers would be in today's dollars, taking inflation into account, using the Consumer Price Index.

The results?

$1,725,934.60 cap.

and

$55.23 top ticket

Oh, if only a major Broadway musical could be done for $1.7 million. And if only the tickets were only $55.23.

Wonderful Town in 2008 would probably be $10 million, more than 5 times the 1958 version when adjusted.

We've got our own version of inflation. Expense inflation or Enflation as I call it.

Should we be surprised that recoupment is more and more delayed when our expenses are increasing so dramatically?

Yes, it's the stagehands. Yes it's theater rent. Yes, it's health insurance. Yes, it's advertising. Yes, it's *everything*. And, as producers, we have to look at everything.

Interestingly enough, the article also mentioned a weekly nut for *Town* of $44,000 (a weekly "nut" on Broadway is a term used to described the amount of money required by a show to pay all its expenses, or the show's breakeven). Converting that to current dollars gets you $337,516.10. That's closer (I'd guess that a new revival would cost about $500k/week give/take).

This is a down and dirty statistical analysis, and inflation indexes don't measure improvements in quality which come with price tags (although, if we can't financially support it, maybe we shouldn't buy it - would you buy a brand new computer with the best technology if you knew you might be out of work and lose your house in 3 months?).

However, even with these rough numbers, if I were looking to start addressing where our biggest Enflation has occurred (and I am), I'd start with the upfront expenses.

At $15 million dollars a musical, we're starting ourselves so far in the hole, it's hard to get even halfway out.

And then we look like A-holes to our investors.

March 28, 2008

How many projects are you working on?

If you're like me when I got started, your answer is "one". And here's why you need to go out and get a few more right now.

The development of a show is like walking through a mine field. Something could explode at any time. You could fail to get the rights, an author may quit, you may lose funding, and so on. You could literally be working on a show for years and have it end just like that! (insert finger-snap noise here)

Having multiple projects gives you an insurance policy for your career (and your mental state) if a project does disintegrate during development.

See, I know you guys. Once you get an idea, you run with it like you're in the Boston marathon, right? You write scripts, develop marketing campaigns, t-shirt slogans, etc. That's great, but you have to be careful. Don't get yourself so emotionally invested that you can't move on if you have to quit the race, due to no fault of your own.

True story . . . I had an idea to do an evening of monologues and songs based on the book _Mole People_. I wrote half of a script. I started contacting songwriters. I was really pulling it all together . . . before I had finalized the rights agreement.

Then guess what happened. When the Author changed agents, and her new ten-percenter and his ten-dollar haircut refused to give me the rights because they were holding out for an HBO film deal (never came, by the way). Go on, guess.

I lost the rights. And I cried.

I did too much. I went too far. I wasn't just emotionally invested. I was emotionally obsessed. And when one of the mines went off, I was destroyed. A year and a half wasted, and I had nothing to show for it. If I had another project to work on, it wouldn't have been such a heartbreak.

Cy Coleman used to say developing shows was like planting a garden. You plant a whole $@%&-load of seeds, water them all, then stand back and see which grows first.

I guess that's why, even when he died, he was working on a number of projects. He's probably in tech for three of them at the same time right now.

Be focused, yes, but diversify your project portfolio. You wouldn't put all of your money into one stock. Don't put all of your heart into one show.

March 29, 2008

The new casting director: reality television

One thing everyone agreed on: The *Grease* reality show, *You're The One That I Want*, sucked . . . hard.

What no one could agree on was whether the idea of casting through a reality television series was a blemish on the beautiful Broadway process, or if it was a marketing coup.

The argument is about to resurface with the upcoming *Legally Blonde* reality television show on MTV.

Sorry to say but there isn't a black or white answer on whether or not it's appropriate. Like most things in life, you have to weigh the many factors surrounding the decision before making it. The big question . . . what show are you casting?

Grease makes sense. It's immensely popular with the public and everyone on the planet has done the show. In fact, when I worked on the revival of *Grease* in 1994, I mentioned to Jim Jacobs, the author, that I had played Kenickie in a summer theater production (that's me in the photo). He looked at me, smiled, and said, "Ken . . . I haven't met anyone who HASN'T done the show."

So *Grease* and reality television go together like rama-lama-ding-dong. If I was the producer of *Grease* and I had the opportunity for a television show, I would have hula-hooped at the chance.

If I was producing *Hamlet*? No. *August: Osage County*? *Spring Awakening*? Not gonna happen. It doesn't make sense.

Legally Blonde? On the same network that aired a live version of the show? You bet your Bundy I would.

For the show that it's appropriate for, it's a marketing bonanza. And not only for the show, but also for Broadway in general.

Because as much as *You're The One That I Want* did suck (hard), even sucking on television means millions and millions of people every Sunday night hearing the words Broadway over and over, and hearing how people dream about getting there.

And that's good for all of us.

(Oh, and no comments on why I'm standing on a 1969 Volkswagen Beetle in a production of *Grease* that is supposed to take place in 1957, because I have no flippin' idea. Summer stock, baby. Summer stock.)

March 30, 2008

What's your average?

Someone congratulated me the other day on the recoupment of my three shows. "You're 3 for 3! You're batting 1000, Ken! Congrats!"

Obviously, my three shows make me very happy . . . but batting 1000 doesn't. That's not what it's about.

In fact, I'd rather by batting .750 . . . if that meant I was 15 for 20.

The "P" in producing doesn't stand for perfect.

Don't hold yourself back from starting to produce for fear of not being perfect. Because at the end of the day, it's not about 1 show or 3 shows. It's about your body of work.

Want some proof? Look at this guy's resume. There a whole bunch of flops in there (including one that lasted for two days).

But how can you find them among the 42 Tony Awards and 134 nominations?

Do you think Manny cared about being perfect?

I've gotta go now. I have to see what I can do about *reducing* my average, because I think the "P" in producing stands for productive.

March 31, 2008

Tired of hearing me type?

Thanks to Paige Strothman, you can hear me talk instead!

Check out an interview I did with Paige on her podcast here.

Paige has also done interviews with Henry Krieger, Seth Rudetsky, and more.

Oh, and she's still in high school.

Imagine how many subscribers this podcast will have in 10 years if she keeps it up (and she will).

Success is about stamina. If you want an idea to be big, it's going to take time. Start now.

Imagine if you had been the one to start collecting email addresses of people who wanted discounts to theater tickets ten years ago? It might not have reaped many rewards then . . . but now? You'd be selling email blasts to people like me for beaucoup de bucks and you'd be able to email blast for your own shows for free.

The sooner you start, the sooner you succeed.

APRIL 2008

April 01, 2008

Even Opera reviewers suck.

A review of *La Boheme* at the Met from today's NY Times:

"Metropolitan Opera audiences have loved Franco Zeffirelli's production of *La Boheme* for its overstuffed, hyper-realistic sets ever since the company first staged it in 1981, and critics have disparaged it for nearly as long . . ."

It turns out that the Zeffirelli "Boheme" has had more performances than any other productions in the Met's history . . .

27 years of La Boheme, despite the bad reviews.

Even at the fancy-schmancy opera, what the people want always wins.

I have to respect the Times for calling out the fact that the reviewers and the people have two very different agendas. So why do we still worry so much about them?

Is *Wicked* not enough of a poster child to demonstrate that reviews don't matter as much as we think? Just read these wonderful quotes from their round of reviews.

Here's my feelings on reviews:

Have you ever played Monopoly?

Great reviews are like "Advance to Go, Collect $200" cards. They send a surge of sales your way quickly, and allow you to sell tickets to your early weeks of performances without advertising. They let you skip past that hotel on Boardwalk so you can have time to build your own someplace else.

But then it's up to you. If the people don't enjoy it, they won't keep coming. And there may be some backlash. (*Thom Pain* anyone?)

Bad reviews are like "Go to Jail" cards. You don't get a chance to collect an easy $200, but you'll be out with a few rolls of the die (or maybe you have your own card up your sleeve) . . . IF you can wait it out.

How do you wait out the jail time?

Make sure your show has an economic model that can withstand those first few weeks when the people don't rush to see it because some guy who wouldn't be friends with them in high school even if his Dad owned an amusement park told them not to.

Stay in jail until your word of mouth takes over.

And don't create shows to please one guy or girl. Create shows that please millions AND one guy or girl. You.

April 02, 2008

Talkin' Broadway stops them from Talkin'.

The infamous and original broadway web chatter site, talkinbroadway.com, issued a statement recently, letting all their chatterazzi know that they no longer will publish "reviews/reports of dress rehearsals/gypsy run-throughs."

They've got good intentions here. But they're making a mistake. As I learned from social media guru, Warren Ackeman at Affinitive, the more you tighten the reins on your online audience, the more likely those reins are going to break. Does TB really think their passionate peeps won't find another place to chat? They're gonna scurry to find one fast. Like roaches when you turn on the light.

I'm sure there are producers all over town celebrating Talking Bway's new policy. But that just means they're not confident in what's gonna be on that stage.

You can't produce with fear about what people are going to say, no matter who they are or what sites they visit or when they come.

And, remember, if your show is fantastic, you'll WANT those people talking about your show as early as you can get them.

So Talkin' Broadway, thanks for trying to protect us from the bullies. But don't worry, we can take care of ourselves.

And if we can't, we're definitely in the wrong business.

BTW, if any Talking Broadway regulars are reading this and want to write reviews/reports of dress rehearsals/gypsy run-throughs, might I suggest BroadwaySpace.com. ;-)

April 03, 2008

"How do I find a Producer for my show?"

Writers often ask me how they should go about finding a Producer.

The search for Producers is not unlike actors looking for agents. Sure, you can send in unsolicited manuscripts like an actor sends in headshots, and hope that yours falls into the right hands. But the chances of that happening are the same as winning the lottery . . . twice in a row.

The best way to get a script through the door is through a recommendation. Have someone else that the Producer knows (and respects) be your mule and march the script across the border of the Producer's office for you.

Even better than that is getting your show up on its feet. Plays and musicals were meant to be performed, not read. So get them up and get people there, by any means necessary.

The other thing I tell writers is not to worry so much about getting a Producer on board early. If you've got one, great, but if not, don't sweat it. I know it may seem like a Producer is an answer to all of your administrative and financial problems, but that's not the case. That's like saying a babysitter is better at taking care of your child than you are.

So, I tell writers the same thing I tell the actors looking for agents. Just keep doing great work and the right people will take notice. When you are ready for an agent or a producer, one (or several) will be banging down your door begging for the chance to work with you.

Isn't it better to have people begging than begging yourself?

April 04, 2008

Favorite Quotes: Volume VI

"It is my instinct that the theatre has always survived on mavericks - people with a passion for the theatre who go their own way."

> - Cameron Mackintosh

Cameron is the modern maverick. He's the last one (that I know of) that did it all on his own. You don't see a lot of other names above the title mucking it up (to use an expression from his homeland) on his shows.

Could it be that his solitary vision is one of the reasons his shows were so successful?

You better believe it.

I don't care if you have one name above your title or a hundred, there better be one designated person leading the charge.

There are never two Generals in a battle. Never two teachers in the same class. Never two Presidents, dictators, CEOs, and so on.

That doesn't always mean *you* have to be the lead. There is nothing wrong with sitting second, third or last chair.

As long as someone, preferably Cameron, is sitting in the big chair.

April 07, 2008

The 'In The Heights' Prequel

I saw my favorite flop this weekend.

I braved a borough and traveled to Brooklyn to see the BAM concert of *Capeman*, which featured Mr. Simon himself.

It was a wonderful celebration of a musical that didn't work on Broadway, and still has its flaws. But those flaws are found in some of the most beautiful and unique music we've heard on Broadway in the last decade (Encores, if you're reading this, put down that script of *Flora The Red Menace* and call Paul).

As I listened to tunes like "Satin Summer Nights", I forgave so many of the problems with the piece (most notably that the lyrics tend to be more narrative and do not further the characters arcs).

What made me forgive? Three words. Mel. O. Dy.

In the commercial musical theater medium, melody is so very important. Common sense, right? Then why do so many of the young and upcoming composers avoid it like an STD? This not only goes for those fresh out of school, but also to those composers who have been anointed by the New York Times as being the future of musical theater (Has anyone realized that Michael John LaChiusa has never had a hit? Doesn't it seem odd for him to be teaching Graduate Musical Theatre Writing at NYU?)

In their search to be the next Sondheim, so many seem to forget what artists like Paul Simon, Elton John, Billy Joel, Andrew Lloyd Webber, Marvin

Hamlisch, John Kander and Richard Rodgers knew so very well.
A strong melody is like a drug to an audience. It opens their mind.

And then, once they have smoked a little of what you've offered, you can say whatever you want to them. And they'll believe you.

April 08, 2008

Could universal health care revolutionize the theater?

As I listened to Barack and Hillary talk about UHC a few weeks ago, I selfishly started to wonder what universal health care would do for the Broadway and Off-Broadway industry.

One of the biggest expense issues we face on and Off-Broadway is not union mandated minimums. It's union mandated benefits.

Even after some fancy maneuvering in the last AEA negotiation, producers are still required to pay $153 per week, per actor, for the AEA Health Plan. That's $612/month or $7956/year. That kind of cash would buy a few health plans on the individual market.

Imagine 30 actors . . . that's $238,680 a year.

And that's only one union. Add stagehands, musicians, company managers, press agents, ushers, etc., etc. and you're easily up to $500,000 a year, or 5% of the capitalization of a $10 million dollar musical.

What happens to that cash if everyone is covered by some sort of UHC? Would the unions allow us to put our employees on a National Plan and save money?

From what I have read, both Barack and Hillary's plans provide everything that I have heard union reps say is necessary, including the most important element, portability (the ability to take your insurance from job to job, since the length of a run of a show is so unknown).

So will all that money go back into the shows? Or will the unions see that as a "giveback" and ask that it be paid directly to the employee or put in the pension funds? Ooooooh, the drama is building already!

If a Democrat gets into the big house, and actually passes his/her plan, all hell-th care is going to break loose, and we could witness one of the most radical economic reforms in our industry to date.

April 09, 2008

The war of the revivals. Who has the advantage?

The biz is buzzing about the battle of the two major heavyweight revivals this year. Who will take home the Tony for Best Revival of a Musical? Will it be the mother of all mother-daughter stories, *Gypsy*? Or was the wait worth it for R&H and *South Pacific*?

And, more importantly, does *Pacific* have an advantage over Gypsy because it was produced by a Non-Profit?

I decided to look at some numbers to see who was taking home the most trophies on Tony night, NPs or commercial producers.

We start our research in 1994, because that was the first year there was a delineation between revivals of musicals and plays. It used to be one big category.

Since then, 5 of the 14 awards given out for Best Revival of a Musical were produced by non-profits or 36%.

Best revival of a play? 7 of the 14 winners were producer by non-profits or 50%. Sorry my pundit friends, no clear cut favorite here based on these numbers.

Still, does *Pacific* have an advantage because it could afford to employ more musicians, employ more actors, previewed as long as a new musical would preview, etc. because they weren't relying on ticket sales to fund the production?

Yes, they have an advantage. But they only have it because they wanted it. And the commercial producer could have taken the same risks, if they could convince their investors it was worth it.

I've seen NPs under-produce shows and look cheap, and I've seen commercial producers overproduce and have almost no regard for the bottom line (*Show Boat*, anyone?).

Either way, it's a choice the producer has to make, no matter who is paying the bills. And whoever has the most guts usually wins.

In this case? It's South Pacific. The scarcity rule plays here. By keeping *SP* off the boards for so long, they've created something super-special that yet another production of *Gypsy* can't beat.

April 10, 2008

More stats on who and what are winning Tonys.

In yesterday's post we only looked at revivals. Let's look at new shows today.

In the last 20 years, there has only been 1 New Musical Tony Winner produced by a non-profit (and that new musical was *Contact*, which featured popular music on tape and no singing).

In the last 20 years, there have only been 3 New Play Tony Winners produced by non-profits.

Obviously you can see what business the Broadway non-profits are in, in this city: revivals, which are generally regarded as safer choices.

Seems odd, doesn't it? I know the mission statement for each theater is different, but you would think that non-profits would be the ones taking bigger risks, wouldn't you?

And people crack on commercial producers all the time for not taking enough risks with new material.

We do it more often and better on Broadway than anyone else.

Off-Broadway however? Give props where it is due. The only new plays are done by non-profits.

April 11, 2008

Paper got them in the paper.

Earlier this week, The Women's Project announced they would give away 1000 free tickets to their latest play via "download" as their way of "thrusting the medieval enterprise of theatre into the Internet age."

I'm not sure of all of that, but it sure sounds good in a press release, doesn't it? And, that press release went far and wide, including a juicy mention in the Times and on blogs all over the web (present company included).

The WP did one of my favorite things. They took a problem and turned it into a positive.

Obviously, the show wasn't selling.

Obviously, they wanted to put butts in the seats to generate word of mouth.

Obviously, they would have comp'd the 1000 seats anyway (which would have taken a lot of work).

But they got creative, and with this aggressive move, they accomplished the above goals, and got the press to take notice of a new Off-Broadway play.

Also, if you look at their free ticket sign-up site, you'll notice that they are surveying *and* collecting snail mail and email addresses (I'd bet money that when they run out of tickets for this promotion, there will be a very nice email blast with a discount offer sent to the people who didn't get in on time).

Congratulations to The Women's Project for their courage. It paid off.

They papered without papering, and got press that was worth a whole lot more than a paid ad.

April 14, 2008

The Beatles: the best cover band ever.

The Beatles appearance on the Ed Sullivan show is one of the greatest moments on television, and one of the greatest moments in the history of popular music.

If you haven't seen it, do yourself a favor and watch the video below. It's thrilling.

The first song they do is "All My Loving".

The second song they do for this monumental moment?

"Til There Was You" from *The Music Man*.

Oh how things have changed.

Wouldn't it be cool if The Jonas Brothers covered "Mamma Who Bore Me" on *The Tonight Show*? Or if 50 Cent covered a song from *Curtains* on SNL?

That doesn't happen anymore. In fact, what's ironic is that pop music used to look to us for material.

And now, with the advent of the jukebox musical, we look to pop music for material.

Come on, pop singers, watch below and see how cool the Beatles look while singing Meredith Wilson. If they can do it at the beginning of their careers in this country, surely you can too.

April 15, 2008

Comps cost money.

If you've ever gotten a free ticket to see a show, you cost the Producer money.

With ticket printing costs and liability insurance, you could be looking at fifty cents to a dollar per comp, not to mention the labor associated with filling the orders, etc.

Doesn't seem like a lot, right? Well, one of my favorite sayings is that *a lot of a little equals a hell of a lot.*

It would not be unheard of for a Broadway show to have 10,000 comps during the first year of a run (think papering for previews, trade deals, etc.)

That's $5k - $10k. That's some expensive paper, isn't it?

So what if we took a lesson from mail order companies that offer FREE products as long as the customer pays for the "shipping/handling"?

Here's my proposal that I'm going to institute at my shows this week: Charge $1 processing fee for each comp to cover your costs. And, if you can get that fee up front, you'll also get a stronger commitment from the consumer to actually show up for the show, as comp ticket attrition is one of the biggest problems with papering.

The takeaway? When producing a show and looking to cut expenses, a lot of people just look at the big things. Don't.

Termites aren't very big, but put a whole lot of them together, and your house will be history.

April 16, 2008

Overheard at the Broadway League conference: Day 1

This week, members of the Broadway League from all over the country have converged upon the Hilton Hotel in Times Square to discuss the state of our state.

With panels on yield management, research, as well as creative conversations with the team from *Cry Baby*, *A Catered Affair* and more, it's the best opportunity the industry has to get together, share information and work towards bettering our industry and our art. And, like most conferences, some of the best stuff happens away from the panels, during the coffee breaks and cocktail receptions which provide networking for industry professionals of all levels.

If you're a member, you should go to the conferences, held twice a year. If you're not a member, you should consider joining.

In case you couldn't make it to this year's conference, don't worry, "ya got me, baby, ya got me." For the next three days, I'll bring you my favorite sound byte of the day.

Today's tidbit comes from Brian Mahoney, Director of Ticket Sales for The Shubert Organization, or I as refer to him, The Swami of Statistics. Brian sits on decades of data on customers, buying habits, lack of buying habits, and more. And he knows those stats better than most people know their own height and weight.

In today's panel about maximizing revenue through inventory control, Brian spoke about premium tickets. And here's the fact that deserves some consideration:

Guess what show on Broadway sells the most premium tickets.

Wicked? Nope.

Jersey Boys? No siree Bob Gaudio.

Brian revealed that the show that sells the most premium tickets is more than 20 years old . . . *Phantom*.

So *Phantom*, despite it's lack of scarcity when compared to those other shows, sells more of the money seats.

Phantom premiums are cheaper than the others, but that's not what sells them. I agree with Brian when he surmised that it's *Phantom's* foreign audience that buys a chunk of these tickets.

Isn't that interesting, because in Las Vegas the <u>high rollers</u> are also not from this country.

"About 80 percent of Las Vegas's biggest whales are from Asia..." (<u>NY Times</u>)

Hmmmmm . . . good info to have if marketing your premium seats, don't you think? Thanks for the tip, Mr. Mahoney!

More from the conference tomorrow.

Oh, and a $15 iTunes gift card to the first reader who "comments" the name of the musical that the lyric I quoted in the 4th paragraph is from. Remember no cheating (click on the high roller link above for a reminder of that definition).

Yesterday's winner and a correction.

Wow. I've got to start coming up with harder questions. You guys killed that one and gave me grief for making it too easy! :-)

$15 iTunes gift certificate to Gil for correctly identifying *On The Town* from yesterday's post. Gil - check your inbox!

Oh, and A. Scott may have found a snag in my post yesterday. I mentioned (in a little bit of dramatic buildup) that *Phantom* sold more premium tickets than *Wicked*. Swami Mahoney may only have been looking at Telecharge figures, which would exclude *Wicked* and other Ticketmaster shows. I'm going to do some investigating to see if I can clarify the stats, but if *Phantom* is outselling *Jersey Boys*, then it has to be pretty close to the green girl, if it's not beating her.

But thanks A., for the astute observation!

(Update on the above: In his statement, Mr. Mahoney was referring to Shubert houses only. I misunderstood his quote to mean all Telecharge houses. So at this point, we have no actual data that suggests *Phantom* is outselling *Jersey Boys*.)

April 17, 2008

<u>Overheard at the Broadway League conference: Day 2</u>

Day 2's comment comes from the creative conversation with the three women of *Cat On A Hot Tin Roof*: Anika Noni Rose, Director Debbie Allen, and everyone's favorite Cosby mom and Tony Award speech-giver, Phylicia Rashad.

The quote? From Mrs. Cosby herself . . .

"Directors do not control me."

Now, you can imagine the "oooohs" this remark drew from the crowd, especially with her director/sister only two seats away.

But Phylicia Rashad settled us quickly and explained what she meant.

"Directors do not control me . . . but I do *take* direction."

What Phyl was trying to say was that while a director can tell her exactly where she wants her to go, and the director can poke, prod and give suggestions to help get her there, a director ultimately has no say in the exact techniques that she uses. And frankly the director shouldn't care, as long as the performance ends up where the director wants it (in fact, I'm a big believer in secrets - actors shouldn't reveal what works for them).

Here's an analogy. You're having a birthday party at 9:00 PM at the local Chuck E. Cheese. You tell your best friend that it's imperative that they are there at 9:00 PM for the cake and ice cream. You can give your friend directions, buy him a GPS, or send him a Google map if you want. But ultimately, your friend is going to figure out how to get there on his own, by the route that works best for him.

And as long as he gets there at 9 . . . you should care less.

Now, if he gets there at 9:10, but brings you the best present (aka performance) ever, what do you do?

You compromise, because it's not your ego, and it's not your actor's ego that's most important. It's the audience.

April 18, 2008

Overheard at the Broadway League conference: Day 3

The third and final day of the conference yielded this goodie:

David Stone, producer of *Wicked*, brought up the recent sale of the theatrical division of Live Nation, which included the majority of their theaters as well as the Broadway Across America brand subscription series in those respective markets.

David suggested that the corporate structure and pursuit of Wall Street type goals (annual growth rates, etc.) by companies like Live Nation was antithetical to our industry.

David's right. As the article linked above suggests, Live Nation ignored the "boring" (as they referred to it) assets of the live theater and focused on concerts and such. I agree we're in much better hands with John Gore controlling 42 Broadway markets across the country. He actually likes the theater, not just big bottom lines. Those are the best Producers.

But does that mean every corporate structure fails on Broadway?

Something tells me that the big ol' mouse that had 3 of the top 5 grossing shows last week (again) would have something to say about that.

Corporations have it tough. But the quality ones that care can pull it off.

April 21, 2008

I'm all a Twitter.

Twitter is starting to tip.

I've heard it more times this week from friends than I have in the last six months.

So I signed up, and will be twitting often. What that means is when you're on this page, you'll be able to see what I'm up to by looking in the WHAT I AM DOING section in the upper right hand corner of this page. I can twit by text, web, phone from anywhere . . . and I will.

The relevance of Twitter to modern day producers of any sort of content is the demonstration that once again, content that is changing constantly . . . and content that is brief . . . is becoming even more valuable.

Check it out . . . and spend some time thinking how to harness Twitter for your shows.

Oh, and here's a great quote about Twitter from the New York Times, after they raised millions (a lot more than a Broadway show, I'm sure) to launch the company.

Its co-founder says that the company was not currently focused on making money and that no one in the company was even working on how to do so. "At the moment, we're focused on growing our network and our user experience," he (Biz Stone, co-founder) said. "When you have a lot of traffic, there's always a clean business model."

Boy did that make me feel a heck of a lot better about a lot of things that I'm doing. Doesn't it make you feel better?

As that freaky voice said, "If you build it, they will come." It doesn't matter if you're writing a show or building a web-based business.

Click on the "follow me on Twitter" link. I promise some fun updates on the day-to-day of what I do. When I'm in a boring meeting or a boring show, or when something awesome is happening, you'll be the first to know. Even before my Mom. :-)

April 22, 2008

3, 2, 1 . . . launch (hey, did anyone check the weather?)

When you open on the big Broad-way, you get one shot. And it's imperative that you know what's happening around you before you pull that touchy trigger.

Look at this quote from Variety about an industry that's much smarter than we are (partly because they have more resources, I will admit, but mostly because they care more about research).

TV network execs who pay attention to the numbers know that young male viewership can dip in the first few days after a blockbuster videogame launches. And home-entertainment honchos avoid releasing big titles aimed at that demo in the same time period.

The current Broadway season is one of the most competitive I've seen since I moved to New York, with 8 new musicals competing for only 4 Best Musical nominations (anyone else remember 1995, When *Sunset Boulevard* won by pseudo-default, because the only other musical nominated was *Smokey Joe's Cafe*?).

Not this year.

What's interesting to me is that up until a month or so ago, there were only 7 potential nominees.

And then, a small show from out of town, with decent but not stellar reviews, no stars, and a minimal advertising budget compared to its behemothic peers, announced that it was going to beat the Tony deadline and open this season. Look out *Little Mermaid, Young Frankenstein, In The Heights, Passing Strange, Cry Baby, Xanadu* and *A Catered Affair,* there's a new show in town! Are you scared? (I bet most of you don't even know what it is, or it will take you some time to come up with it . . . and that feeling you're having is what we call a lack of awareness in the market.)

It sounds like David versus Goliath, right? But it's not. It's David versus SEVEN Goliaths, and I don't think they make a sling shot big enough.

These eight shows are not only competing for just four nomination slots and the television appearance that comes with it, but they're also competing for press, critics, and more importantly, ticket buyers. Just because there are more shows, doesn't mean there are more audiences to go around. Like too many puppies born in a litter, a few of them can't feed, and end up runts . . . or worse.

I'm rooting for the underdog here. I hope something great comes out of this late entry, because I think the team is talented and I do know the players.

But I can't help but wonder what would have happened if they would have looked at what else was happening in the market like our TV execs above, waited 8 weeks and opened *next* season.

They could have been the first to feed, instead of the last.

April 23, 2008

Schadenfreude is not just a song from Avenue Q.

It's also the feeling you get when you read an article **buried** in the media section of the New York Times announcing that The New York Times Company posted a loss for the first quarter of 2007 . . . compared with a profit $23.9 million in the year before.

Holy profit-drop, Batman!

I'd feel bad for them, if it wasn't for the fact that they hold the theater industry hostage with their exorbitant rates (earning them $23.7 million in three months last year!) and fascist policies, most of which aren't written down (they don't allow shows to share ads even if they are in the same theater, etc.).

Another company announced their 1st quarter results this week as well. Their profit jumped 31%.

Which company? I'll give you a hint. It rhymes with schmoogle.

I wonder where the future of advertising lies.

April 24, 2008

Degrees-R-Us.

According to census data, the percentage of the American population with college degrees keeps rising, with 28% of all workers over the age of 25 reporting having completed their undergraduate education.

According to Broadway League statistics, 76% of our audience has completed college.

Here's my bullish thought of the day:

If college degrees are rising, and people with college degrees go see theater more than others, isn't there a tremendous opportunity for the expansion of our audience instead of the decline?

And if there is such an overwhelming correlation between higher education and attendance at the theater, perhaps our audience developmental programs should focus on colleges and universities around the country.

Here's what I would do for the next survey. I'd find out if there are certain schools sending more people to Broadway shows than others. If we found a few, I'd develop partnerships with those institutions to continue to expand on what we know is working already.

I call this sort of technique fan-the-flame marketing. You find out where the spark of your audience is. Then you go blow on it, until it turns into a roaring fire.

April 25, 2008

Cry-Baby opened last night. So, did HE like it?

Only one way to find out: www.DidHeLikeIt.com

April 28, 2008

Advice From An Expert Vol. 1: The Swami Speaks!

I'm lucky enough to have some pretty cool and influential readers of The Producers Perspective out there, so we're going to start a new series that highlights some of their comments and suggestions about issues we discuss here.

The first refers to a post that I wrote at the start of the Broadway League conference regarding the show that sold the most premium. I quoted Brian Mahoney, "The Swami of Statistics", who wrote in recently and wanted me to make sure I made everyone aware that when he referenced *Phantom* as being the top premium ticket seller, he was comparing premium ticket sales for shows in Shubert Houses only.

Since I had The Swamster on the e-horn, I asked him for a few words of wisdom regarding seating and pricing to share with all of you. Here's what he came up with, and I couldn't agree more:

All seats are not created equal. The public knows this and so do we. What applies to real estate applies to selling tickets: Location! Location! Location! We should remember this when establishing the parameters for discounts and not discount the first class section. We should look at a theatre as if we were running an oceanfront resort: you discount the garden view rooms not the ocean front and ocean view rooms. People who pay full price should get better seats than those buying at a discount.

Some killer analogies in there. There is so much for us to learn from the travel industry. My tip of the day? Sign up for all the travel discount sites you can . . . watch and learn how they get rid of their perishable inventory and maximize their revenue.

Thanks to Brian! Until the next expert speaks . . .

April 29, 2008

Theater things that don't make sense: Vol. 1

Today we start a new series identifying some things that are just plain odd.

Not right or wrong, just odd or out-of-balance.

Many of these things are a result of how the business was born, how it's structured, and who has the power. Many are archaic "industry standards" (I hate that phrase, BTW. How can anything be standard in an industry with a failure rate as high as ours? Obviously the standards suck, so why keep using them?)

Many of these things may never change . . . unless enough of us Producers start jumping up and down all at once and start demanding it.

You guys game? I thought so.

Ok, here we go . . . volume #1.

Did you know that if you produce a show in any Broadway or Off-Broadway theatre in New York City or any major touring house across the country and want to sell merchandise (t-shirts, CDs, etc.), you will be forced to a pay a commission to the theater owner? (10%, 15%, even higher in some markets!)

Now, did you know, that in the same contract, you will be told that the theater owner has the right, whether you like it or not, to sell drinks, concessions, etc.. and you get no participation in that, even though it's your audience buying the $4 Kit Kat and $5 bottled water.

Either give us a piece, or allow us to sell it. Producers have so few ancillary revenue streams. If we had more, our risk would be reduced.

Why do you think Steve Wynn can spend $100 million on a show in Las Vegas? Because he has additional revenue streams that help support it: hotel rooms, restaurants, souvenirs, and oh, I don't know, gambling?

We may never get a piece of the bar, but we should never stop searching for additional ways our content can make us money.

April 30, 2008

Who will say, "It's an honor just to be nominated" this year? Guess right and win.

The nominations are pouring in! The Outer Critics, The Drama Desks, The East Lansing Twitterers of America Club, and on May 13th (insert dramatic music here), The Tony Awards!

Nominations and awards are important. After a focus group on *Altar Boyz*, we learned that the #1 compelling piece of information that we could tell people to get them interested in buying tickets was that we were the "winner" of the Outer Critics Circle Award for Best Off-Broadway Musical. It didn't matter that they didn't know what the Outer Critics Circle was . . . they just knew that we won something. And that something piqued their interest.

So the people that get nominated, especially for the "Big 3" (Best Musical, Best Play and Best Revival of a Musical - the only awards that can have considerable impact on a box office), are one step closer to having another tool in their marketing toolbox.

Who will it be?

The real interesting category is Best Musical. The fight for the Big One is almost as unprecedented as our upcoming presidential election! As I've mentioned before, this is an extremely competitive year, with 8 new musicals duking it out for 4 spots. That means a lot of producers are going to have nothing to do on June 15th.

Here are my picks, in order of how sure I am:

1. *In The Heights*

2. *Passing Strange*

3. *A Catered Affair*
   and

4. *Young Frankenstein*

It's the 4th spot that's the wild card. There are a lot of middlin' musicals out there this year. Will Disney finally get a break? Is everyone over Mel Brooks and his cockiness? Will the critically revered but box office beleaguered *Xanadu* triumph? What about *Glory Days*? And don't count out *Diet Hairspray* aka *Cry Baby*.

What do you think? Am I right? Wrong?

Here's my challenge to you. If you disagree with me, go ahead and make your differing prediction in the comment section. If you get all four nominations right and I'm wrong? Free $10 Starbucks gift certificate. To every one of you who gets it right.

But you must make your prediction by Thursday at 6 PM, and only one prediction per person!

MAY 2008

May 01, 2008

"You're a theater guy, so what's all this talk about a documentary?"

Another good question from a reader who caught my "twitter" today about reviewing the operating agreement for the documentary that I'm shooting.

People used to ask me if I would ever do film. My answer was always the same: "I won't do film until I run across a project that tells me I must do it as a film."

Not everything should be a play or a musical. Whenever I'm contemplating doing a show, I ask myself (and you should ask yourself), "What will make this project so unique that it becomes more *special* on stage than in any other medium (book, film, etc.)?" If there's another medium that would be even more effective, you have to consider that.

Theater is a non-realistic art form. Film is a very realistic art-form. In film, if you're on a street, you show the actual street. In theater, if you're on a street, you show a semblance of a street. It's what you do with the lack-of-a-street that makes the stage special. Back to the doc . . .

3 years ago I came across a band called Red Wanting Blue, one of the top unsigned bands in the country. 12 years, 8 albums, thousands of fans . . . but still no record deal. Yet they keep going, and going, refusing to give up. And let me tell you, if you think the life of an actor is hard, it ain't nothing compared to the lives of 4 guys climbing the ladder of the music industry (just wait until you see this footage).

On top of all of this, their music is amazing. And commercial. And one day, in the middle of pitching them the idea of writing a musical about a band just like them, I found myself saying, "Think about writing something similar to your story. What I want is your story." And then I realized, I really did want <u>their</u> story, up close and personal, as they change tires in negative 45 degree weather in Montana and pee in jars to save time in the back of their freezing cold van as they tour the country reaching for the brass ring of a record deal.

So we're filming it.

This Sunday, the band is headlining at The Mercury Lounge in New York City. I'll be rockin' out in the audience myself this weekend, so come . . . and you'll get a chance to see some of the most passionate people I've ever met.

Oh, and I'll buy you a drink. Click here for more <u>info</u>.

May 02, 2008

Why did I decide to be a Producer of this Broadway show?

We all know the odds: 4 out of 5 Broadway shows don't return their investments. So for those of us nutty enough to want to do it, how do we choose the right project?

What do we look for when putting our record and reputation on the line? A good score? A reasonable economic model? Passionate creative team? Producing partners you admire? A show you can say you're proud to be a part of even if He doesn't like it?

Yes.

But that's not all.

For me, there has to be all of those things . . . and something else. Something unique, something remarkable, something purple. Something that can cut through the noise of the other 30+ Broadway shows screaming for attention in the 12 block stretch that is Broadway.

Something that advertises and markets itself, so you don't have to.

And that's why I just recently signed on to be a Producer of *13*, the new Broadway musical by Jason Robert Brown and Dan Elish and spearheaded by one of the most prolific and respected producers on Broadway (and on **television**), Robert Boyett.

So what does *13* have that made me call Bob to see if he was looking for partner like me? Yes, it has all of the above in super-spades (wait until you hear this score), but it also has this . . . a cast of 13 teenagers. No adults.

And a band of teenagers. No adults.

Now that's something that gets attention, don't you think? It's the special little spark that makes us stand out from the crowd without having to buy our place in the front with full page ads, stars that cost $35k/week, etc.

Producing a hit, like having a successful marriage, is super hard. You wouldn't marry someone that just looked good on paper would you? You'd wait until you met someone with something really special before making that huge commitment. Something that others didn't seem to have. Something that made this person stand out from the crowd.

That special spark is no guarantee that you'll be married for 50 years or that you'll run for 50 years. But add it to everything else and I'd bet on it.

Oh wait. I am.

A game I like to play . . . look at the <u>longest running shows</u> on Broadway or any big hits. Find their SS (special spark)? What did *Cats* have? *Annie*? *Mamma Mia*? *The Producers*? Find it in these shows . . . then find it in your own before you get down on one knee.

Stay tuned, readers . . . lots of Producer Perspective ahead as *13* readies to bow on Broadway in September.

May 05, 2008

<u>**Advertising and asking for anything: Why they are the same.**</u>

Conventional marketing wisdom says it takes <u>five impressions</u> before a consumer is primed for purchase.

The same is true when you're a producer and your job is to get people to join your team, whether they are a director, a writer, an investor, or an intern.

Translation? Getting anyone to do anything is all about follow-up.

A talented up-and-comer was asking me for some advice yesterday and she told me how she wanted a director to read her script, but was dismayed because she had sent the director an email and hadn't heard back.

She sent just one email. And was praying for a positive response. That's like placing a 1/4 ad in Time Out and expecting to sell out for weeks.

It's easy for us to take this kind of lack of response as a personal slight, but it's not. The director is a consumer just like everyone else, and you've got something to sell. If companies like Apple or *Altar Boyz* gave up after one impression, no one would sell a thing.

Does this mean that you should send four more emails? No. Think of asking for anything just like a media plan: *Vary your media.* Email (online marketing) didn't work? Try another form of direct response, like a phone call (telemarketing). Or go to a party where you know the person will be and make sure he/she sees you (billboard). Have a mutual friend mention you to him/her (word-of-mouth).

But don't just give up and think no one wants your product.

Instead, think of every impression you make as getting closer and closer to your goal.

And the best thing about follow-up impressions? Unlike 1/4 page Time Out ads, they are free.

Oh, and they actually work.

May 06, 2008

<u>The Enron of Broadway</u>

Early in my career, I worked for one of the most powerful commercial theater companies in the world.

I also worked for one of the weakest commercial theater companies in the world.

Ironically, they were one and the same: <u>Livent</u> - the producers of *Show Boat, Ragtime, Kiss of the Spider Woman, Fosse, Barrymore,* etc.

In just over a year, we went from opening our own theater on 42nd St., to having our paychecks stamped <u>Debtor In Possession</u>.

I was reminded of Livent when I read this <u>article</u> that announced that the trial of Garth Drabinksy, my former Tony Soprano, had begun.

The allegations and the indictments on both sides of the border are pretty serious (if Garth stepped into Buffalo he'd be arrested). I won't get into too many details about what I know, because frankly, I don't want any of those Mounties thinking they should call me to testify.

But let's just put it this way. During the big horse race of *Lion King* versus *Ragtime*, there was a lot of concern about whether we were out-grossing the animals on Pride Rock. Frankly, from what I recall, a lot of the *Ragtime* grosses that were published around that time were just like the best friend I had when I was five. Made up.

That's not the point of this post.

The point is, after everything that has happened, Garth is still at it. He's produced television. A theater piece that won awards last year. For the love of God, he's a consultant!

You should print out that article and hang it by your desk. If Garth can bring down a company, face jail time, not be allowed in the US and still soldier on? Then surely a bad review or a lost investment is not going to stop you, is it?

Garth called me about a year after Livent went tummy-up. He said, "Kenny, there will never be anything like the shows that I did on Broadway ever again."

I told him he was right. Because he was. His passion and super-ego produced some of the most beautiful shows we've ever seen by some of Broadway's greatest artists. The problem was that the industry couldn't support shows like *Show Boat* or *Ragtime* the way he built them. He built mansions on cliffs. And the cliffs couldn't hold them up.

Criminal charges aside . . . is it crazy that I miss the guy? I'd probably still get him his double whipped latte if he asked me . . .

May 07, 2008

You gotta spend money to make money, right?

Not always.

I consider myself very lucky to have worked on the last *Gypsy* revival starring the beautiful Bernadette Peters. It was directed by the cool Sam Mendes, and produced by the gentlemanly Robert Fox (*Boy From Oz, Pillowman, The Hours, Atonement*). It was a first class revival, with first class people, and I loved it.

Unfortunately, it closed after a year and a half. We got great notices and people loved the show, but for whatever reason, we failed to become a must-see (*Nine* won the Tony that year).

A few years later, here comes Arthur Laurents and Patti Lupone in another revival about the celebrated stripper, and people are buying so many tickets you'd think the show hadn't been revived four times, had two movies and been seen in every dinner theater around the country . . . twice.

After seeing *Gypsy* so many times during my tenure, I thought I would have been bored watching the new production. But I wasn't. It's a great production of a great show with great performances.

Here's what's I noticed: The set was smaller in this production. The ensemble didn't have as many costumes. There definitely weren't as many vari-lites in the air. And, what the . . . they didn't even use a real dog or a real lamb!

And yet this production is set to out-perform ours. Doesn't seem fair, does it?

There are probably a zillion reasons why (please feel free to comment your thoughts), including many that we couldn't control. But having two productions of the same show done in different styles this close to each other is a great test case.

It once again proves that a show's success isn't based on whether or not you build custom made boots or you get them off the rack, or whether you get the super-premium lighting package or just the basics. Or even whether or not Momma Rose had a real dog in the first scene.

Do you think those are the sort of things people talk about when leaving your theater?

Should we have done anything different on the previous production? Nope. It was a stunning stylistic choice and unfortunately it just wasn't as successful as we had hoped.

But it does demonstrate that spending more doesn't always make you more. In fact, you can afford to spend less, if you're confident you're giving them more elsewhere.

This also works in the reverse.

Why do you think Wicked is the biggest spectacle we've seen in awhile?

May 08, 2008

Speed dating for producers.

My biggest advice to new producers is to follow the <u>famous Nike philosophy</u> (one of the most successful advertising tag lines ever), and get out there, find a show and produce it.

The rebuttal I hear most often is "Where do I find a show to Produce?"

Well, here's one option.

The <u>New York Musical Theatre Festival</u> is holding their annual Next Link Networking Party next weekend. It's like speed dating for producers, writers, designers, etc. looking to get involved with a project that will go up at NYMF in the Fall. Bring your business cards, your passion and a goal . . .

Tell yourself you won't leave until you find a show that you want to produce.

Tell yourself you won't leave until you get a producer to read your script.

Tell yourself you won't leave until you do something . . . anything . . . just set it and Nike it.

See? It is like speed-dating. The goal is the same. (Wait for it. Wait for it. Good, you got it.)

May 09, 2008

I'll take the option that sells less tickets.

I got in a conversation about print versus online advertising today, and I posed the following SAT-like question to my adversary . . . got your #2 pencil ready?

At the very beginning of a campaign, one Producer spends $100k on a print ad that sells $100k worth of tickets.

Another Producers spends $100k on Google ads that sells $50k worth of tickets.

Which one is more valuable?

A. Print
B. Online
C. Neither
D. Multiple choice questions suck.

My answer? B (and D.)

Obviously this is an oversimplification because we don't know all the specifics, but here's my general thinking . . . sure, you may have sold less tickets, but online statistics have taught you a helluva lot more that you can use in the future (even on print campaigns).

You'll sell more because you initially sold less.

It's education and it has a cost.

Why do you think med school is so expensive? Because those schools know after you pay them a buttload of cash you can use that knowledge to earn an even bigger buttload.

May 12, 2008

The science of storytelling.

I saw a show this weekend that was, um, a little hard to follow. But so many of the problems with the show could have been corrected had the authors listened to Mrs. Apostolu, my AP Chemistry teacher.

As writers and producers we need to remember that stories aren't created out of nothing. They are put together. Made in a lab from our own version of the periodic table of elements.

You can't make salt without Na and Cl.

You can't make water without 2 Hs and an O.

And you can't make a story without the perfect combination of character and conflict.

Whenever I forget how to balance that chemical equation, I go to this chemistry **textbook** . . . or, to mix metaphors, the best blueprint for script writing there is.

May 13, 2008

The Tony nominations are in: we were all wrong.

The nominations were announced this morning, and here are the four shows with a shot at the fat trophy this year:

Cry Baby
In The Heights
Passing Strange
Xanadu

Ok, ok, so in my prediction, I knew I was hanging out on a limb by choosing *YF* over *Xanadu*, but the shock of this set is *Cry Baby* getting a big nod over *YF* and *A Catered Affair*. I can't help but think that Brooks backlash had a big part in the *YF* snub, but the ignoring of *A Catered Affair* (in so many categories) will be the talk of Joe Allen's for days to come.

Unfortunately, the nominators fooled all of you as well. Only one of you chose *Cry Baby* as a nominee (Kudos, BDG), and most of you chose *Affair*.

But since it was such an odd year, I'm going to get everyone that took a shot at the nominees the Starbucks card anyway. So check your email and have a couple of frappuccinos on me.

Here's some insider Tony nomination trivia: The Edison Cafe (aka The Polish Tea Room), which has been the preferred diner of Broadway muckety-mucks for decades (and was featured in the Neil Simon Play *45 Seconds From Broadway*), becomes a conference room at 1 PM on the day before the nominations. The cafe closes up, they black out the windows, and the nominators meet there to make history . . . probably over matzoh ball soup.

Love to hear your thoughts on all of the nominations, so let the commenting begin!

May 14, 2008

Theater things that don't make sense: Vol. 2. Interested?

Do you get excited when you get a big tax refund?

You shouldn't. It means that you just gave the government an interest-free loan for the year. If you're a smart saver, you'd be much better off doing some recalculating of your weekly withholding. Why?

Because the money is always better off in your pocket than the government's, because you can do something with it: invest it in a stock, a show, or just let it sit in your savings account earning a few percent in interest.

What does this have to do with theater?

Well, when a show like our non-nominated friend *Young Frankenstein* announces that they have an advance of $15 million dollars, have you ever stopped to think where that money is? And how much interest it's earning? And who is getting that interest?

On a hit show with a $10 million dollar advance, you could earn a 2.4% annual yield or $240,000 with a crappy Chase savings account. That could be 30 - 50% of the costs of running your show for a week.

And imagine the interest rate you could demand if you took a bunch of advances for Broadway shows and put them together! Well, that's what happens. And imagine what an aggregate $35 - 50 million dollars earns.

Advance ticket sales are not held by the Producer. Since the theatre owner controls the ticketing agent (and may actually be the ticketing agent), the theatre owner controls the interest. They are earning money on the money people have paid to see your product. Doesn't compute, does it?

Cash management is the key to big business. There's a reason why one of the most successful businessmen I know recommended a book to me called <u>Buy Low, Sell High, Collect Early, Pay Late</u>. There's a reason why the on-trial bosses at Livent never offered direct deposit (checks never get cashed right away, which means money sits in their account).

There's an argument out there that Producers shouldn't hold on to advance sales, because they might try to dip into the money to cover losses or expenses, and because the shows come and go so quickly.

This is true, but it's also true for every company out there.

You pay for your plane tickets in advance, don't you? You don't see a third party holding on to the funds until after you travel before delivering it to the airline.

You buy stuff online that doesn't arrive for weeks from companies with only a web site, but credit card companies give the merchants the money sometimes as early as the next day.

Once again, traditional business methods that allow companies to get a leg up aren't allowed on Broadway.

At least one of the major theater owners splits the interest with the Producer, but not the others, that I know of.

Should they? Maybe. Or maybe they'll argue that there are costs with keeping track of all that cash and costs of doing the ticketing that service fees don't cover, and that $240k has to pay those administrative fees (cough, cough).

So I'm not saying it doesn't make sense that we don't get the interest (although I encourage all of you to ask for the split - we need every ancillary revenue stream possible).

I'm saying that it doesn't make sense that we don't control the ticketing . . . and then the interest just happens to come along with it.

May 15, 2008

Advice From An Expert Vol. 2: A Gamblin' GM speaks

I jokingly twittered from a casino in Palm Springs last week wondering if the odds on the craps table were better than the odds of investing in a Broadway show.

Well, craps and Broadway are no joking matter to my good friend and uber-General Manager, Mark Shacket, who is currently in office at Alan Wasser Associates, one of the largest General Management firms on Broadway.

Mark worked it out . . . so I thought I'd include his musings on the subject as volume II of our Advice From An Expert series! Enjoy!

-

_- - - - -
-

CRAPS - EXPECTED LOSS

If we assume the following things:

- that a typical craps table rolls the dice every 30 seconds
- that the point or seven hits every 5 rolls (meaning each "cycle" from the coming out roll to the end of the session is 5 rolls on average)
- that you play the pass line bet with maximum allowed odds every time, with max odds 3X-4X-5X (House edge: 0.37%)
- that you make 2 place bets every "cycle" (Average House edge: 4.06%)
- that you make a hard way bet every other "cycle" (Average House edge: 10.10%)
- that you make 2 prop bets every "cycle" (Average House edge: 12%)
- that your craps session lasts 2 hours

then the expected loss for your 2-hour session is 37.48%.

BROADWAY - EXPECTED LOSS

If we assume that for every 10 Broadway musicals produced, the following results are achieved:
- 0.25 musicals are HUGE hits (Wicked, Phantom): 1000% return
- 0.75 musicals are big hits: 250% return
- 1 musical is a hit: 130% return
- 5 musicals lose some money: 60% loss
- 3 musicals lose everything: 100% loss

And we assume for every 10 Broadway plays produced, the following results
are achieved:

- 0.25 plays are HUGE hits: 250% return
- 0.75 plays are big hits: 150% return
- 1 play is a hit: 120% return
- 5 plays lose some money: 60% loss
- 3 plays lose everything: 100% loss

then the expected loss for your average Broadway investment is 36.88%.

(It should be noted that the above assumptions are based on little more than
my whim.)

Therefore, Broadway has a slightly better expected return than craps (36.88%
loss for Broadway vs. 37.48% loss for craps). Ken's question was which has
"better odds", and these figures suggest Broadway investing has better odds.
But not so fast! Broadway investing may have a better average return, but the
mean return is far lower. What does that mean? Let's look at an easy-to-
understand example:

The New York State Lottery paid out 54.7% of their receipts in prize money.
Does that mean that if you play the lottery regularly that you can expect to
make a return of $0.547 on each dollar? No! In fact, your return will almost
certainly be far less than that. Consider how much of that 54.7% payout is
paid to the small handful of multi-million dollar jackpot winners. That will most
likely not be you. So playing the lottery may have an average return of 54.7%,
but the mean return (what the majority of people experience) will be much
lower, since they don't share in the big payouts.

The Broadway investment analysis above assumes you can invest in every
Broadway show evenly, which you can't. Broadway's average loss is
mitigated in large part by being able to invest in the huge hit. In fact, if you
remove only the huge hits from the equation, the expected loss on Broadway
jumps to 52.50%! But because investors can only put their money in select
shows, there is a good chance that they will never find the very rare, huge hit.
Note that 8 out 10 times you invest, you will lose 60% or more. So
the average return on Broadway may be slightly higher than on craps, but the
expected return (i.e., the mean return; what most investors will experience) is
much lower. Broadway is therefore a far RISKIER investment than craps,
even though the overall average expected loss rate is lower.

What can we learn from this? Well, first, only invest in hits. But there's another important thing to remember: When you're rolling the dice on the felt, you have absolutely no information about what the next number rolled will be. But when you're rolling the dice on a Broadway investment or producing opportunity, you have plenty of information to consider. Who is the producer and what is their reputation and track record? How does the budget look to you? What does the current marketplace look like? Are there other similar shows on the boards and how have they performed? Who is in the cast or on the design team? Is the script well-structured? Is the show marketable? Read, learn, and study everything you can about your investing or producing opportunity and you will be sure to have more than your share of the success.

- - - - -

Thanks, Mark! See you at the tables!

May 16, 2008

I don't care who Cubby is, I want to know who his parents are.

Because whoever created Cubby Bernstein has come up with the most creative viral marketing campaign I've seen on Broadway in awhile (Cubby has already received mentions in The NY Times, Playbill, etc.)

And Cubby is even twittering! Can you believe it? A Broadway campaign that is WITH the times!

Rumors have it that Cubby is the brainchild of Douglas Carter Beane and the folks at the other roller-skatin' musical, Xanadu (a check of WhoIs.net is of no help in determining who Cub's biological parents are).

(update: episode 2 confirms that this is Xana-oriented)

Cubby has our attention. And now let's watch and see how effective he is in doing his job.

The fun stuff should be just beginning . . .

What would I love to see? Cubby sitting in a seat at Radio City on Tony night next to the Producers of Xanadu. Take this all the way, guys. Take it all the way.

May 19, 2008

<u>**1-800-Get-A-800#**</u>

You've heard me whine like a 13 year old who can't get tickets to *Wicked* that one of the greatest obstacles we have as theatre marketers is that we'd don't have easy access to our customers.

The easiest place to get your customer's permission to speak to him/her on a consistent basis is when they make their purchase.

Since Producers don't control the purchase point, we can't get the customer's information (email, address, phone) and we can't ask that customer if they'd like to hear from us again. In fact, we have to purchase the right to communicate with them again through ultra-expensive email blasts sold by the ticketing agent. Doesn't make sense, since many of these people are our customers in the first place, right?

Right. But that's the way it is, and we're not the only industry with this problem (think Book publishers and how their products are primarily sold through Amazon.com or Barnes and Noble).

Since this problem isn't going away anytime soon, we have two options:

1. Take advice from a William Finn lyric and "Bitch, bitch, bitch, bitch" and get nothing accomplished.

or

2. Stop being a Cry Baby and find alternative solutions.

Producing on Broadway is like being a contestant on a Japanese obstacle course game show. You're going to see giant encumbrances every few feet. Things that don't make sense. Things that are scary. Things that look like they were created to make you fail. (Watch the video below!)

What separates the Producers from the game-show-losers is whether you let those obstacles scare you into doing the same old thing over and over, or whether you look for ways around those obstacles.

Example . . .

Problem: We can't communicate with our customers.

Sometimes when I'm faced with problems like this, I flip it around and try and get the opposite to happen.

If we can't communicate with our customers, then let's find a way to get our customers communicating with us.

Here's one easy-breezy solution:

Get a Vanity 800 # and put it on all of your materials. Thanks to internet technology, it's a lot easier and a lot cheaper than you think. Check out this company which handles all of my numbers (1-877-RAD-PROM, 1-888-MY-1-TIME, 1-877-ABOYZ-411, 1-877-OFF-IS-IN, and a few more).

800 #s build consumer confidence. They give the perception of a larger company. And people will call you. They'll call for information, to give you feedback, to ask for directions (I don't understand big companies who bury or don't publish their 800 #s on their website, trying to avoid customer contact. If you don't want to talk to your customers, then that means you're afraid to talk to them, which means you have no faith in your product).

They'll call because they need something. That's when you can get what you need from them.

And as Malcom Gladwell points out in *The Tipping Point*, the people that call these #s are usually exactly the people that you want to talk to, because they've got to be pretty passionate about your product to be calling.

Will this *one* idea get you over the wall and to the finish line? Maybe not.

But coming up with ideas and ways to deal with the obstacles that stand in front of us is a heck of a lot better than just staring at the wall and cursing at it.

What ideas do you have to establish a direct line of communication with our customers so that we can rely less on third parties? Comment away!

May 20, 2008

There are two kinds of stars.

One that sells tickets, and one that doesn't.

And believe it or not, the one that doesn't sell tickets isn't necessarily a bad thing.

Have you ever wondered why a show cast a certain celebrity? Have you ever said to yourself, "Why on earth would (insert Producer's name here) cast someone from an 80s TV series when they have no talent?"

Here's are the two types of stars in our universe:

1. There's the type of star who sells a ticket regardless of the show, i.e. Madonna in *Meet Me In St. Louis*, or Jim Carrey in *Barnum* (my casting dream). Obviously the costs associated with this type of star are high, because guess what? If you know the star is going to sell tickets regardless of the show, then the star's agent knows it too.

2. The second type of star is the one that may not sell tickets right away, but one that gets press, and therefore gets the show editorial content which they may not have otherwise received, i.e. Jason Priestly in *Falsettos* or a Survivor finalist in *The Crucible* (my casting nightmare). This type of star is often used in "stunt casting" to help get a show back in the papers. They are also intended to be the straw that breaks the customer's back when the customer is deciding whether or not to make a purchase. They add value to the show because of their name recognition so the customer can run back to Wichita and say they saw a show with "That guy from that show with the zip code. You know, the old version of the OC." These stars are much more cost effective, since they are not in as high of a demand, and because they usually are looking to use Broadway as a booster rocket for their career.

When you see celebrities in shows, try and determine whether or not they are Star #1 or Star #2.

And when you're doing a show, try to not use one at <u>all</u>.

May 21, 2008

<u>**"How do I get started with Producing?"**</u>

Another common question I get from readers is how they should get started in producing.

Here's my answer on getting started in Producing . . . or in anything . . . in the form of a Kenism.

Newton used to say, "For every action there is an equal and opposite reaction."

I say, "Producing is like racquetball."

When you connect with that rubber ball in that white-walled room, it's going to come back at you. Whether you like it or not.

Sometimes, you'll hit a winner, sometimes you'll hit a dribbler. Sometimes, that rubber ball is going to hit you square between the eyes, like it hit John Candy in *Splash*.

Or sometimes, that ball is going to hit you square in the ball (or the lack thereof).

But if you serve it up, something will happen. Without a doubt. Energy responds to energy.

So maybe when you serve up your first show, it won't move to Broadway. But maybe you'll meet a playwright that will hit a winner in the third game of his match. Or maybe you'll discover a key strategy that you'll use in your next game that'll break a tie. Or maybe you'll get an agent to represent you that will get you in a tournament.

No matter what happens . . . the ball will come back if you hit it against the wall.

The key is . . . to serve.

There's no coincidence that the hardest part of racquetball is the serve. It takes the most strategy, the most strength, the most finesse.

The key is to remember that the ball will come back, even if you don't serve it perfectly. There's a wall there. The ball is rubber. It's got no choice.

And if you love the theater, then neither do you.

Just serve it.

May 22, 2008

Will that be cash or cash?

You won't hear that line when you're standing in line at the TKTS booth anymore if the current test, taking place at the South St. Seaport location, is successful.

Yep, that's right, the "trailer" (as it's commonly referred to), will take credit cards when the new location opens in Duffy Square (a year and a half behind schedule).

My response to this adoption of credit card technology? Welcome to 1983, TKTS booth!

Ok, sarcasm aside, I am thrilled that thousands of theatergoers will finally be able to pay with plastic instead of paper. But why the decades of delay? This is a perfect example of our industry lagging behind the technological times, and suffering for it.

In *Influence* (my favorite sales book of all time), Cialdini discusses credit cards in depth, and cites studies that demonstrate that just accepting credit cards and displaying a credit card logo got consumers to spend more money . . . in cash! People spend more when they use credit cards, it's that simple (NYC cabbies take heed - you will get bigger tips, so stop telling me your machine is broken). Why do you think cruise lines don't accept cash on board but only let you put expenses on your cruise charge card (one of my employees is on a cruise right now - I should ask for her expert opinion as to whether she would have ordered that many Daiquiris if she paid in cash).

Add that to the zillion other reasons people like to use credit cards (postpone payment, get rewards, avoid ATM fees, loss prevention, fraud protection), and it's no brainer that it crushes the few potential concerns the naysayers have had: transaction times might be longer (I'd like to see data on that, because it seems issuing change and having a buyer dig out bills would take longer than a swipe), there is a cost (happily borne by the shows and TDF can probably turn a deserved profit), and my favorite . . . that paying with a credit card is too easy for the consumer and that they should have to go through some inconvenience to get this discount (as if standing in line for hours isn't enough).

Here's my response: When people want to give you money for your product . . . take it!

Why make it more difficult? Especially when you're selling a product in an extremely competitive and economically challenged market. Selling bottles of water in the desert and there ain't an oasis in sight? You can restrict your method of payments to gold bullions or tea leaves for all I care. But selling perishable inventory without any other major revenue streams?

In 2008, the consumer's experience and the ease of that experience is vital. We can't be snobs anymore and expect them to pick us over the countless other entertainment options in this city (it was only in the 80s that we started allowing people to know their seat location before making their purchase. Can you believe that? Who do we think we are?)

We need to get over ourselves.

In 2008, the consumer is in "charge".

May 23, 2008

Who's right? The audience or the judges?

Last night's Idol shocker reminded me of two things:

1. Always set your DVR to record 5 minutes past the end of a show that broadcasts live (I literally heard, "And the winner is . . . " and my screen went blue).
2. Judges and audiences don't always see eye to eye.

The three witches of Idol basically handed the title to David Jr. before the votes were in. But America ignored the cutesy charisma of the 17 year old and gave it to the real rocker.

Who was right?

And is there a winner's curse?

Avenue Q bested *Wicked* for the Tony way back when, but which one would you rather have invested in?

Little Mermaid wasn't nominated this year but *Cry Baby* was . . . which do you think will run longer?

Jersey Boys won, and it's still winning.

Is there any correlation?

What would happen if we let our audiences decide our winners, just like on American Idol?

Broadway.com wants to find out with its Idol-like Audience Awards. You get to pick your choice for Best Musical, Best Play, and even non-Tony categories like best breakthrough performance and favorite onstage pair (which has a little too much of a high school superlative feel for me).

Let's watch closely this year and see the deviation between the two. I'll post the results when both are in.

Vote for your choices here.

Speaking of awards and surveys, we'll be having our own Producer's Perspective Tony Pool which will be announced on June 1st. No Starbucks cards this time. We'll be goin' a bit bigger, so stay tuned!

Oh, and when you're voting for the Broadway.com Audience Awards, pay special attention to the categories of Best New Off-Broadway Play and

Favorite Long Running Off-Broadway Musical, especially if it's your FIRST TIME taking a survey like this since you were an ALTAR BOY (Oh just vote for 'em, already, will ya?).

May 26, 2008

How to paint a face and sell a show.

Wicked is not a show that advertises much. It doesn't have to. That's why, whenever they do anything, I pay attention.

Here's what I've noticed: heavy on the outdoor, a bit of radio during tight times, occasional full page NY Times ads that look like editorial announcements . . . and street fairs.

That's right, Elphaba lovers, nestled between the roasted corn-on-the-cob and the 1000-thread count sheet vendors, you'll find a booth selling the most successful Broadway musical of the last 20 years (at least).

Selling is not the right word, because you're not going to find Ticketmaster operators trying to get you to upgrade to premium tickets at their booths.

What you'll find is an opportunity to take a "Which Witch Are You" personality quiz, a chance to sing your favorite *Wicked* tunes (Oh the poor roasted corn and bedding vendor guys who have to listen to the final notes of 'Defying Gravity' sung by 9 year olds who didn't make the cut at Stage Door Manor), and my favorite . . . a free green face painting.

That idea makes my face go green . . . with no paint necessary.

The hardest thing about a street fair is getting someone to come to your booth, when the buttered corn on the cob is cooing at them from the booth next door. By offering something for free that you'd pay 15 bucks for at Six Flags, *Wicked* gets families to run to their booth, stand in line, and absorb all the marketing messages the staff can muster.

My favorite part? There is no stickier or more visible impression you can make at a fair like this! That face-painted family is going to be reminded of that experience and the musical that goes with it all night long. And it's not a random freebie. There's a girl with a green face in the dang show! It makes total sense.

So should you all go out and get a face painting kit? No. But when you think about it, the street fair is the perfect analogy for any cluttered advertising environment . . . like the famed pages of the A&L section in the NY Times, for example - lots of people wandering through, flipping, browsing, not really sure what they are looking for . . . waiting for something to grab their attention.

How can you get your audience to stand in line to be marketed to, without making them feel like you're hitting them on the head with a selling sledgehammer?

May 27, 2008

<u>When a dozen roses are not as good as one.</u>

I've gotten a bit of a rep for being a marketing stuntman, with my "<u>Virgins Get In Free</u>" promotion and the "<u>Backstreet Boys Boy Band Battle</u>", and so on.

Someone asked me recently what got me started with these out-there attempts to get attention. It took me a week to come up with the answer . . .

Her name was Molly.

Molly was a short haired figure-skatin' freshman from Northern Massachusetts who went to my high school, and I thought she was cuter than Dorothy Hamil in a sun dress.

Every Valentine's Day, my student council had a Sweetheart Sale on roses. For a buck, they'd put a rose in the locker of your crush.

Sweet, huh?

And the perfect opportunity to let Molly know that I was dreaming about her triple-toe loops.

So I bought a rose, right?

Nope.

I bought 12.

Seems inconsequential now, but it was the equivalent of taking a full page ad in the New York Times announcing my affections for that bobbed beauty.

Funny, but it was all the things I look for when advertising and marketing a show these days:

- <u>It got attention.</u> Word leaked out about what I did even *before* she opened her locker. It was the talk of the halls and all eyes were on her as she stepped up to spin her combo lock. My French teacher called me "tres romantique" the day BEFORE Valentine's Day.

- <u>It was a lot of buzz for not a lot of bucks.</u> $12 bucks. Big whoop. So I'd have to put off buying the *Cocktail* Soundtrack that week. Jammin' to Kokomo would just have to wait.

- <u>No one else was doing it.</u> My conservative prep school buddies were too shy (and too smart?) to get more than one rose for the object of their affections. I stood out. And made the other guys look cheap.

- <u>It was timed for a second impression.</u> There was a dance that same night. I could follow up on my flowers with a face-to-face (hopefully cheek-to-cheek) slow dance to George Michael's "Careless Whisper".

It was planned perfectly, and it was executed perfectly.

And then she rejected me. And I was the laughing stock of the school. My French teacher came up to me the next day and said, "Pauvre Serge." (My French name was Serge. Don't ask.)

<u>Lesson #1</u>: When you plan guerrilla events, stunts, gimmicks, etc, remember who your audience is. Molly didn't want a dozen roses, unless they were thrown to her on the rink after a couple of choreographed double axles. She was a freshman. She didn't want the kind of attention I gave to her. Maybe it would have been different if I would have given her just one?

So I failed.

Ok, I sort of failed.

A few days later, Molly's friend Lara came up to me after AP Chem and told me she thought my adolescent dorkiness was cute. And we dated for a whole ten months!

<u>Lesson #2</u>: Just because your first audience doesn't want what you're selling, doesn't mean that there isn't a secondary audience waiting in the wings. And that audience might be more suited for you anyway.

Gosh, I wish I knew where Molly was now. And I wish I remembered her last name.

Which brings me to . . .

<u>Lesson #3</u>: You will forget your failures.

May 28, 2008

Favorite Quotes: Volume VII

"Advertising is a tax you pay for unremarkable thinking."
　- Robert Stephens,
　　Founder of <u>Geek Squad</u>

It doesn't get much clearer than that, especially considering that when I needed some computer work a few weeks ago, guess who I called first?

And when the technician arrived, guess what my first question was . . .

I'll give you a hint. It wasn't, "Can you give me an Exchange Server?" Not even, "Can you solve all the problems with Vista?"

It was . . . "Did you come in the car?"

Read the full article about this comment <u>here</u>. Special thanks to Cedric for pointing this one out.

May 30, 2008

Win the new iPhone! Play the Producer's Perspective Tony Pool!

All right, let's see who's got game! It's time to pick your winners for The Producer's Perspective Tony Pool.

I've picked prizes that I think are essential for all Producers out there:

<u>GRAND PRIZE - The new iPhone!</u>

Unfortunately, I wish I had a handle on when it was coming out, but I don't. Rumors are swirling that it'll be announced before the Tonys (June 9th), but whenever it comes out, the winner (and me!!!) will get one!

<u>1st PRIZE - $50 Dinner at Angus, where all the Tony Award winners (and losers) hang out.</u>

<u>2nd Prize - Pick any 2 books from my recommended books on my blog, plus a 4 pack of Red Bull.</u>

A few rules:

- Only one entry per person.

- All questions are weighted the same. It's just like an 8th grade exam. The person with the highest percentage of correct answers wins!

- Only one winner per prize. There is a tie-breaker.

- Polls close on June 15th at 12:01 AM.

- IMPORTANT: Only Producer's Perspective <u>email subscribers</u> are eligible. You MUST subscribe to the feed via the feedburner email box to the left in order to win. Make sure you sign up today!

- Employees of Davenport Theatrical and <u>Gerry Schoenfeld</u> are ineligible (There's no real reason to make Gerry ineligible, other than that it makes me feel like I have just a thimble's amount of power to say he can't play with us)

- If Gerry Schoenfeld doesn't like that last rule or any rule (or the color of my shirt, for that matter), I reserve the right to strike it faster than they struck the *Glory Days* set.

Happy voting!

JUNE 2008

June 02, 2008

A Purple Elephant?

Seth Godin would be proud.

It looks like Rodgers and Hart were great songsters and marketers, based on Edward Albee's reminiscence of his first Broadway show, in this Sunday's Times.

"The first Broadway show I ever saw was in 1935 . . . and it was a musical starring a small elephant and Jimmy Durante. It had a score by Rodgers and Hart, and it was called *Jumbo*. It had in it such songs as "My Romance" and "The Most Beautiful Girl in the World." It probably hooked me on theater, but I'm sure the hook was the small elephant."

What would Edward Albee remember if he saw your show today?

It doesn't have to be wildlife, but it has to be something.

(Do you think Durante would be peeved that the elephant got billing before him in Albee's quote?)

June 03, 2008

What's the best part of a meal?

The dessert.

Chefs save the good stuff, the sweet stuff, for the end. The dining experience is designed to leave you with the taste of sugary goodness in your mouth as you pay the bill and head home.

I saw a show last week where . . . well . . . the lettuce on the salad was a little wilted. The entree was overdone. But the chocolate mousse of an ending was good enough to make me forget the taste of what came before it. I found myself telling a friend that I liked the show, when in actuality, I just liked the dessert.

It made me realize how important *last* impressions are.

I've seen some of the most creative chefs in the business work magic with the final few moments of their meal/musical.

For example, I thought the last non-star driven (aka <u>Craig Bierko</u>) revival of *The Music Man* was pretty dull. But it was hard not to perk up when the entire cast played "76 Trombones" on brass instruments in the curtain call . . . and then they dropped a giant American Flag (for real, yo).

It was hard for an audience not to applaud for that mound of whipped cream shoved in your face.

Despite the cheesiness of that pile of sugar, the lesson is the same. Make sure the taste you leave in your audience's mouths at the end of your show is a good one. I'll leave it to you to decide how sweet it needs to be.

It varies depending on who's sitting at your table.

June 04, 2008

<u>Love means never having to say you're sorry.</u>

I love the theater.

So you don't have to apologize for it, even when it's in its rawest forms.

You know how you can love your significant other more when they've just woken up and have bed head? Or your baby when they've just used the potty for the first time?

Well, that's how people that love the theater feel when they see theater, even when it's a "baby" (reading, showcase, workshop, etc.)

What the #$*& am I talking about?

When your baby is getting out there for the first time, your audience knows what they are in for. We know what to expect.

If we're going to see a reading, we know you're not going to have full costumes, and that the actors only had a few hours of rehearsal . . . just like if we are going to a one-year old's birthday party, we know that the kid is going to be in diapers, that the parents really planned the party and that there are going to be a bunch of other one-year olds at the party screaming and poopin' their brains out.

The parents don't have to stand up and give a speech before the party begins explaining that the cake will be bigger when the kid turns 18.

And you don't have to give a pre-show speech explaining why the music stand represents a desk and what the show would have been like if you had more rehearsals and more money.

Don't apologize for it. Don't make excuses.

Let the show do the talking and save what you've got to say for after the show in the lobby.

June 05, 2008

What do a Producer and a Politician have in common?

(Insert good punchline here.)

Ok, now that that's out of the way, here's what I think a Producer and a Politician really have in common.

Both have to shake hands and kiss babies.

Modern CEOs of any type of company, from a company of actors to a company of accountants, can't hide from their customers anymore. Corporate America lost the trust of its consumers some time ago, thanks to the idiots of Enron, etc.

It's time for us to come out from behind the desk and let the people know that there are humans behind the product, especially if that product is an artistic one that generates emotional responses from its audience.

Dave Thomas knew this, which is why his commercial campaign for Wendy's was so successful.

How can you be like Dave?

Go to the theater. Hang out in front of your box office. Write your next email blast discount offer as if it's from you. Introduce yourself to audience members. Or, gulp, have a blog. (These ideas are especially useful for not-for-profit executive directors or artistic directors who have subscribers or repeat visitors.)

In short, communicate with your audience directly, instead of acting like the Wizard of Oz.

And, let your audience communicate with you . . .

Remember a few weeks ago when we talked about how it was our job to find new ways to collect an audience's information?

Well, here's a great way to do it.

Don't bury your contact information on some lost page deep within your website (don't you hate when you can't find a company's phone number or email address?). Remember, you WANT your customers to talk to you. Don't make it hard for them to do anything that they want, whether that's buy tickets or talk to you.

Put an email address on the home page, or close to it. And don't make the email address something like info@mysupershow.com. Make it more personal like producer@mysupershow.com or yourname@mysupershow.com and encourage people to write to you by saying something like "Questions or comments about My Super Show? Email the Producer at . . . "

Then, do something really radical . . . respond to the people that write in. People that take the time to write are the ones you need to respond to. They are your super-fans that will spread great word of mouth like a 15 year old boy spreads mono, or they are your super-complainers that need the chance to vent to a person, so they *don't* spread their word of mouth like a 15 year old boy spreads mono.

Not only will you increase your brand loyalty, but, well, would you look at that . . . you just found out who your audience was. You're one step closer to getting all of their information and being able to communicate directly with them, without the need for a third party. And once you have that info you can continue to communicate with them about your current project . . . or your next one.

I know this may seem like a lot of work, but this <u>guy</u> <u>does</u> <u>it</u> (or makes it seem that way, which is almost as good), so I'm sure you can find a way as well.

June 06, 2008

<u>Comps cost money - The Update!</u>

On tax day of this year, I wrote a <u>blog</u> about the price of comps and how I was going to start a policy charging a service fee to combat two issues: expense and attrition.

Well, no new idea is ever complete until you test it. Good idea? Bad idea? No one knows until you put the idea into action and look at the results.

It has been nearly two months since we instituted the $1/comp policy, so what happened?

- Attrition is down. Over 96% of all the comps that were reserved and paid $1/ticket redeemed their tickets.

- We have received only ONE complaint from a customer about the $1 payment. All of the other customers have given their credit cards to us without any issue, and we've covered the cost of the comps, with a little left over.

Oh, and that ONE complaint? It was from a company who we know for a fact SELLS vouchers that we give them on trade for profit, despite the fact that our vouchers say they cannot be sold. Money that could have gone to us is being diverted to them instead.

So just like that, a policy that some thought would create havoc and make a lot of people peeved went by unnoticed . . . except by a thief.

It was a big success, right?

Not so fast. Don't forget that time is moolah. Processing credit card orders, getting numbers from customers, etc. all take time from my staff, which means they lose time from other activities that might be more profitable.

So we're not done just yet. We've got to find a way to automate the process so that it's less labor intensive. Or we have to raise the price of the comp. ;-)

You come up with great ideas all the time, don't you? What's stopping you from putting them into action. And once you do, how can you tweak it to make them better?

Here's my three step process to new initiatives:

- Have the idea.

- Put it into action.

- Examine the reaction.

June 09, 2008

Kermit was right.

It's not easy being green, especially on Broadway, where we power more and more Vari-Lites and burn more and more <u>paper</u> each and every year. David Stone, the Producer of *Wicked*, and therefore maybe the "greenest" producer of us all (in so many ways), has taken the lead in trying to prevent

Broadway from falling too behind in the eco-movement, since we are usually so far behind in every other movement.
Wicked is sponsoring the event below, which is open to all, so check it out if you can. And a jolly-green giant sized thank you to David and the others involved for forcing our sometimes wasteful industry to band together to fight an issue that affects us all.
While I don't believe that David's involvement is anything but altruistic, I would be remiss if I didn't mention how *Wicked* supporting a "green" initiative on Broadway hits the sweet spot of marketing. It just seems to make sense . . . and supports a social cause.
The real press worthy initiative will be the first Broadway show that announces they are entirely green.
(Producers of *Hair*, are you reading?)
See you at the event.

WICKED invites you to join representatives from
THE BROADWAY LEAGUE, THE NEDERLANDER ORGANIZATION,THE SHUBERT ORGANIZATION, JUJAMCYN THEATRES,ACTORS' EQUITY, LOCAL 1, IATSE, LOCAL 802
at The Gershwin Theatre, on Tuesday, June 10
12:00 – 1:30 pm
For a Town Hall Meeting On Making Broadway Green
Special Guest Speaker: Allen Hershkowitz, Ph.D.
Environmental adviser to the Oscars, the Grammys, Major League Baseball and the NBA

Over the past few years, many industries have made strides to improve work practices and make changes that better our environment. We hope you will join us, and other members of our community, for an interactive industry-wide town hall meeting to discuss how we can all come together as an industry to affect change and become a leader in this movement.

June 10, 2008

Twitter under fire. How do you avoid the flames?

When I thought Twitter was about to <u>tip</u>, I had no idea that they would get major socio-political plugs on CNN not <u>once</u>, but <u>twice</u>.

And obviously, neither did Twitter.

A few weeks ago, the site experienced more than just the usual growing pains of a new company with a lot of new attention, thanks to a major database crash because of "too many connections" (isn't that their goal?).   Bloggers everywhere have been lamenting their twitter troubles and competitors are seeing a hole in the twit-osphere.

The last time I saw a revolutionary new company not be able to keep up with its demand was a little website called Friendster.

Will Twitter be trounced by the next MySpace? Only tweets will tell.

How does this relate to Producing?

When developing a show, you have to be ready for the ridiculous to happen.

What would you do if an investor saw a reading and was ready to hand you a check for 10 million dollars? What would you do if Time Magazine wanted to do a feature on your show for its next edition? What would you do if Tom Cruise expressed interest in your script?

We all daydream and wish upon stars and "secret" for this kind of attention. But what separates the Friendsters from the MySpaces are the companies and producers that turn that attention into a spotlight on how they are ready for the big time. Instead of a spotlight on how they can't keep up.

Are you ready?

June 11, 2008

Patton would be proud. It's a Producer Boot Camp!

TRU (Theater Resources Unlimited), one of the few institutions dedicated to the training of new Producers, has just announced the their first ever "Producer Boot Camp," a weekend of seminars dedicated to getting the new Producer producing!

This two-day weekend intensive will feature a number of seminars about everything involved with getting your show off the ground, with a specific focus on producing at the AEA Showcase, Off-Off Broadway or festival level.

They've got some great some great panels planned about budgets, marketing, contracts and more led by speakers like Jed Bernstein (former President of the League of American Theaters and Producers) and Jeremy McCarter (chief critic of NY Magazine).

I'll be giving a talk as well about "New Models" of producing and how I got my shows started by starting small.

Hope to see you there.

June 12, 2008

Advice From An Expert Vol. 3: Listen to those who can't.

Volume three in this series started out as a "Question From A Reader", but as you'll see, this reader has a lot more answers than I do on this issue, so we turned Jay Alan Zimmerman into an expert!

- - - - -

OPENING DOORS & INCREASING AUDIENCES

I'm an author/composer, so guess how many Tony nominated shows I saw this year.

Answer: zero.

Obies? : zero.

I used to see shows in previews and opening night, but can't anymore because I've become deaf.

Which totally s*@#!s for me AND producers.

There are over 30 million Americans with hearing loss and millions more with other disabilities, and this group is growing daily due to aging, overuse of amplification, and unnecessary wars. Add to that the millions who speak languages other than English, and you're missing out on a lot of potential customers by not having your show accessible to all.

What we need is something as simple as the 3-foot-wide door.

You may not have noticed the widening of doors since Bush 1 signed the ADA, but now wheelchair users can go through them just like you. Currently the deaf are shut out from most shows (all the fringe festivals, events like NYMF, one-night concerts) forced to wait years until the producers decide to have a captioned night via the TDF TAP program (which also requires that I be free that night and buy a ticket 3 months in advance.)

Sound Associates has developed one promising system called the "i-caption." Basically, a handheld PDA shows a PowerPoint slide show of lyrics and dialog, which is synced to the show via a wireless connection. Supposedly four Broadway shows use this system, but when I took my family to *Hairspray* for Christmas it was broken and we had to leave and get a refund.

It's so easy to convert a script into PowerPoint. Why not make scripts or caption slide shows downloadable from show websites? Then I can print it out to read with a flashlight, or bring it on my laptop, or on the new iPhone I'm going to win from this site (without seeing the shows). Eventually every theater should have a wireless sync via Bluetooth, which could be used both by your crew and for captioning.

Becoming deaf made me so mad I wrote a <u>musical</u> about it. The producer of the DC production, Commit Media, made it accessible not only to people with hearing loss but to wheelchair users and the blind.

Including this audience made a big difference in filling the house. You can sell-out too.

Just make your doors a little wider.

June 13, 2008

<u>Sorry Rent-Heads . . . no day but tomorrow.</u>

While the characters in *Rent* can live the words of a *Godspell* tune and live day by day by day by (repeat ad naseum), your job as a Producer is different.

Your job is to look at tomorrow, and then take steps today to make sure you're around tomorrow.

According to <u>Riedel</u>, the producers of *Young Frankenstein* have looked at their forecast and have realized that they need to make some significant changes in order to maintain economic viability. That's what big business does.

What is unique about *YF*'s situation is that they are going after the actor salaries.

Contract re-negotiations on Broadway are always difficult, as, naturally, everyone wants to see an increase after a job well done and after a year of service.

Your job as a Producer is to figure out how much you can afford, based on several factors including:

- The economic forecast of the show and . . .
- The cost of replacing the actor.

Failing to secure an actor during a renegotiation means you have to replace him/her. And that can be expensive. It's your responsibility to do that math. Add up the costs for rehearsal space, casting, rehearsal musicians, new photos, rehearsal salaries and, gulp, new costumes! An additional $1000/week or $52,000 (plus benefits, etc.) in additional salaries may sound like a lot, but depending on the role, $52k might easily be eaten up in replacement costs.

However, new cast members sometimes gets new press, repeat customers (casting is one of the few things we can do in the theater to update our content), etc.

Up to you to choose wisely.

YF is doing the fiscally responsible thing for their investors . . . however, it ain't gonna look that way to the artists when they hear they're getting a cut instead of a bump, no matter how much they are being paid now. One of biggest issues we have in our industry is that businessmen and artists have a hard time speaking the same language, which creates a natural adversarial relationship. It's hard for each party to even understand what the other goes through every day.

What would I do to make sure this bad medicine goes down smoother?

Take it myself first.

Riedel suggests this as well, and I have to agree. And it would be the first thing I'd say in a negotiation. "I'm reducing. We're all reducing. So we're asking you to reduce as well."

Much harder to counter that argument.

And sometimes you gotta take the shot in the arm, to show your kid you're willing to endure the same pain.

June 16, 2008

Take II: And the winner of the Tony Pool and the iPhone is . . .

Whew!

While grading your tests, two things happened:

1) I found our winners, and 2) I remembered why I never wanted to be a teacher. And it wasn't just because my high school English teacher told me that he got so stressed teaching that he used to think of students as he chopped wood after school . . . and he didn't even have a fireplace.

Ok, enough of that awkward intro, here are the winners of the first annual Producer's Perspective Tony Pool!

GRAND PRIZE: The new (say it with me) iPhone!

Dial it up, MARYBETH IHLE, and get ready to switch to AT&T because you won! And no tie breaker necessary!

1ST PRIZE: $50 to eat at Angus, where after a few Blue Hawaiians, all the Tony losers will be giving the speeches they never got to give.

Angus changed up his menu recently (I'm starting a petition to bring back the sirloin steak salad), and ERICA RYAN will be eating for free soon enough (and signing my petition soon after).

2ND PRIZE: 2 Books off the PP recommended list and a 4 pack of Red Bull

Shotgun that Producer juice so you can stay up all night reading, LUCY YU, because your hot Tony pickin' just slid you into the money.

Thanks to the rest of you for playing. This was the first annual PPP, which means there'll be one next year too, giving all of you who picked Xanadu to win another shot (Sorry, Cubby, that means you too).

And can you imagine what the iPhone will be like next year?

My portion of this blog is over. Now, I'm turning it over to you.

I want to know what YOU thought about the Tonys! Comment away below, just end your comment with a DidHeLikeIt-type thumbs up, down, or mixed.

Because whether or not the actual ratings were up or down last night, it's your ratings that I'm much more interested in.

June 17, 2008

Theater things that don't make sense: Vol. 3. We need you. Pay up.

This year's Tony Awards featured more performances than previous years. Why? Because the producers of the Tonys know that performances are what America wants to see.

Our fans in Ohio and Florida would much rather watch the original cast of *Rent* or see a number from *Young Frankenstein* (whether or not it was nominated) than watch the acceptance speech for Best Sound Design of a Play. Wouldn't you?

That's why I watched from the suburbs of Massachusetts in the late 80s. In those pre-YouTube days, I used to record the Tonys on our VCR so I could watch them over and over again. And it worked! The Tony performance of *Secret Garden* got me to buy tickets . . . twice.

What you may not know is that those Tony performances cost money. A LOT of money. A performance by a big musical can easily cost $200k - $300k. The cast members get a week's salary (up to a cap), new sets and props have to be built (we had to build an entire new set of desks for *Millie's* "Forget About The Boy" appearance in 2002), there are dresser costs, recording session expenses (the ensembles are tracked, the principals are live), transportation costs, stagehands costs, and so on. It adds up!

Since The Tonys need these performances to attract an audience, to build ratings, to get advertisers, to make money, you would think that they would pay for the appearance, right?

Nope. The Tony Awards give each show a stipend to offset the costs of their performance, but they don't pay for the whole thing. How much? A whopping $20k. And that's for nominated shows. Non-nominated shows pay full freight.

So we provide the content for them to make money, and we pay for the bulk of it. Seems crazy, right? And did I tell you that they get to approve of the number?

You're probably saying, "The ratings are so low, we're lucky we even get a show." It's true, sort of. Thank God for CBS's commitment to The Tonys, but they're not doing this for charity or because a CEO somewhere was smitten by a performance of *Shenandoah* when he was 7. I was once told by an insider that while the numbers of viewers aren't exceptionally high, the TYPE of viewer that watches the Tonys is why CBS does the show year after year. The Tonys, as you can imagine, attract a very concentrated group of highly educated, more affluent consumers, which means they can charge top dollar to top brands.

Why do we pay these high costs year after year? Simple. When are you ever going to get the opportunity to get a three minute national commercial for your show to your target demographic for $200k. It's like a blue light special for TV time!

So we'll keep paying, and for the shows like *South Pacific, In The Heights,* even *Young Frankenstein,* it's a no-brainer.

But what if you're *Cry Baby? Xanadu?* All of a sudden that Tony nomination isn't the greatest thing that has ever happened to you, is it?

Because you have to pay for it.

June 20, 2008

A whole new world.

For those of you following me on Twitter, you know that I've been watching a lot of Sorkin lately. I was in the middle of the third episode of *Sports Night,* when I realized that once again he was taking me somewhere I had never been before . . . and there was no magic carpet required.

In *West Wing,* he took his audiences behind the scenes of The Oval Office, a place steeped in mystery and excitement and high stakes, and something the world doesn't really know much about, because we're not allowed access.

In *Studio 60,* he took his audiences behind the scenes of *SNL,* a place steeped in mystery and excitement and high stakes, and something the world doesn't really know much about, because we're not allowed access.

Sports Night? Same thing. *A Few Good Men?* I'd never seen a military trial for murder with words like Code Red before, had you?

Sorkin opens doors that are usually closed. The subject matter alone is enough to excite the audience into tuning in, and then his twists and turns keep you there.

And when he's done, you feel like you've learned something about a subculture that you knew nothing about before. You feel like you're on the inside. You feel like a *Soprano* (another great example of this device).

Works in the theater too: *A Chorus Line, Wicked, Rent* . . . heck, even *Cats!*

Your audience is Jasmine. You are Aladdin. Take her somewhere.

And listen, that girl has been around, so don't show her the usual sights. Show her a subculture.

June 23, 2008

"I've got a rep to protect."

Truer words have never been spoken, even if they are a quote from my favorite horrible movie <u>sequel</u> ever.

(Side note: Way back when, I tried to get the rights to this movie . . . twice. I wanted to do a *Rocky Horror*-type late-nite version, and spoof the 1000-thread count sheet out of it. Have the actors on bikes instead of motorcycles. Have the audience do the sound effect of the bomb shelter alarm. And you all know you could sing along with all the tunes, you cool riders you. FYI, I was denied the rights and was told that the authors had NO interest in a stage version . . . ever. Harsh, right?)

Back on topic . . .

Speaking of bomb shelters, I recently walked by the giant disaster area of a construction site in the middle of Times Square that will *someday* be the new TKTS booth.

Construction began <u>two years</u> ago, and was supposed to be completed just six months after that! Yet it still remains unfinished (despite this <u>blog</u> that says it would be done last Saturday) and is the ugliest of eye sores in the most heavily trafficked area in our city. If I were a NYC government leader, I'd be having a fit and fining someone up the you-know-where big time, because one of our main tourist attractions looks like a junk yard . . . and that's gotta have an adverse effect on the people paying to visit our fair Times Square.

End rant. Back to the point.

As I walked by the site, I noticed a sign posted on the ugly garbage bag-black walls, boasting the name of the "Construction Management" team of <u>D. Haller, Inc.</u> It's a business card, slapped right on to the side of the walls that have been up for a year and a half longer than they should have been.

In all fairness to D. Haller, I don't really know what the hold up is. Rumors in the industry are that the stairs were constructed overseas and were delivered late. And winter weather had a part.

So maybe the year and a half delay, and the damage to the city's brand, and the disruption to one of the theater industry's chief economic infrastructures, isn't D. Haller's fault. Or maybe it is?

The fact is, it doesn't matter.

Cuz if your name is on something, whether it's a construction site or a Broadway show, it doesn't matter who's fault it is. It looks like yours.

So, If things go wrong and your stairs aren't delivered on time or it's too cold in the theater or your box office is rude to a customer, you better have the answers and a solution, or be able to stir up some sheet in order to find one.

Otherwise, you'll never have to worry about producing a sequel to anything.

Let's have some fun. As a little test, I'm going to call D. Haller in the AM and find out what in the name of Michelle Pfeiffer is going on. Tune in tomorrow. I'll let you know exactly what they say.

June 24, 2008

Free tickets to the A-Train Plays!

The Off-Broadway Alliance, previously known as The Off-Broadway Brainstormers, are sponsoring a benefit performance of the _A-Train Plays_, aka _How The &#$@ Did They Do That In 24 Hours_, this Wed., June 25th at 8 PM at New World Stages.

Christine Pedi and Cady Huffman are just a few of the Bway stars that are coming out to walk across a metaphorical tight rope with no net this year.

I'm a member of the OBA, and I grabbed a few freebies just for you!

First 10 readers to email me get 1 ticket. It's a great show, and a great networking opportunity as you'll be in an audience with a ton of folks from the Off-Broadway community (I'm sure the Time Out Lounge at New World will be hoppin' afterwards).

If you don't get 1 of the 10 freebies, you can still go, and because you're a PP reader, I can get you in cheaper.

Here's how to save $20 and get in for only $30.

1. Click here or visit www.BroadwayOffers.com and use code APBOB608.

2. Call 212-947-8844 and mention code: APBOB608

3. Print this blog entry and bring it to New World Stages, 340 West 50th St. (between 8th and 9th Aves.)

All the proceeds go to the OBA to help fund initiatives for the Off-Broadway community like 20at20, market research, and more.

Choo-choo, catch the train!

Wait, subways don't go choo-choo.

Ah, crap, I mixed the metaphoricals again.

June 25, 2008

Update on the TKTS booth: Does hanging up on someone give you a good "rep"?

On Monday, I told you I would test the rep of the men behind the management of the renovation of the TKTS booth to see if someone would take responsibility, and also give a citizen some information.

Here's how it went down:

Call #1: D. Haller

Ring, ring . . .

D. Haller: "D. Haller."

Me: "Hi. My name is Ken Davenport. I'm a NYC resident and I have an office in Times Square and I'm calling about the construction project at Duffy Square that seems to be incredibly behind schedule. I was wondering what the delay was?"

D. Haller: "You have to call Ellen Goldstein at the Times Square Alliance about that. Her number is 212-452-5208.

Me: "Ah, ok. But aren't you the construction management firm?"

D. Haller: "You have to call Ellen Goldstein at the Times Square Alliance."

Me: "Ah, ok . . . but can you tell me . . . are you the construction managers."

D. Haller: "Yes, we are the construction managers but you have to call Ellen Goldstein at the Times Square Alliance."

Me: "Huh. Ok. Thank you."

Call #2: Ellen Goldstein at the Times Square Alliance

Ring, ring . . .

Ellen Goldstein: "Ellen Goldstein."

Me: "Hi Ellen. My name is Ken Davenport. I'm a NYC resident and I have an office in Times Square and I'm calling about the construction project at Duffy Square that seems to be incredibly behind schedule. I just got off the phone with D. Haller and they said . . .

Ellen Goldstein: "They tell everyone to call me about this. I'm not the right person to talk to about this."

Me: "Oh, ok, well, can you tell me who I . . .

Dial tone. She hung up. End of conversation. Hmmmmm . . .

Call #3: D. Haller

Ring, ring . . .

D. Haller: "D. Haller."

Me: "Hi. I spoke to you earlier about the construction project in Duffy Square and you said to call Ellen Goldstein. She said she was the wrong person to talk to and then she hung up on me."

D. Haller: "Really? Huh. Well, let me put you on with Billy."

I don't really know who Billy was. But he was definitely the Boss.

And Billy was great. After asking me if I was a reporter, he confirmed that the project was supposed to take only six months. He told me it wasn't a management problem, and that the design of this project was extremely ambitious (something confirmed in the TSA's own description). Did you know that the design actually was honored by the New York City Art Commission for excellence in design?

I asked when he thought it would be done. He anticipated it would be completed by the end of the summer.

Billy then apologized for Ellen hanging up on me and he said I deserved info as does everyone else who lives in this city.

What did I learn in my day as a faux-Geraldo?

- The person that answers the phone is like a soldier on the front lines. Arm them with the right info so they can deal with "incomings".

- Don't hang up on people. Duh. Cuz they might have a blog. Or write a user review. Or tell their friends that your show sucks, and you won't have a chance to give your side of the story.

- Speak to the boss. Go to the top when you want the real answers, even though they may not be the ones you want to hear.

- And my favorite lesson of the day? Just because something wins art awards and is praised up and down as "significant", doesn't mean it's practical.

Whether or not you're building a TKTS booth or a Broadway show for a market as complicated as the one in Times Square, there has to be a balance between art and construction.

June 26, 2008

Advice from an expert Vol. 4: a 'wicked' good investor speaks

Do you ever find yourself cruising the Bway grosses and trying to calculate the weekly profit of *Wicked*? And then do you ever wonder who the lucky Mother Ozers are that invested in The Green Machine?

Well, I found one sitting in the corner of Angus, waiting for his helicopter to take him to the Hamptons and trying to decide between a new Ferrari or a yacht.

Ok, I exaggerate. He wasn't at Angus.

When I asked him what it was like to be in such a monster, he said, not surprisingly, that before he started receiving his almost-set-your- Rolex-by-them monthly profit distributions on *Wicked*, he had lost a lot of money in quite a few flops.

He was a reader of my blog, so he knew my affinity for baseball analogies, which is why he smiled when he said . . .

"But investing in the theater isn't about having a high batting average. It's about having a high slugging percentage. I would much rather strike out twice and then hit a home run, than get three base hits." He paid for dinner.

June 27, 2008

If you wanna sleep, don't have kids.

I ran into a new mommy and daddy the other day. I asked them how it was going and if they were getting any sleep. "None," they both replied . . . And then they smiled.

They love their kid, so they didn't care if that silly little schmoopie didn't sleep a single winkie.

I don't get a lot of sleep when I'm working on new stuff. I bet you don't either.

And I also bet you don't care.

If you do care, don't be a parent or a Producer.

June 29, 2008

20at20 returns . . . with a vengeance.

Next week, 20at20, a project of The Off-Broadway Theatre Alliance, returns.

And this year, it's bigger and better than ever.

There are a bunch more shows for you to see this Fall for only $20. So check it out. It's only around for 2 weeks, starting 9/2 and ending 9/14.

What's cool about the program is that it started as a simple idea. And 2 years later it has generated more press for Off-Broadway than any other Off-Broadway promotion that I know of, and has generated more revenue than any other Off-Broadway promotion that I know of.

Ideas are easy. Execution is what it's about.

Your 2 challenges for the next week?

1) See at least 1 show during 20at20.

2) Take a simple idea and execute it.

When you finish challenge #2?

Do it again.

June 30, 2008

TKTS Update: A "comment" from the President (of the TSA)

If you don't read the comments on my blogs, then you're missing out. I pride myself on having some serious smarty-pants readers (including the ones that disagree with me).

And if you don't read them, you missed a comment from Times Square Alliance President, Tim Tompkins, about our <u>search</u> for more info on the TKTS booth.

It's an important comment, so I'm pulling it out and putting it up on the mainstage. Here's what Tim had to say:

> I want to apologize for one of our employees having hung up on someone who was asking questions about the Duffy Square project. That wasn't appropriate or professional.

> If anyone has questions about the project, they can call Minerva Martinez at 212-452-5213.

> There is no doubt the project has been a real challenge, partly because of bad luck (the lead glass contractor went into bankruptcy last year) and partly because it is a very ambitious and innovative project from an architectural and engineering point of view. All that we ask is that people reserve judgment until it is completed; at that point we hope people will see it as an iconic and wonderful gathering place which allows people to enjoy both Times Square and the theater in new ways.

Thanks for the response, Tim, and for acting the way a President (and a Producer) should. Taking responsibility, giving accurate information on where to get answers, and giving us a positive spin on a difficult situation is something we all can learn from.

When you're in charge, something inevitably will go wrong. Without a doubt. Will you be ready?

Because how you react when things go wrong, is the most important thing to get right.

JULY 2008

July 01, 2008

Shows that happen in Vegas, stay in Vegas. And vice versa.

If you've been following my recent road trip on twitter, then you know that I've gone from Columbus to Nashville to Las Vegas, baby, where there could be more live entertainment in one concentrated district than anywhere in the entire world.

As I was scootin' around Sin City in my rental car, I saw a sign advertising the earlier-than-expected closing of *Spamalot.*

Another one bites the desert.

Vegas has been binging on Broadway the last few years, eating up Tony winners like *Avenue Q, The Producers* and *Spamalot* and puking them right back up like they were bad tomatoes.

The closing of these shows seems to be a very hard thing for a lot of very smart folks in charge of Vegas entertainment dollars to understand, including the Wizard of Oz-Vegas himself. No matter how many millions are lost and how many times they swear they'll never touch a Broadway show again, back the Vegans come (yes, I'm hijacking that word), much to the delight of Broadway producers and authors who earn some nice up front advances and/or fees.

And believe me, I've wanted to sell my shows to Vegas for years. It just sounds sexy, right?

It may sound sexy, but more often than not, it ain't successful. And success beats down sexy every time.

Why don't most Broadway shows work in Vegas? Here's an easy way to think of it. Reverse the flow.

Would a Liberace Impersonator work here? How about Dirk Arthur's Extreme Magic? Or a topless revue that features the sinking of the Titanic and destruction of the temple of Sampson and Delilah?

If those shows wouldn't work here . . . why in the world do we think that our shows would automatically work there.

"But Ken! *Mamma Mia* has done ok! *Phantom* seems to be doing fine! And so is *Jersey Boys*!"

True that. But those aren't Broadway. Those are brands. (And it's interesting to note that while they are all doing fine, these shows haven't replicated the enormous success they have in other markets).

So what do I think it takes for a show to work in Vegas and keep people from the slot machines?

- Brands are beautiful.
    - In a town where tourists turn over ever 48 hours, word of mouth is hard to come by, so pre-existing knowledge of what you've got to offer is essential. They've got to come in knowing you.
- Who needs English?
    - Vegas is a global destination and having a show that crosses language barriers gives you a showgirl-size leg up on the comp so you won't have to comp.
- Spectacles are spectacular.
    - The city of Las Vegas is a spectacle by itself, so it makes sense that people want what brought them there in the first place. Get synced up with the city.

One thing that doesn't matter? Price. I threw down $168-and-change to see the Beatles-infused Cirque du Soleil experience, *Love*.

What did I think? Well, I'll just say this . . . jukebox musicals are hard, even if produced by a company that grosses $630 million/year.

July 02, 2008

A profile of a one-hit wonder woman.

As a guy that produces a show about the 80s, I know about one-hit wonders all too well. They get bad reps for being "lucky" and "in the right place at the right time."

Here's a fantastic profile of a one-hit-wonder in the producing world. The difference between Ms. Craymer and Vanilla Ice is that she never wanted a second hit. She was satisfied enough with the chart-busting monster she developed the old fashioned way - with passion and perseverance (think what you want about the show, but its success demands that we study it).

The article is an incredible outline on how to produce, no matter what you're working on, whether it's the Dancing Queen of all jukebox musicals, or a new adaptation of *The Tempest* set on the moon starring Tickle-Me-Elmo.

The article stresses the importance of:

- Developing relationships with the creatives

- Finding a project you're passionate about

- Understanding the appeal of that project without trying to make it something that it isn't

- Being a control freak

- Being prepared for great personal sacrifices

- Bringing work in-house

- Staying true to your vision, despite financial temptation

- Being a control freak again

Alright, enough with the bullet points. Here's the article.

Oh, and before you think that I'm up at night reading British papers, this article came to my attention thanks to the surfing-saving e-clipping site, BroadwayStars, founded by a reader.

July 03, 2008

"The end of Broadway . . . blah, blah, blah."

The NY Times review of the strangely suspenseful *Legally Blonde* reality show ended with this old chestnut . . .

. . . I'll still be watching, even if a victory by either one takes us another step closer to the end of Broadway as we know it.

Really? That's the conclusion? That old hackneyed "end of Broadway" whine that is usually saved for closing time at Marie's Crisis?

Despite what I think of the NY Times as an advertising vehicle, I still think their articles are well written and edited, which is why I was shocked to see this cliché slip through the editorial cracks.

Here's my issue with it . . .

The review seems to be preaching about the commercialization of Broadway musicals, as if the medium is too sacred a cow to exploit in this manner. This isn't the first time members of the press and many others have made this argument over reality shows, star casting, discount promotions and more.

My point is not whether it's too commercial or not too commercial, or whether reality shows have a place for the theater or not. We'll save that for another blog.

My point is that . . . is the New York Times really surprised that the Broadway musical looks for commercial opportunities?

Look at the roots of the American musical. The <u>first musical</u> was born by accident, because a ballet company was ousted from their venue by fire, and shoe-horned into another show down the block. Vaudeville, minstrel shows, burlesque, etc. were all the precursors of the American Musical, and you can't get any more commercial than the magicians, animal acts, acrobats, etc. that made up those acts (I'd bet your yankee-doodle-dandy that George M. Cohan would have done a reality show).

The commercialism of Broadway isn't the end of Broadway . . . it's just doing what it has always done. We shouldn't be surprised, and we shouldn't predict the end of an art form because of it.

Instead, we should be even more proud of the *Show Boats* and *Spring Awakenings* that actually manage to get done, challenging the "quo" without alienating the audience.

July 04, 2008

<u>While we're talking about the Times . . .</u>

In a <u>recap</u> and coal-raking of this year's Tony Awards, New York Times reviewer, Charles Isherwood, said:

The pleasure of the Tony Awards, for me and probably for most theater lovers (and, seriously, who else watches?) is a chance to see artists we admire rewarded for their work, to see them acting joyous, excited, flustered, grateful, maybe a little foolish - in short, human, divorced from the stage personality, without the mask of character to obscure them. The glow of that kind of happiness is always touching. The highlights of all Tony telecasts, for me, are the acceptance speeches . . .

Huh. You guys are theater lovers. Is that why you tune in? I wasn't sure I agreed with him . . . so I did a poll on BroadwaySpace. Here are the results as to why a few hundred Broadway lovers tune in to the Tonys:

45% To See The Performances

30% To Find Out Who Wins

10% To Hear The Acceptance Speeches Of The Winners

6% To See The Host

9% To See The Celebrities

The Tonys took a lot of knocks this year for recycling past Tony winners, including non-nominated show performances, presenting awards pre-telecast and showing edited acceptance speeches.

We have to remember, the Tonys are a television show, and the biggest branding opportunity Broadway has every year. If we want long speeches and catered egos, then let's hand out the hardware of a catered lunch.

No, the ratings didn't go up, but the quality of the experience for those same number of viewers did.

July 05, 2008

Bonus post! Free Screening Tickets to "The Rocker"

A special rain-soaked Saturday post!

20th Century Fox gave me a few screening tickets to *The Rocker* to distribute to my readers. I guess they know that all of you . . . well . . . rock!

Want a pass? Email me. I have 10 . . . and they are valid for 2 tickets each.

The screening is Wed., July 9th at 7 PM in NYC.

Rock on, and I hope that no one blew their fingers off with fireworks yesterday (How I escaped my youth with all of my extremities, I have no idea).

July 06, 2008

Oopsie. Sorry, email subscribers, I am alive.

All of you email subscribers must have thought I was taken hostage by The Times Square Alliance since you went over a week without an update from TPP.

Don't send out the Broadway Delta Force just yet. I'm still here . . . and this entry is an apology for the clog in our feed that prevented delivery to you since last Wednesday.

We've removed the clogging contaminants (some stray Microsoft code) and you should have received an email yesterday with a flood of 8 posts catching you up.

Sorry again. We've got an early warning system installed now to prevent that from happening again.

And if I ever am taken hostage, watch my Twitter. I'll tweet for help.

July 07, 2008

Theater things that don't make sense: Vol. 4. Size envy.

Why is it that most of the companies that service Broadway Producers have offices that are bigger than most Broadway Producers'?

Shouldn't the people that produce the shows be the ones with the fancy addresses and the giant conference rooms and the late-nite catering?

Most of the offices of my peers don't rival the offices of the ad agencies, the general managers, the accountants, the lawyers, the lighting rental companies, etc.

In fact, the only Producers' offices I know that can measure up, are offices that also include in-house service agencies like General Management, Marketing, etc.

Unfortunately funny, no?

As someone once said to me, "There's no money to be made in Broadway. But there is money to be made OFF Broadway."

Something tells me that he wasn't talking about producing shows at theaters under 499 seats.

There are several rational explanations for this phenom, the main one being that it's easier for those service industry specialists to serve multiple clients, than it is to produce several shows (especially in a market that doesn't care about competition).

But we can rationalize it all we want. If our service industries had smaller offices, then they wouldn't have to charge so much, and if they didn't have to charge so much, then our shows would recoup faster.

And if our shows recouped faster, then the producers and investors would be more encouraged to take more risk.

And when you take more risk, everyone gets rich . . . in more ways than one.

July 08, 2008

House seats shouldn't be on the house.

Every show on Broadway holds a certain number of seats off-sale to the general public called "house seats". They are reserved for the authors, producers, cast, theater owners, etc. and are generally released 48 hours prior to each performance if not used.

(Ticket buying tip: if you're looking for great seats to any show, go to the box office 2 days prior to the performance you want to attend looking for any house seat releases.)

It is also industry standard to allow other people in the industry, from agents to ad agencies, to purchase house seats, even if they aren't working on that specific show (i.e. I can have my assistant call for house seats to *The Little Mermaid*).

When I started out, each GM office had a "house seat hotline" that was open from 3 - 5 PM, Monday to Friday, and anyone could call and purchase great seats to any show at regular prices with no service fee. There was even a way to hold these tickets on a "48 hour hold" which reserved the tickets, didn't obligate you to buy them, and if you didn't purchase them, they were just let go 2 days prior as previously discussed.

We've gone to email and fax now, so house seat requests can come in 24 hours a day. And believe me, on hot shows like *South Pacific*, they do. Every friend of a friend knows someone who works somewhere close to Broadway and wants a couple of tickets to the hottest show around.

House seats are a job that sometimes falls to the Assistant Company Manager, but many times, a person in the General Manager's office assumes the responsibility.

You know what that means?

It means that house seats cost shows money. The GM has to put someone on salary. In triplicate house seat forms are created. Phone calls, faxes, mistakes. Money, money and time and money.

Should we get rid of house seats? No. But why not add a service fee to offset the costs and inconvenience?

If we charged $5/order to the people that had no connection to the show (I'm not suggesting that we charge those that work on the show), we could pay for the staff member and expenses associated with house seats.

And what if the buyer didn't want to pay? Well, then they can call Telecharge like anyone else. I hear the same locations would go for double regular price. But something tells me that just like the $1 comps, the buyers would suck it up and pay.

I'm all for being nice to the people in my industry. But I'm all for being nice to my investors first.

July 09, 2008

The stats on adapts.

Musicals aren't a very original art form, everyone knows that. From *Show Boat* to *Shrek*, most are based on pre-existing material.

But it feels like it's getting worse, right? Especially if you've read any of the *TOS* advertising, which is billing itself as one of the few totally original new musicals.

Well, let's look at the last three decades and see what our authors are up to . . .

In the last 10 years, 64% of all musicals were adaptations.

In the 10 before that, 68% of all musicals were adaptations.

And, in the 10 before that, it was 60%.

Relatively consistent, right? And no sign of a trend in either direction.

But here's a trend that you can't deny.

In the decade starting 30 years ago, 6% of all musicals were based on movies.

In the decade starting 20 years ago, 11% of all musicals were based on movies.

And in the most recent decade, the percent of musicals adapted from movies was 19%.

Most of you probably could have guessed this trend, but can you guess why?

Is it because we've run out of classic novels to adapt? Is it because *Rent* tipped our audiences away from the epic British pop-era to crave more modern stories and scores? Is it because we can't get our hands on the rights to contemporary novels because the movie companies use whatever petty cash they have to wrap up those rights for years?

Who knows, but the fact is that the movies are on the marquees. Is it the sign of the <u>end</u> of Broadway as we know it?

Nah. Adapted musicals are the majority, and it doesn't matter where they come from, as long as they keep coming and as long as audiences keep coming to see them.

July 10, 2008

<u>The real stars get stepped on.</u>

I stepped on Big Bird today. And Thomas Edison. And even Pat Sajak (I enjoyed that one).

Yep, while in LA I took a walk down Hollywood Boulevard on the wondrous Walk of Fame. It's quite a big deal, you know. They have a big to-do when you get your star. And then people take pictures of it (even if they don't know who you are). And it gets a Wikipedia <u>entry</u>.

And it's brilliant marketing.

Why don't we have we have a walk of fame? Anyone out there reading that controls that bit of real estate known as Shubert Alley? Or what about down our namesake street itself?

Seems like the perfect place to put down some permanent markers for our biggest stars, no? (We actually have a theater hall of fame, but it's at the

Gershwin Theater, so only the *Wicked* audiences get to gaze on the names of the inductees).

I know what you're saying . . . that most people don't know our stars like they know Hollywood stars, so it wouldn't be as exciting since we don't have an "Elvis".

But that's my point. By creating a public and permanent honor we are saying to the world, "Hey, these people are significant, so you should pay attention . . . and take pictures".

You don't think that people would? Then try this:

Go out into the streets. Stop on the sidewalk and look up . . . at nothing. Soon enough, someone will walk up next to you, stop, and stare straight up in the air wondering what the heck you're looking at.

You can't *tell* your audience to pay attention. You have to *do* things that demonstrate that your art form <u>deserves</u> attention.

Do that, and your audiences will pay attention . . . and full price.

July 11, 2008

<u>Like a pea, I'm in a pod.</u>

I was honored to be asked to join the popular Broadway podcast <u>Broadway Bullet</u> as a regular contributor. This week marks my first p-cast, and in it I talk about my definition of a Producer's job.

I'll be contributing a "column" for each episode, which comes out twice a month.

So if you want to shake it up and hear me talk instead of reading what I type, give it a listen.

I promise to try and be as good for you as a plate of peas.

July 14, 2008

<u>Some things are the same, no matter what coast you are on.</u>

They've got movies and we've got theater.

They've got two seasons and we've got four.

They've got Panda Express and In 'N Out Burger and . . . well, we don't.

There are a lot of things that make the left and right coasts very different.

But there are some things that make it seem like we're in the same time zone. Like selling.

Meet MJ. I did . . . on Hollywood Boulevard trying to sell what is in his soul (his music) to anyone that would stop and listen.

At first, I couldn't believe how much he reminded me of Duane from this previous post of mine.

But then I remembered something . . . the science of selling is the same, no matter how many seasons you have.

July 15, 2008

Me and the geeks chattin' about investing in Broadway.

I was asked to be a guest on "The Wall Street Geeks" BlogTalkRadio segment on Sunday night.

The segment served as an intro to investing in the Great White Way for all of their Wall Street savvy investor listeners. Host Michelle Price asked me some great questions, including one which led me to my favorite new analogy.

Tune in and listen to me compare the process and timetable of returning capital to investors to an overflowing pool.

Thanks for having me, Geeks!

July 16, 2008

When I think about you I test myself.

No one likes taking tests.

Blood tests, Scholastic Aptitude Tests, Life Expectancy Tests . . . none of them are fun (I'm a goner by 63, BTW, in case anyone wants to send flowers now).

But, in order to stay healthy, go to college, and find out what we're doing wrong in order to start doing it right, we take tests.

You've heard me preach about the importance of testing in advertising and marketing before, so this post is nothing new. And frankly, a lot more important and successful <u>people</u> have preached about it since the beginning of modern advertising itself, so it shouldn't be anything new to anyone selling anything.

That's why it's so shocking that testing in the commercial theater is as rare as a 5th row seat to *Jersey Boys*. What other industry would spend 10 to 15 million dollars on developing a product and not test it before going to market?

But this isn't about them, this is about you.

How can you test your advertising or your Act II? What do you do if you can't afford one of the companies out there that offer these services, like the super-smart peeps at <u>Live Theatrical Events</u> (no coincidence that they are a Nielsen company).

Here's my rule of thumb and forefinger . . . when anyone, anywhere, pitches me a product or service (especially one that I can't afford), I immediately go to Google and see if I can find out a way to do it myself.

Enter <u>SurveyMonkey.com</u>, the online survey system that lets you design custom surveys and it promises to have your answers to you faster than you got your SAT scores.

If you took my Producer's Perspective Tony Pool, then you used a SurveyMonkey survey. Or if you attended a reading of *My First Time* and got an email the next day asking for feedback on tag lines, the set, etc., then you used SurveyMonkey.

Test. Then take your results and stir them in with your gut instincts. And cook up a response that'll increase the life expectancy of your show.

And so . . . I'd be a hungry-hungry hypocrite if I didn't test myself!

So here it is, folks, The Producer's Perspective survey! Your chance to rate how I've been doing over the past year and give me feedback on what else you want from the blog!

<u>Click here</u> to take the anonymous survey. Results to be revealed on a future blog.

July 17, 2008

Sequels suck. But just for us.

Squeezing successful products for every penny of profit may sound like a greedy, grubbin' producer sort-of-thing to do, but the exploitation of products that have penetrated the market successfully is what allows producers to reinvest in more new product.

When most industries squeeze their products for more profit out pop sequels.

How many *Rocky* films were there? How many Lestat books?

How many iPhones do you think there will be? Yep, even technology has sequels.

But plays and musicals don't . . . or not successful ones, anyway.

Bring Back Birdie, Annie Warbucks, Best Little Whorehouse Goes Public, etc. Bomb, Bomb, Ba-bomb (although that last one had some great Carol Hall tunes . . . and a real horse on stage).

There has never been a successful musical or play sequel in the modern theater (the thought of a play or musical sequel just sounds brie-zy, doesn't it?).

In a year and a half, we're going to see the biggest challenge to the "sequels-suck" theory, when the longest running musical in history puts up its version of "what happened next".

The question is, will it, like *Rocky II*, sit next to its predecessor on the shelf? Will both shows be up at the same time?

Not if I was producing both (and I bet they won't have the same producers). I'd slide out the old for the new. The one thing that *Phantom* has to fight history is that it could seamlessly present its sequel, instead of waiting 20 years.

But I wouldn't be producing it. Given the opportunity to do a sequel (with all the economic baggage that will come with it) or something new, I'd go for the original.

Now, if I had an opportunity to produce *Rocky 7*, that's another story.

July 18, 2008

The sequel to sequels.

So *Les Miserables II: One Show More* is out of the question.

Ditto to the sibling sequel *Thoroughly Modern Molly*.

If we can't sequelize our shows, is there anything else we can do to extend their life?

Movies release remastered versions with bonus material.

Books reprint 2nd and 3rd and 10th editions.

iPhones have software updates.

What can you do to re-energize your audiences into coming back to your show? Recast? A new song or scene appears? Talk backs? A new special effect? A new sound system?

Some of these are pretty drastic (and pretty expensive), so before you go asking your authors for a new tune for Act II, let's look at those other industries and what they do.

Remastered, 2nd editions and software updates all have one thing in common. They seek to improve their product. They don't just make it different. They make it better.

What would you do if your show was running 20 years to make it better?

July 21, 2008

Don't get caught in your wet suit.

Part of the documentary I'm shooting involves interviews with celebrities that work in difficult industries, face failure every day, but never give up, despite long odds and longer hours.

I've been fortunate enough to interview Seth Godin, Dr. David Sidransky, Doyle Brunson, "Rudy", and more (You're going to love these things when we're done).

I also wanted to interview the founders of Google, Larry Page and Sergey Brin. I knew it was a long shot, but hey, the risk/reward ratio was pretty good. It took me about 3 minutes to shoot an email off to the press dept., and if it got through, it'd be like hitting the lottery on my birthday after getting an opportunity to invest in a tour of *Wicked*. In my pitch letter, I made sure they understood that we could do the interview in as little as 15 minutes.

Two days later, I got an email back from Google's press department saying that Larry and Sergey's schedule "leaves next to no time for media opportunities."

Hmmmm, really? Not even 15 minutes? Sounds like a "He's Just Not That Into Me" excuse to me. I would have much rather had the truth, because I don't care if you founded Google or you founded America . . . everyone has 15 minutes if you *want* to give it.

So . . . I couldn't let them get away that easy. :-)

I FedExed Larry and Sergey a copy of *The 4 Hour Work Week*, which teaches readers how to be more effective with time management, so they have more time to do the things they want to do, while still making googles of dollars. (I also just happened to know that they had hired the author of *4 Hour*, Timothy Ferriss, to speak to their employees.)

I included a letter that quoted their press rep's response, and told them I was sending them the book "to help put a little more space in your week. You've given me Google. I'm giving you time. Seems only fair. When you're done reading it, give me a call so we can set up the interview."

And guess what happened??? Guess who just called me?????

Ok, truth is . . . they didn't. But wouldn't it have been cool if they did?

Think I was too much of a smart a$$? Think I was risking pi$$ing off powerful people? Think they really are too busy and that their time is really too tight???

Look at the photo below . . . it was featured in an article in the NY Times last week about how Google missed profit expectations (That's Sergey in the wet suit. It looks like that suit is the only thing that's tight for Sergey).

It's ok that they didn't want to do the doc. You're going to get lots of people telling you they don't want to be a part of your projects.   When Google isn't interested, go to Yahoo, and then AOL . . . and you'll find someone eventually who you connect with. Keep Googling.

But when the situation is reversed, and people are asking you for things? Make sure the people doing the talking for you aren't blowing smoke up your server.

Tell people you're not interested. And tell them why. The truth always comes out, and you don't want to feel like you've been caught *without* a wet suit.

July 22, 2008

Theater things that don't make sense: Vol. 5. Regional theaters as authors.

The regional out-of-town tryout is a popular way to develop new works headed for Broadway, especially expensive musicals.

Shows like *Jersey Boys, Thoroughly Modern Millie, Light In The Piazza, Color Purple* and more, were all incubated out-of-town.

So how does this work?

Traditionally, Producers of shows with commercial dreams cut deals with these theaters to put them on their season.

The deal usually includes an up-front "enhancement" payment for line items that are above and beyond the regional theaters customary budget (most wouldn't normally do musicals of such size and scope, so they may need costume help, additional sets, per diem for the creatives, etc.). This fee can easily be several hundreds of thousands of dollars if not more. But, it makes sense that the Broadway producers would pay for it.

In addition to this fee, it is also customary that the theater gets a royalty, usually between 1 and 1.5%. (To put that in perspective, the minimum for an author of a musical (bookwriter, composer, etc.) according to the APC is 1.5%.)

This is what doesn't make sense to me.

As producers we're forgetting the incredible value we're giving these theaters. We've gotten desperate looking for development deals, and we're giving away what little we have left of the store, before the store has even opened.

A world-premiere of a brand new musical on its way to Broadway is of tremendous value to a regional theater. It brings audiences, subscriptions, fund raising opportunities, publicity, and more. Think about it: if you were the AD of a regional theater, what would you rather have . . . a self-produced revival of *No, No, Nanette*, or a brand-spankin' new musical on its way to Broadway? You'd pass on the "Tea For Two" in two seconds.

Yet not only do we enhance the production (making the show more attractive for the theater's subscribers), we also pay them like they were an author for the rest of the run of the show?

It's like someone inviting you to their house dinner. You bring the wine, like a good guest should. Yet, after you leave, they expect you to send them a bottle every week until you move away.

Yes, the development work done at regionals is crucial and at a lower cost, but it's costing us too much to do it. It seems that even the theater owners out of town have found a way to squeeze us content providers.

The good news is that there are almost 2,000 regional theaters around the country. We just have to do the work to find the ones that want us, instead of the ones that just want to make money off us.

July 23, 2008

Survey says! It's nice to meet you.

Thanks to all of you who completed my survey!

You gave some terrific feedback, and it was just cool to find out a little more about you. Sometimes I feel a little like nutty Norma Desmond typing to all you "people out there in the dark", so it's nice to know that the lights are on and there are a lot of people home.

Want to know more about the other folks reading?

GENDER

60% male
40% female

AGE

3.6%   18 and under
21.4% 19 - 25
23.2% 26 - 30
24.1% 31 - 40
16.1% 41 - 50
10.7% 51 - 60
.9%   61+

TOP 3 PROFESSIONS

33.9% Producer
25.0% Writer
22.3% Actor

WHERE DO YOU LIVE

93% in the US
51% of those living in the US are in NY
5% are from Texas

Our Far-Away reader award goes to our reader down under in Australia.

Neat, huh?

Data is real. It forces you to focus. It gets us out of the ethereal and into the actual. It establishes a baseline, which you can then use to improve.

Who can you survey? Here are some ideas:

Survey your regional theater audience about what shows it wants to see next year before planning your subscription season. I'll bet you 2 boxes of Domino's chicken kickers you'll sell more tickets.

Survey your actors about the directors and choreographers they want to work with. I'll bet you double or nothing you get more people to show up for auditions.

Find the data. Use it to focus. And use that focus to improve whatever it is you do.

One more stat:

MY FAVORITE SUGGESTION ABOUT WHAT TO WRITE ABOUT

"I also enjoy the entries that spark discussions in the comments, as your readership seems to boast incredibly smart people who, whether they are challenging or agreeing with your thoughts, respond with respectful and well thought-out comments."

Damn straight, my readers are smart. I kind of want to challenge another blog in an smart-off or an arm wrestling match or something.

My comment on that comment is to continue to comment! I've read so many Oil Barrels of Wisdom (so much more valuable than pearls) from all of you. This blog was created to try and turn the Titanic that is Broadway. It's going to take time. It's going to take effort. But if we're all here grabbing the wheel, then over time we just might find a way to smoother waters.

Um, to the one person who told me in the survey to ease up on the analogies in his/her feedback, don't read that last paragraph.

Oh, wait, crap.

July 24, 2008

Merch madness.

I fell in love with the movie *Better Off Dead* (and its leading lady, <u>Diane Franklin</u>), when I was 14.

In addition to using my allowance to buy the movie on VHS (which cost $79.99 at the time), I also bought the poster and the soundtrack. They didn't have *Better Off Dead* t-shirts . . . so I created my own with a silk -screen press I made in shop.

When a consumer is crazy about something, they want to re-experience it in any way they can. They want to show it off.

They want to buy merch.

As marketers, we're always looking to find our most passionate customers. Sometimes we forget to look in the most obvious of places.

Our most passionate people are standing in line at our merch stand.

People willing to fork over $65 for a zippered *Wicked* <u>hoodie</u> are also the ones most likely to tell their friends that they "just have to see that show!" These are the types of people that are the keys to any successful word of mouth campaign (for Fyiero's sake, they're willing to pay to wear an over-priced sweatshirt probably made in a sweatshop featuring your logo!).

Like the <u>800# idea</u>, reaching out to your merch buyers is another way around Ticketmaster and Telecharge, allowing us to talk to our BEST customers directly.

So, how do you take advantage of it?

Collect contact info at your merch stand. Create partnerships with your merch company so that they give you access to the people that buy merch online (or start your own merch company). Offer a gift certificate for tickets that they can buy for their friends. Stuff the merch bags with flyers. Train your sellers to sell the show as well as the shirts.

Merch stands are mines of golden customers. And they're there in our lobbies.

Now if only Diane were in the lobby . . .

July 25, 2008

Where's the Tony Award ticket police when you need them?

Shortly after a show opens on Broadway, all 800 or so Tony Voters are invited to see the show, even if it's months before the nominations are out.

As many have reported, one of the biggest challenges facing Tony hopefuls is the same challenge that faces our presidential hopefuls: voter turnout.

I've had to work the phones on a few shows, trying to make sure every one of those voters had seen the show I was on at the time. On *Ragtime*, the alleged book-cook, Garth Drabinsky, used to call me himself at the end of every day to get an update on the % of Tony Voters who had seen the show (We never broke 70%).

It's definitely an issue that needs addressing.

But I want to address the opposite issue. What happens when they do come . . . and it's not them.

Tony Voter ticket fraud occurs more frequently than Donna Murphy misses shows. Voters call in for tickets, and then pass them along to their friends, their assistants, and so on. Sometimes it's because they've seen the show already (opening night, etc.) and other times it's because they just don't want to see the show.

I've been in plenty of a box offices and watched as freckled-faced AMDA students came up asking for their Tony tickets, claiming to be people I knew that were in their 70s.

What do you do? Turn them away? Risk irritating an actual voter? (I did turn someone away once.)

800 voters. At 2 tickets each, that's 1600 tickets or the equivalent of a full house at The Marquis Theater. That's about $100k worth of revenue that we give away, or 1% of the capitalization of a 10 million dollar musical.

If we're taking money out of the pockets of the investors and good locations out of the hands of the public, then we need to insure that the people sitting in those prime orchestra seats are the actual decision makers.

How? It's time for all Tony voters to be issued photo identification by the League, just like a college ID, that is updated every year with a "validation sticker" (it's important the shows are not the policeman on this issue, for fear of voter backlash). That ID has to be shown in order to pick up your tickets, and those tickets can only be picked up at the box office, 30 minutes prior to showtime.

Will it solve the problem? No, just like underage drinking, it will probably never go away. But, required IDs do make it a lot harder for people to get their hands on the good stuff.

Ironically, instituting this policy will cause voter turnout to drop because those already low turnout numbers are counting for tickets used . . . not valid tickets used.

But let's let it drop, because then we'll realize how important that first issue really is.

July 28, 2008

"Well, we're moving on . . . down!"

Off-Broadway shows have always graduated to Broadway.

But in the last 5 years, we've watched a bunch of Off-Broadway shows graduate early. Like smarty-pants Juniors with a lot of AP credits and perfect SAT scores, shows like *Avenue Q, Spelling Bee,* and *Title of Show*, have moved on to the big time and the bigger budgets, instead of staying Off-Broadway, like they would have 15 years ago when Off-Broadway was more fertile ground.

The logic behind the skip-a-grade mentality? If you have a commercially viable product, and if you're raising one million bucks, why not raise two or three, and get the built-in marketing machine that comes with a Broadway address (Tony Award eligibility, press attention, tourist attention, more advertising dollars, etc.)

Here's my question:

Could it work the other way? Could what goes up, also come down?

If Producers shoot for Broadway for the branding that comes with it, then after they get it, could they ever retreat to where they came from, or where they belonged in the first place?

I'm not talking a 'hit' and run here. I'm talking the shows that are at the end of their Broadway runs, whether that's a few weeks after the Tonys or a few years.

Could *Spelling Bee*, with its brand firmly in place after its Broadway run, have moved to a smaller theater Off-Broadway? What about when the hard-workin' *Xanadu* decides to call it quits. Could it move and take a majority of its audiences with it, with a minority of its expenses? Or what about those great plays that get expelled prematurely, like the acclaimed *Journey's End*. Broadway-ending grosses of a couple hundred grand a week would be like Xmas weeks Off-Broadway (certainly those grosses would drop, but then again, so would expenses).

Deals would need to be struck with the unions to ever attempt such a transfer, but if it's a close-or-move situation, why wouldn't they be reasonable?

There'd be a zillion other challenges: new design, tech costs, limited marketing dollars, and so on. It would take the perfect storm of a show to ever give it a shot and a producer with some serious poobahs.

But someone will, and someone should. As a Producer, it's your job to do the due diligence on this and any other idea that could extend the life of your show.

Downsizing is part of every other business, why shouldn't it be a part of ours?

July 29, 2008

Get your philosophy on . . .

I got an email from a 17 year old reader from Miami, FL who is taking classes at my alma mater this summer. We'll call him David . . . because that's his name.

One of David's classes is called "Theatre in New York" and it's a class "dealing with the philosophy of performance, particularly in relation to theatre seen both on and Off-Broadway. The class culminates in a presentation where I, as part of a group, must answer the question, "What is Theatre?""

David's group has decided to ask all sorts of folks in and out of the biz for their answer to that question.

Tough question, right? At first I tried to come up with a clever answer like the urban mythical Harvard applicant who when asked on his application to "Use the space below to describe yourself" answered with one word. "Brief."

Here's what I came up with.

What is Theatre?

Theatre is the only art form that exists in the present tense.

Film was.

Books were.

Theatre is.

What is Theatre to you?

Use the space below to comment your thoughts. To quote our good friend, David . . .

There are no parameters, no rules. It can be as long as you want, as short as you want, as specific as you want, as broad as you want. We thank you for sharing your time to help us with our project (and our grades).

July 30, 2008

Closing the circle on the customer.

When a customer buys a ticket to a Broadway show for the first time we have an opportunity as an industry. An opportunity to close the marketing circle on that customer and never, ever let them leave.

When a customer buys a product, they are much more likely to buy a second product that is similar in nature.

In other words: Sell one show, and it's easier to sell a second, and a third, and so "fourth".

It's our job as producers to close that circle on the customer, directing them to other shows, even if those shows are our competition.

So how can we close it?

- Could the theater owners put videos in the lobbies of box offices (and bathrooms?) showing video loops of all the Broadway shows (maybe only in their theaters, if they wanted to keep their circle smaller).

- What about similar shows teaming up to recommend each other with a sign at the exit that says, "If you loved Rent, you'll love Spring Awakening".

- Or my favorite . . . the endorsement: When political candidates bow out of a race, what do they do? They endorse someone in their own party. They may have lost, but the party lives on. When shows close, couldn't they "endorse" a show that's still running? (I got *Brooklyn* to send out an email with this message on *Altar Boyz* years ago - I offered them a commission on any tickets sold on the offer they sent to their subscribers).

Producing theater in NYC is competitive. I've had Producers tell me I shouldn't be blogging on some of the subjects we've discussed. They think I should save my ideas for myself, because keeping business practices private strengthens a business. They think I should just sell my shows.

My feeling? Circles, when closed, are round. If a customer isn't going to see my show, as long as they see another one, I don't mind.

Eventually, they'll come a-round.

July 31, 2008

Why you and your career are like teenagers.

Provided you're "eating right", you're growing every day.

I know it may not seem that way. At times you may feel like you're not going anywhere, that you're making no progress, that you'll never be "tall enough to ride this ride". I feel this way all the time.

But remember when you were a kid and every time you saw grandma or your parents' friends they always said, "My oh my, look at how you've grown!"

And remember how you didn't know what in the name of growth spurts they were talking about because you didn't feel any different?

It's hard to feel growth from the inside. But trust me, grandma and everyone else can see how you're changing.

So keep eating your veggies (studying) and getting your exercise (doing shows), and you'll be one of the big boys soon enough.

And unlike a teen, there's no end to how big your career can grow.

AUGUST 2008

August 01, 2008

Stop! Thief!

Someone stole The Prom logo. Again.

See for yourself. Here's mine. Here's <u>theirs</u>. Amazing, isn't it?

It always makes me laugh when people blatantly rip things off. And, believe it or not, this is the third time that it has happened. Imagine if someone stole your car . . . three times.

I used to get mad. Really mad. So mad I'd actually pay my attorney $1,000 to write a <u>C&D</u> every time it happened (that's another form of robbery, but we won't get into that . . . yet).

I don't get mad anymore. Because I realized something . . .

There are two kinds of people in the producing world, whether you are producing theater or thermostats: <u>Creators</u> . . . and <u>Copiers</u>.

And the people who copy aren't usually malicious. They're just lazy. And that's just sad.

So what am I going to do about the logo thief? I'll call tomorrow morning myself and introduce myself and ask them to remove it. They will.

Because they're not stupid. Just lazy.

Unfortunately, as long as there are Creators, there will be Copiers. You'll have them too.

Just do yourself a favor. Protect and defend yourself, yes, but don't waste too much time (or money) on them, when you can be spending that same time (and money) creating.

Keep creating and the Copiers will never catch you.

August 04, 2008

<u>Update: The thief has been caught and released due to good behavior.</u>

As I promised in my <u>last post</u>, I called the logo-offenders first thing yesterday morning. A woman named Chrissy answered the phone.

After a brief explanation of the situation, I urged Chrissy to look at her logo, and then look mine.

"Oh my, well we certainly did use your logo, didn't we."

She apologized profusely, thanked me for not sending lawyers after her and said that her designer must have "Googled 80s prom" and promised to have it down ASAP (it is gone - the link from Friday's post doesn't even work anymore).

So no drama this time, which unfortunately makes for an uninteresting blog topic. But it makes for a much more efficient business.

(BTW, while I had Chrissy on the phone, I urged her to considering licensing The Prom as a sit-down production. We'll see!)

Special shout out to my former intern Megan Shea for catching my logo-borrowing friends.

Oh, and speaking of Copiers, there is one on Broadway right now, which I saw last night (this one did get sued by the "original" . . . and the original lost).

What did I think of the show? Imagine making a Xerox of your favorite picture when your toner is low.

That's what you get when you copy.

August 05, 2008

If life gives you limos, make lemonade.

At _The Awesome 80s Prom_, the show starts on the street, with the characters mingling with the audience members on the way in.

The Captain of the Football team and Head Cheerleader even arrive in a limo.

Fun, right?

Thanks to being buddies with the former car service provider of Brian Stokes Mitchell, Eartha Kitt, and Harry Connick Jr, I only paid $50 for the 30 minutes of service.

Cheap, right?

It was the best deal since TDF, until the driver skipped town a month ago and left us limo-less.

We searched everywhere to find a comparable deal. We even tried offering a limo driver who dropped off <u>audience</u> members at the show $50 to moonlight and take our cast around the block (it worked but it was incredibly awkward).

The best deal we could find was a driver who agreed to do it for his two hour minimum of $150.

That's a $100 increase per week . . . or $5,200 per year for a show that only operates once a week. Yikes. That wasn't going to work.

Or was it . . .

It took my crackerjack staff just one 15 minute brainstorming session to come up with a fine example of creative producing, and turning a negative into a positive . . . cash flow.

Here's what they said . . .

Sure, we had to pay the guy $100 more . . . but, we were also getting another hour and a half. If there was a two hour minimum, then in the name of George Michael, we were going to use that two hours.

Yep, you guessed it . . . *The Awesome 80s Prom* now has limo service.

My also crackerjack street team sells Prom tickets on Saturday afternoons in Times Square. Or, should I say, they try and sell them. It's a difficult pitch when you tell the customer they have to take the subway (scary!) far from Times Square, to see it.

But it's the easiest pitch when you tell them that if they buy, they also get a free limo ride to the show (and a bottle of champagne courtesy of the driver).

Over the past 8 weeks, prior to the limo service, the street team has sold ZERO tickets to the Prom.

This past Saturday, the first day of shuttle service . . . they sold 7 at $25/each for a total of $175. That's right, math whizzes . . . what used to cost us $50, just made us $25! And even better . . . we gave 7 customers a truly memorable experience that they will talk about.

Do that every week and we just made another grand over the course of the year.

I could have made out with every single member of my staff after we hatched this plan.

While it's not a huge chunk of change in either direction, it's an example of the type of creative producing that is necessary in our competitive world.

They only thing that really pi$$es me off? That I didn't think of it a long time ago.

Don't wait for a limo driver to ditch you before you look at every thing you're doing on your shows. Is there anything you can do to add to your audience's experience and reduce your cost?

When you start examining your operation, make sure you look beyond the dollars. Because what looks like more money at first glance, may actually make you more money when you look closer.

August 06, 2008

Kenny got in trouble! Kenny got in trouble!

Busted.

By a 20 year old volunteer usher named Tibor (ok, his name really wasn't Tibor - he just reminded me of a Tibor I knew once).

My offense?

I was trying to take a picture . . . for all of you.

Here's how the felonious photo went down. I went to see *Hair* in the park last night (a perfect setting for an imperfect musical), and grabbed my iPhone to snap a photo of what I thought was a post-curtain call party.

See, Director <u>Diane Paulus</u>, served up a sweet Donkey-show style <u>dessert</u> for us, filling the stage with audience members and turning the Delacorte into a dance club - 60s style.

It was something to see

And it was certainly something to take a photo of.

I know the rules. But certainly they couldn't apply to this, right? This was a beautiful free-for-all. If the insurance agents let it happen, surely the unions would allow a photo or two.

Wrong. As I snapped, I heard Tibor's bellowing war cry of "NO PHOTOS!" and then he demanded to watch me delete the photo! Wow. Tough love, huh?

So I don't have a photo for you today. Because Tibor stole it from us.

Yes he was doing his job. But he also did the show a disservice.

Why do we take photos? We do it because we think whatever is happening is worth sharing with other people.

The act of taking a photo is literally loading a word of mouth weapon. And your audience is your army. The more ammo they have the better.

I'm not giving people carte blanche to take photos during the 4th scene of the 2nd Act of *Phantom*. Taking photos is not appropriate in many situations - for the safety of the performers and to prevent distractions for the rest of the audience.

But as a Producer I look for every opportunity to get photos on my audience member's cameras so they can fire them all over MySpace, Flikr, Facebook and yes, their blogs.

What can you do to make sure your audience members are taking home "legal" digital memories of their experience? Have a "cut-out" in the lobby they can take a picture with? Have your cast come out and sign autographs in costume right after the show comes down? Or ask the union for a special waiver for the post-curtain call party that occurs on stage with 150 non cast-members?

Or just tell Tibor to take a pill. Because what he didn't realize was that as he waited for me to delete my one photo, the woman in front of me was capturing some video on her cell phone.

There are times to follow the rules. And then there are times when there are so many rule breakers, that you've got to realize that maybe your rules are too restrictive.

August 07, 2008

Favorite Quotes: Volume VIII

Want a show to happen? Book a theater.
                    - Anonymous Producer

I talk to a lot of people with shows, and people with ideas for shows and people with shows about ideas for shows. Are they good? Who knows. Most haven't been done yet.

Every time I find myself wallowing in development hell on a project, I book a theater. Sometimes for full production, sometimes for a reading, sometimes for something in-between . . . but I book a theater. For a performance. Where people are going to sit and watch what I've done.

Oh crap. There are going to be people coming to see what I've done!

And presto, all of a sudden things start to happen.

You'll have to get a cast. You'll have to raise the money. You'll have to finish Act II. You'll have no choice. The theater is booked and there are going to be people coming to see what you've done.

Creating art from scratch ain't easy. You know what is easy? Sitting on it forever trying to make it perfect.

But you can't. You gotta get it out there. Because the truth is . . . it's not art until the world has seen it.

So get off your Act II and book a theater.

August 08, 2008

Halftime shows for shows?

I've been thinking a lot about sports lately.

Maybe it's because I'm sore from my basketball game last night. Or maybe because we're getting close to the pennant race and my BoSox are gonna make another run for it.

Or maybe it's because of the email I got from one of you about my traumatic Tibor post. The email asked why it was ok to take photos of a professional athlete like LeBron James at a basketball game, but we weren't allowed to take photos of actors in a curtain call?

Interesting point, right? With all due respect to my Broadway actors, the images of LeBron and his peers are probably worth more than the ensemble of *Hair*, don't you think?

But that's not what this post is about. The point is, I have sports on the brain.

What else do they do in live sporting events that we could learn from?

They overcharge their beverages. So do we.

They have uncomfortable seats. Check.

They have halftime shows. Hmmmm?

Why do we have an intermission anyway? To sell F&B? To build tension in the story? To change the sets? To give the actors a break? To give the audience a break?

All of the above.

Sporting events also do something very interesting during their act break. They have cheerleaders and musical performances and audience interaction (the $1,000,000 half court shot), oh my! It's a bit circus-like, but it keeps the audience revved up, and actually enhances their experience. *And it's in the style of the entire evening.*

What do you do during your intermission to enhance the experience?

Don't take me literally. I'm not saying we should keep the curtain up and have the *Spring Awakening* cheerleaders do a pyramid onstage to a remix of "Totally F*cked".

But I bet if you thought about it, you could figure out some sort of intermission activity that would be appropriate, and add to the experience and excitement. And give people something to talk about.

Like . . .

People are always peering into the pits during intermission. Maybe it's an usher standing by the pit asking if anyone has questions, and talking about how important live music is to the Broadway experience.

Maybe it is a continuation of what's going on onstage in a lesser form (a couple of those *Hair* hippies hanging around in the stands would have made sense).

What about some video of early television shows during intermission at *The Farnsworth Invention*?

Maybe it's too much. I don't know. But I do know this.

If you were buying a $100,000 full page ad in the New York Times, you'd spend time and money making sure you were taking advantage of every column inch in the best way possible.

Well, your most important ad is what happens in your theater every night. And there are 20 minutes of column inches going to waste every night. You've got your audience captured. Give them something else to do, other than get frustrated at the long lines at the bathroom.

Because that's certainly not going to get the audience in the S-P-I-R-I-T for Act II.

August 11, 2008

A Social network is like a nightclub.

It doesn't matter what it's called.

It doesn't matter where it is.

It doesn't matter if it's big or small, or if it serves tapas or not.

The only thing that matters?

Who's <u>there</u>.

When Lindsay, Britney or Paris-ey show up at a club, there's a long line past the velvet rope of people dying to get in.

A couple of Broadway biggies have signed on to <u>BroadwaySpace</u> in the past couple weeks, and our membership and traffic jumped as a result.

This social proof theory about community building applies to both online and offline communities, like . . . community theaters . . . and regional theaters, and any theaters.

Are the leaders in your community coming to your shows? The mayor, the biggest business owner, union leaders? Are they talking about it? *Are they talking to you?*

We got lucky at BroadwaySpace. All of our folks just showed up. Maybe because we serve some killer tapas.

If your leaders aren't showing up to your space, whatever it's called and wherever it is . . . what can you do to get them there?

August 12, 2008

How advertising and waging war have changed.

In the early days of modern warfare, we dropped big bombs. We didn't care who or what was nearby. We weren't confident that we'd actually hit our targets, so we just tried to hit everything and everyone close by. We'd show everyone how powerful we were just by the size of the cloud.

It worked. But it was also wasteful.

These days, we have something even scarier than big bombs. We have missiles so smart they could hit the computer I'm using right now and take out the intended target and <u>only</u> the intended target (I just moved 6 feet to the left).

We have technology to pinpoint exactly what our targets' habits are; when they're strong and when they're vulnerable.

We can plan our attacks to be less wasteful while at the same time be more effective.

Advertising has changed in the same way.

Old advertising was about big bombs as well, like full page ads in the New York Times or giant television buys.

But if you've been a waging a war in the last few years, you've seen the effectiveness of those bombs drop, while the expense has gone up.

The future, no, the present of advertising is about more focused, targeted strikes that can have more of a *concentrated* effect, by using technology to find out what, where, when and why to shoot before pulling a trigger.

August 13, 2008

<u>Spitzer screwed you too.</u>

Long before he was paying $5k a pop for a night of illegal entertainment, Client #9 decided to wage war on those charging $1.50 a pop on top of a ticket to a night of legal entertainment.

Yep, our un-clothed crusader had a thing for facility fees.

In 2003, Elliot wrote a <u>missive</u> to several entertainment venues in the city, including Radio City, Madison Square Garden, and yes, Broadway Theaters, warning them that charging $1 or $1.50 or $4.50 in addition to the ticket price was illegal.

For a moment, Producers and General Managers thought the facility fee (aka the additional profit center fee) might vanish, because no one was stronger than The Spitz.

Haha. Nope.

Here's what happened.

Before Spitz, the consumers were given information like this:

$99 ticket + $1.50 facility fee = $100.50 total cost.

Spitz said this was not truthful advertising. So after he stirred up the muck, Producers were forced to give the information to the consumer like this:

$100.50 ticket

Can you see how we got Spitzed?

We all know our consumers constantly complain about our high prices. At least the first scenario allowed us to explain that it wasn't the Producers charging this extra buck fifty.

An even bigger problem is that for those of us who use psychological pricing. If we want a price under $100, then we have to further reduce by the facility fee. In the above scenario, a $99 ticket would only net us $97.50.

Somehow, while Spitzer was taking a swipe at the theater and facility owners, the Producers got smacked instead.

Oh, and P.S., The Altar Boyz are taking back their endorsement.

August 14, 2008

How do you make your show recession proof?

Simple.

Make it great.

There's a lot of talk in town these days about whether or not Broadway and Off-Broadway will be affected by our "current economic climate." (don't you love that phrase? Climate. Ooooooh. It's so . . . weatherly.)

One producer even said to me . . . "Man, if only it was like last summer."

Well, let's take a quick look at this summer as compared to last summer.

The last four weeks of grosses this summer had 6 members of the million dollar gross club.

Over the same four week cycle last year? Three weeks had only 5 members and one week had 6.

The great are doing even greater.

So, are the $12 gallons of <u>gas</u> and the thousands of foreclosures around the country affecting this little corner of the country? Of course . . . we've seen at least <u>two</u> big shows pull the plug before taking the plunge. And there are even rumors of another. But before you panic, take a look at those shows . . . do you think the market was really craving either one?

During droughts or famines, it's unfortunately the less fortunate that are to go first.

So don't waste your time worrying about whether or not this is the right time to do a show, or the wrong time to do a show, etc. <u>Market timing</u>, in the stock market or in the show market, is never a smart thing. There are some stocks that are soaring right now . . . and there are shows that will soar as well.

Whether yours will be one of them or not only depends on one thing.

How great it is.

And getting it great is always your charge, no matter what kind of climate we're in.

August 15, 2008

How to write a great headline.

When searching for effective forms of advertising, I tell people to simply look and see what affects you. You are exposed to over <u>5,000 </u>marketing messages every day (and growing). Surely there have to be some good ones in there somewhere, right?

Writing headlines, or subject lines, or lead copy, is one of the most important forms of advertising messages. <u>John Caples</u>, literally wrote the <u>book</u> on this subject, after he created the most famous headline in history, "They Laughed When I Sat Down At The Piano but When I Started to Play!", and revolutionized the biz.

One of the best tips I ever got in searching for headlines was to look at the covers of women's magazines.

8 Love Truths You <u>Must</u> Learn

How Dirty <u>Is</u> His Mind?

Get Healthy In A Hurry!

Interesting, huh?

Well, I found a new place to search for great headlines.

And *you* probably go there every day. In fact, the name of the site includes one of my favorite advertising buzz words, "You".

YouTube.

What's making YOU click on videos? When you're killing time in your cubicle you-tubing "people falling down" on the 'tube, which ones grab your fancy based on the headline? My favorite?

<u>If you watch this 100 times you'll still laugh.</u>

This one was so popular, it was copied as many times as Caples.

You're responding to marketing all day long, even when you don't know it. Figuring out what makes you do the things you do will help you figure out what will make other people do the things you want them to do.

August 18, 2008

<u>**I can't do that.**</u>

I can't.

There's no way. As much as I'm a big believer in hard work and passion and perseverance, there is no way that I'm going to win 8 gold medals in swimming.

I just wasn't built that way. But Michael Phelps was.

At 6'4", 194 lbs and a wingspan that an eagle would envy, the man is a just a couple of gills short of being a fish. And no one is gonna catch him.

I would be a fool destined for failure if I thought that if I worked hard enough, one day I'd be able to out-butterfly him.

Does that mean I should give up my dream of working in swimming, if that's what I was passionate about?

No way. There a zillion things I could do to work in and out of the pool. I could coach. I could design a more aerodynamic suit. I could negotiate the zillions of dollars in endorsement deals that Phelps is going to get.

I could figure out what my greatest talents were and apply them to the world in which I wanted to work.

If you want to work in the most competitive of worlds, including the Great White Way, you've got to be objective about what you can do, and yes, what you can't.

Maybe you weren't meant to act, but you were meant to direct. Maybe you weren't meant to direct, but were meant to design. Or maybe you were meant to write, or produce, etc., etc.

If the theater is your hobby, do whatever you want, whenever you want, wherever you want.

If it's your profession, and you *have* to work at the top, then you owe it to yourself *and* to the biz to find out if you belong in or out of the pool.

And then, wherever you are and whatever you do, kick like a son-of-a-fish.

August 19, 2008

I'm addicted to Speed.

The tweets are true.

Earlier today, I twittered that I had signed on as one of the Producers of the 20th Anniversary revival of David Mamet's *Speed- The-Plow* , starring *Entourage's* Jeremy Piven, *Mad Men's* Elisabeth Moss and Broadway's Bobby-baby, Raul Esparza.

I'll admit . . . Seems like a strange choice for the Producer of *The Awesome 80s Prom, My First Time, Altar Boyz* and *13*, doesn't it?

Sing it with me now: "One of these things is not like the other things . . . "

So if this show seems so far from my "style", why am I doing it?

Well, there was a super long list of "pros" that got me to opt-in for my 2nd show that'll open this fall, including the lead Producer, Piven and Mamet himself.

But one of them was simply that it wasn't my style.

In poker, the best teachers will tell you that it's important every once in awhile to "vary your style of play." If you're a very conservative player that only bets when you've got the nuts, bluff once in a while. If you're an aggressive player, play one or two hands tight every couple o' rounds.

Shaking up your style forces you to get out of your comfort zone. And most importantly, it keeps you learning and growing so that you're ready to play in any game at any stakes, no matter who is dealing.

So I'm varying my style of play . . . with a play.

And with this cast and this play, it feels like I've been dealt a couple of pocket aces.

Stay tuned . . . gonna be a fun fall.

August 20, 2008

No refunds. No exchanges. Except . . .

Sometimes, people don't like my shows. Sometimes, they even leave before they are over.

What can you do? You can't please everyone. And frankly, I bet people walked out of *Oedipus Rex* during previews (incest, violence . . . makes *Spring Awakening* look like "Hee-Haw").

Sometimes those people ask for their money back.

Then what do you do?

The theater has always printed its harsh "No Refunds/No Exchanges" policy right on the ticket, as if to say, "Don't even ask or we'll beat you with a stick."

Most people don't ask. And frankly, they shouldn't. You don't ask for a refund if you don't like a movie, or if you're unhappy with the exhibits hanging on the wall at the museum. You're paying for an objective experience, and taking a risk right along with everyone else.

The problem is that the cost of a theater ticket is a lot more than a movie or a museum, so I'd wager that we get more refund requests than both combined.

You can't give customers their money back just because they didn't like the show. But in today's customer service The "Don't Ask For Your Money Back Or The Box Office Treasurer Will Beat You" policy doesn't work either.

It's your responsibility as a Producer to temper your customer's unhappiness as much as possible, to try and reduce the volume of that customer's word of mouth. Because it most certainly is not going to be good.

So what can you or your able-minded box office do?

If people are leaving early, I do just about anything short of a tap dance to get them back in the theater to see the full show. Both *Prom* and *Altar Boyz* are shows that take a few minutes to get groovin' and snap judgments aren't good for any show. I even promised one couple I'd take them out to dinner if they sat through the show and then still wanted their money back (they ended up buying *me* dinner . . . and even expressed interest in investing in a show in the future).

When people won't stay, I always offer those people a chance to come back to see the show again. Most refuse, so I offer them vouchers that they can give to friends who they think might like the show more. I even suggest they give the vouchers away as Xmas gifts (you save them money and you become a hero).

If that fails, I offer them free tickets to another one of my shows, or a steep discount.

T-shirts? Drinks?   I keep going to additional offers like a never-ending flowchart.

Maybe they won't take me up on any of it, but they see that I'm trying to do everything I can to provide them with some value. The effort alone usually softens their temper.

And if it doesn't? And they are still as mad as ever and they still want their money back?

I still won't give it to them.

Why? Because people like that are going to speak poorly about your show no matter what you do.

You could triple their money back, and they'd still talk about you like you *Oedipus-ed* your mom.

August 21, 2008

Please call your lawyer. Part I.

A <u>friend</u> of mine was cutting a deal with a promotional partner recently and when he received the contract, he told the potential partner that he'd be get back to him after his lawyer reviewed the paperwork.

The partner told him not to bother and squashed the deal, for the sole reason that my buddy wants to spend his own money on a second set of legal-eagle eyes.

My friend was thrilled . . . because he knew right away that this was not a guy to do business with.

Anyone that gets skittish when you want a second opinion is someone <u>you</u> should be skittish about.

I cut creative deals on my shows. Before I do, I make it a point to encourage the other party to speak to their agents, their lawyers, their pet hamsters, whomever, before they sign on the dotted line.

By encouraging people to get a second or third opinion, they'll trust you more.

And at some point when a discussion comes up about a clause in the contract and they state that it wasn't explained to them properly . . . well, they can't point the finger at you.

August 22, 2008

<u>**Please call your lawyer. Part II.**</u>

It's official.

The phrase, "I'm calling my lawyer!" and its many consumer-screamed derivatives including "My husband/wife/uncle/cousin is an attorney," have jumped the shark.

Listen to this recent mis-use of the lawyer scare card:

At a show in NYC, a woman had to be escorted out of the theater in handcuffs after refusing to put away her guinea pig (?) and for spewing a hate speech. The show that she was (not) seeing inevitably started late. Here's a quote from the show report . . .

"Most of the audience members were very patient and understanding with the exception of one man who threatened to sue us because we were starting the show late."

Remember when this sort of phrase used to get you all sweaty? You didn't want the big bad lawyers to come huffin' and puffin' and trying to blow your house down.

I'd bet some of you have even used this once or twice when you were dealing with a company that wasn't giving you what you wanted (come on, admit it).

All customer service reps, including theater owners, managers, box office staff, etc are going to hear this at one point or another. And for me, when someone says, "I'm going to contact my lawyer unless . . . ", that's the equivalent of them using the "F" word.

When someone swears at me or a member of my staff, they've just given us the right to shut down and stop helping them.

And when someone uses the "L" word, they have also drawn a line in the sand. That's when I say, "Please do contact your lawyer. In fact, here is the name/address/phone/email/fax/skype of my law firm who I have on retainer, and they would be happy to speak to yours at any time. Thank you for taking this uncomfortable situation out of our hands and putting it into the hands of professionals."

That usually elicits a blank stare. And some back tracking.

Odds are that the consumer is never going to do anything. They were just looking to scare you. But you're smarter than that.

And frankly, this is the safest thing to do from a legal perspective as well. If the customer IS looking to pursue legal action, then you want to be very careful about anything you say and take a hint from Miranda and shut up.

However, if they do want to contact your lawyer and you're a show, you've probably got one on retainer getting a weekly fee. Let 'em earn it.

At some point in your career, you will probably have some sort of legal action against you, probably for a 1-800-LAWYER-ish slip-n-fall.

Don't let it scare you. The best and biggest companies in the world get sued all the time. Consider it a sign of success.

Cuz we're not afraid of big bad lawyers in wolf's clothing anymore.

Guinea pigs?

Yes. We are scared of them, so keep those half-rats out of the theaters, will ya?

August 24, 2008

Special Sunday Post: 13 for 13 Tomorrow

The *13* Box Office opens at 10 AM tomorrow . . . and we're selling $13 tickets to the first 100 people in line, so come on down to The Jacobs Theatre!

Read the deets on JRB's website here. I'll see you there!

August 25, 2008

Turn the lights down low. Turn up the Barry White.

And insert bow chika bow bow music here.

Before any sort of main event, it's important to set the mood. And that goes for the theater as well.

When doing a show, it's important that you don't go-for-gusto until you've warmed up your audience for what they're about to experience. You want them to be ready. You want them to be excited.

You want them to call you the next morning for another date.

Rock bands have opening acts. Live talk shows have warm-up comedians. Movies have previews.

What do you have?

Is there music playing while the audience is seated? What kind?

Are your ushers dressed formally? Are they in costume?

Is there a character on stage? Off stage? Both? (Brian Bradley worked up the crowd into a frenzy during the 30 minutes prior to the Alma Mater in the last revival of *Grease* that I PAed.)

Is the curtain open? Drawn? What type of curtain is it? (One of the smallest but most significant changes I've seen to a "pre-show" was on the last *Gypsy* revival, which I CMed. For the first few previews, the audience entered the theater and stared at a blank, dark and depressing stage . . . for 30 minutes. We wondered why they weren't so responsive during the first scene? We brought in the beautiful "grand drape" for later previews and the audience's somberness disappeared.)

What you do in the 30 or so minutes from when your doors open to when your show begins is crucial. You're setting the tone for the entire evening.

So make sure you consider it.

Because you'll never get the reaction you want from your audience, without proper "beforeplay".

August 26, 2008

"How much should I pay for an option?"

A great question comes from one of my readers on the left coast.

What do you do when, after spending years reading every script that comes across your desk and attending every festival in the free world, you finally find the holy grail of new shows!

Clear off your calendar, because you're ready to sink the next few years of your life (and the next few years' salaries) into getting this show off the page and onto the stage!

But before you book a theater, you better make sure you have the right to book a theater. Time to option the property.

But how much do you pay? Is there a third party appraiser? A blue book for scripts?

The antiquated APC from The Dramatists Guild sets the first option for a new musical at $18,000. Is that appropriate for you?

I don't know.

It's up to you to decide the value of the script and make an offer to the author or the author's agent.

I've paid everything from $1 to $1000s when optioning material. The answer to the question from the other coast is that the option amount differs depending on so many things, like:

- What is the project?

- Is it completed or just an idea? A commission?

- Who is the author? What have they done?

- What do you have planned for the project? Broadway? Off-Broadway? Tour? Foreign?

- What is the potential commercial viability?

- How many people are interested in it?

- Was it your idea?

- Etc.

I will say this, when you're thinking about what to pay. Front money or seed money is hard to raise in the theater. Unless you're sitting on some giant corporate development fund, getting people to pay for early readings, workshops, etc. is hard, but that's the money that is oh so necessary.

I often tell my authors and creatives that I try to keep my advances low so that I have more money to put into the shows themselves. The hungrier authors are usually more than happy to forego a few bucks if it means a few more readings, or a few more rehearsals, or few more musicians.

We're all making an investment in the early stages, and we're all better served in having early money go into the show, instead of into a pocket.

August 27, 2008

Why we should have a World Championships of Theater.

Ok, are you ready for this one?

I may have eaten a few too many hot dogs at the Red Sox/Yankee game tonight, because listen to what I'm spitting up:

If the Olympics and Oedipus were born in the same ancient land and only a few hundred years apart, why don't we have a Theatrical Olympics? Or a World Championship of Theater?

Imagine it . . . put together a governing body of judges from around the globe. Committees in each country would put forth their best entries in each of the usual categories (i.e. Best Musical, Best Play, etc.). Those Judges would travel to see each show and pit East vs. West, North vs. South, Hairspray versus Chinese Opera!

It would be the Miss Universe of the theater!

Ok, maybe it is the hot dogs talking. (But www.WorldTheaterAwards.com is available, FYI)

But the point is that awards and competition are important for marketing and for audience development, no matter who the organization is.

Having awards, makes people want to win them.

Having winners, makes people want to see them.

(In an early *Altar Boyz* quantitative focus group, we determined that the most compelling fact that made people interested in seeing the show was that we had won the Outer Critics Circle Award for Best Off-Broadway Musical. I'd bet the actual award that 95% of the people surveyed didn't even know who the Outer Critics were.)

Does your city have community theater awards? What about high school excellence awards? Any state-wide professional theaters going against each other for bragging rights and a trophy?

None of the above? Well, start one.

Maybe we don't need a world champion of theater (although I think we need it more than we need a badminton champion, but that's besides the point).

But we can all always benefit from a little competition, right? Cuz even if you don't win, you can always tell your audience what an honor it was to be nominated.

August 28, 2008

Fun with festivals.

Theater festivals have exploded in size and number over the last five years, just like film festivals.

The Edinburgh Fringe, NY Fringe, Minneapolis Fringe, Toronto Fringe, Midtown International (which announced their award nominations today, coincidentally), NYMF (which gave birth to ABz), and countless others were created to give new plays and musicals an easier entry point to production by covering a portion of the expenses and responsibilities, namely press/marketing and theater rent.

So getting into a festival makes your life easier, right?

Not so fast, fringe-meister.

Getting into a festival is like an actor getting an agent. You've still got to do most of the work, especially if you want to stand out.

Festivals are like buffets. All the shows are lined up next to each other. The quiche is next to the corn which is next to the strawberry Jell-O with the marshmallows.

While having all those choices sound too good to be true at first, they can be overwhelming to the consumer, especially if they are "new" dishes the diner has never tasted before. And remember, you can only eat so many in one sitting.

I mean, think about it . . . how many times have you been to a buffet and found yourself wandering around the bar trying to decide just what you should try.

That's what a festival audience does.

And if you're lucky enough to get on their plate, you're probably just one of many portions.

With so many choices, it's hard for the Jell-O to stand out.

Your job as a Producer in a festival is to make your show seem like a waiter-served entrée that costs a lot more than the flat rate, all you can eat, warming tray heated, slightly stale, other options.

You can't just be one of the choices. You have to make yourself *the* choice; the one that makes them come back for seconds.

How do you do it?

Don't do what the other shows do.

Do more. And do different.

SEPTEMBER 2008

September 01, 2008

The biggest drama of the year.

The biggest drama of the year ain't on a Broadway stage.

This year's biggest drama is on the political stage.

The question is, do elections have an effect on Broadway grosses? As Jerry Lewis says every Labor Day during his telethon when he wants to look at the numbers . . . "TIMPANI"

I took a look at the Broadway grosses tote board from 9/1 through election day since '85 (all available online, btw), and here's what I found out.

In the 5 presidential election years since '85, the grosses during that specified period (9/1 - Election Day) grew by an average of 12.51% and the attendance grew by an average of 8.70% versus the same period one year prior.

In all the other years since '85, the grosses grew by an average of 5.83% and the total attendance grew by only 1.12%.

Yep, election year growth is outpacing non-election year growth.

I was just as surprised as you. Yet another reminder that an assumption is never as good as a calculation.

I cannot tell a lie, however, and I must admit that I don't believe we have enough data to determine if there's any correlation.

Since the League's website doesn't report earlier than '85, I guess we'll just have to see what happens in November.

Stay tuned for an update after this year's biggest drama climaxes.

Even then, we probably still won't have enough data. So, we'll just have to see what happens over the next 5 presidential election years.

You'll still be reading in 20 years, right?

Think any of the shows currently on the boards will still be running?

Oh, and P.S.

September 02, 2008

Favorite Quotes: Volume IX

Continuing with our presidential theme . . . here's a quote from a former President that might as well have been a Producer, because he hit it right on the head.

Nothing in the world can take the place of persistence. Talent will not; nothing is more common than unsuccessful men with talent. Genius will not; unrewarded genius is almost a proverb. Education will not; the world is full of educated derelicts. Persistence and determination are omnipotent. The slogan "press on" has solved and always will solve the problems of the human race.

      - Calvin Coolidge

September 3, 2008

Trim the fat off your meet before you eat.

I don't believe in meetings with more than 4 participants, including me.

Have a lot of people on a project? Cut the meet into smaller pieces and devour them at different times.

You'll get a lot more done and waste a lot less time.

A smaller portion is easier to digest . . . and also makes you hungrier for the next one.

September 4, 2008

Hal gave me the day off.

Ever been in a room and had something to say and then someone beats you to it?

And you just find yourself saying . . . "Yeah. Yeah. What he said."

That's how I felt when reading this **article** about my favorite mentor, Mr. "I had 2 Best Musicals and 1 Best Revival running at the same time" himself . . . Hal Prince.

Some buzz quotes from the famed Producer/Director to whet your appetite:

"There have been a lot of shows, but how many of them do what theater should be doing: 'Astonish me!' "

"And what about the $1.50 'maintenance fee' on each ticket? Why should the audience maintain the theater? Isn't that what the theater owner is supposed to do?"

"I used to produce a show a year. If one didn't work, maybe the next one did. I made a living in the theater. You can't do that anymore. You can't produce a show a year when each one costs $14 million."

Thanks for giving me the day off, Hal.

And thanks for inspiring me to work through the night.

Read it **here**.

September 08, 2008

Theater things that don't make sense: Vol. 6. Publishing isn't only for books.

The R&H library is for **sale**. Asking price is a cool $250 mil.

Why so much?

It is industry standard that when a Producer signs a deal with a team of authors to produce their musical, the Composer and Lyricist hang on to a collection of rights in a paragraph that goes something like this:

The Producer or Bookwriter shall not be entitled to receive any percentage or share of any monies or proceeds derived by Composer and Lyricist from the publication, mechanical reproduction, synchronization and small-performing rights of the separate music and lyrics contained in the Play as written by the Composer and Lyricist, or any rights in or to such separate music and lyrics as are customarily granted to music publishers or from any use of whatsoever kind and nature of the separate musical compositions in the Play for motion picture, radio and television purposes or otherwise, all of which Composer and Lyricist shall be entitled to receive and retain, without accounting for or paying any share thereof to Producer or Bookwriter and the copyrights and all renewals and extensions thereof shall be in the name of and solely for the benefit of Composer and Lyricist.

In other words, the Producer (and when I say Producer, please understand that I really mean the Show and more importantly its investors, which the Producer represents) sees no financial benefit from published song books, from songs used in commercials, from songs on albums of other artists, from muzak in elevators, etc.

As you can see from the R&H price tag, this bundle of rights can be quite valuable.

I don't know the origin of this *industry standard*, but I suspect that it has roots in an era when musical theater tunes were more of an accepted part of popular culture and it was more common to hear these tunes on the radio, on records, and on **television**. The songs had a life of their own away from the show. Irving Berlin, George Gershwin, etc. didn't need a show to get a song out to the world.

Today most composers/lyricists do.

Shouldn't shows share in some of these monies, since the show and its investors (most of which probably did not recoup their investment) were responsible for helping to introduce that show and therefore its music to the world?

Does it make sense to you that a flop musical which lost almost its entire investment had a song featured on a popular television show, and made the composer and lyricist thousands and thousands of dollars in royalties, but the investors never saw a penny? Guess where the producers of that TV show first heard that song? They saw the musical. (True story)

I don't think anyone can argue that the production of a 10 million dollar musical assists greatly in the marketing of that musical's songs.

The show and its investors make those songs more valuable, therefore the show and its investors should be entitled to some portion of those royalties, just like stock and amateur or movie rights, but in a smaller percentage, say 25%, 20%, or even 10%, depending on the songwriting team.

Doesn't the production of the musical make those songs at least 10% more valuable than no production at all?

The Composer or Lyricist would pay an agent 10% for negotiating a deal for these songs, why wouldn't they pay the show that helped publicize them in the first place? (Or better, it's customary for stock and amateur licensing houses to pay commissions to agents, why not push for the publishing house to pay the show a commission or finder's fee so the composer lyricist doesn't pay a penny?)

Before I start getting letters from the Dramatists Guild about how I'm just another producer looking to line my projects, here's what I propose:

The Show and its Investors get a portion of these publishing proceeds ONLY if the Show hasn't recouped its investment. Once the show recoups? 100% goes to the Composers and Lyricists.

Doesn't that seem fair?

I'm not trying to line pockets. All that I want to do is get my money back to my investors as fast as possible. With our unfortunately high "industry standard" failure rate, so many investors see recoupment as a major success.

Getting investors their money back is like a government giving a tax rebate. You give it back so that they'll give it back to you, through reinvestment.

And that benefits all of us, Composers and Lyricists, included.

September 09, 2008

The NY Post gives you a TKTS update

So not only did it take a lot <u>longer</u> to get the new booth up and running, it also took a lot more cash.

And you helped pay for it.

Read more about the 19 million dollar booth <u>here</u>.

September 10, 2008

Advice from an expert Vol. 5: let's search together

One of the industry's up-and-coming marketers, Leslie Barrett, joins us today. Leslie is on loan from her position as the Director of Integrated Marketing at <u>one</u> of our industry's heavyweight advertising agencies. As the Dir. of Integrated Marketing, Leslie insures that marketing and advertising campaigns are working well together.

Leslie and I recently got into a conversation about exactly that, "working well together", and she shared an idea with me on how to combat one of the our biggest online marketing challenges: how do we compete with ticket brokers who can spend a lot more money on online advertising, most specifically <u>Adwords.</u>

Here's Leslie's expert opinion:

- - - -

Search has become such an important part of our everyday lives, it's hard to imagine what we did before the world's information was available at our fingertips.

So, I've been tossing around the idea of cooperative search, where all Broadway shows would bid on the generic terms as a group, ultimately sending the customer to a page that lists every Broadway show (and off-Broadway for that matter) with face-value ticket prices. But I did some rough math, and it just seems too expensive ($3K - $5K per show per week).

Since the secondary market is so highly motivated to sell our tickets (mainly through search), why can't we make a deal, or several deals? The secondary market is a multi-billion dollar industry, and it's here to stay. Let's figure out how to partner with these companies, keep our customers happy, and share in some of this revenue.

- - - -

Leslie's on to something here. I like her co-op search idea, and would go further as to distribute the cost of the program based on its results. Give each show in the program a specific code, and charge the shows that sell the most tickets the bulk of the costs of the program, thereby distributing the costs more fairly.

But Leslie's most radical idea is the one we all have to remember. Reaching across the aisle takes courage, but sometimes our biggest enemies can be our biggest allies. *Godfather* fans will remember that Don Corleone brought all the members of the five families together to talk first.

Then, his son killed them all.

September 11, 2008

Can you create a viral video?

At every marketing meeting I've been to in the last twelve months, someone usually throws out this thought, "What we need is one of them there viral videos!" (That line works best when said with a Will Parker-like Oklahoma drawl.)

Who can disagree with a statement like that! The right viral videos get millions of views, spread a brand's image faster than a speeding kilobyte, and reach every corner of the cornerless world-wide-interweb.

So where can you pick up one of these mini marketing machines?

You can't.

They're not for sale.

Viral videos are not something that can be bought, so beware of those peddling big budget video ideas with the hopes and prayers that customers will distribute them for you . . . for free.

Would you create a TV commercial without knowing it was going to be used?

Would you create a poster without a place to put it up?

Then don't allocate big dollars to a virus that the consumer body may reject.

In fact, the most **successful** viral videos, I know are the ones that look like they cost whatever the price is of a DV tape is these days.

And, most importantly, while fantastically funny viral videos produce millions of views, they rarely produce millions of dollars.

They can spread a message, but they rarely have an immediate impact on your bottom line.

What do you do if you really want one?

Just get one the same way you'd get an actual virus. Walk around and expose yourself to everything. Sooner or later, you'll catch something . . . and hopefully it'll be on a DV tape.

September 12, 2008

"Are you nervous?"

For those of you following my tweets on **twitter** you know that I was in Mexico earlier this week seeing the 100th performance of the **Mexican production** of *My First Time* (BTW, seeing a show that was first read aloud in your living room now performed in another language in another country is a one helluva trip, literally and figuratively).

I got a lot of questions below the border, most of which I embarrassingly couldn't understand (I've got a couple of months before *My First Time* debuts in Spain, so Mom, if you're reading, **this** is what I want for my belated b-day).

The most common question that I understood was about what I was doing next. And the follow up after I told them that I had
a **couple** of **shows** opening up on Bway this fall was always the same:

¿Está usted nervioso?

The answer? Sure, I'm nervous.

There is always a bit of the willies whenever you put something out in the world. If I wasn't nervous, I'd really be nervous.

So don't beat yourself up if your stomach ties itself up as you get closer to a start date on your project.

My advice? Think about opening a new show like a first date.

Be nervous, fine, but be excited. Because just imagine what can happen after that first date.

And no, all you dirty-birdies, I'm not talking about some one-night stand where you get lucky, and someone is screaming your name (like in a review).

While that kind of reaction is fun to brag about to your friends, it's only temporary.

What you want is a first date that leads to something that lasts.

You want your audience to commit for the long term.

September 15, 2008

Exposing myself at The Expo.

This coming Sunday will mark the third (I think) Show Biz Expo, built to bring "everyone in Show Business together under one roof."

In addition to opportunities to audition for Bernie Telsey's office, and to listen to speakers about screenwriting and financing your own independent movie, they are also having a Panel of Theater Producers.

And guess who's on it:

Kevin McCollum, Michael Rego and moi.

Come down and hear what we three amigos have to say about producing (and self-producing). Admission to the expo is free. Just register in advance.

For a full list of the panels they are offering click here.

September 16, 2008

To be a genius, hire a genius.

Microsoft is pulling out the stops in trying to slow their loss of market share to Apple.

In addition to having Seinfeld star in some TV spots, this **article** refers to their challenge of one of Apple's more genius-like moves, the addition of the **Genius Bar**.

The effort to make Windows seem more user-friendly also includes planting "Windows gurus" to help users in Best Buy and Circuit City stores. They could help battle the loyalty boost Apple gets from "Genius Bars" in its stores, Gillen says. "The Apple stores have been pretty successful as a knowledge center that users can get information from. Microsoft has had nothing on the consumer side."

Computers are tricky to understand. Tricky to operate. And it's even trickier to get someone to help you through your problem.

You know what else is tricky to understand? New York City. And the theater. It would help to have some geniuses floating around inside Broadway theaters, wouldn't it?

We've talked about theater **concierges** before (and The League's **"At Your Service"** service is off and running).

But who else could provide some service with a smile to your audiences?

Your ushers.

They meet. They greet. They seat.

Ushers are one of the few staff members that interact with customers moments before and after your show. It's important that they have genius-like skills about your show, your city, and your other shows that they can recommend.

There are a few really nice ushers in Broadway theaters that obviously love the theater and aren't showing people to their seats just because it's a union job with benefits.

There are also a few crabby ones that couldn't be worse customer service reps.

Union or not, the crabs need to go, so the next time you run into one, see the house manager at the theater and file a complaint.

There are thousands of theater-loving students, actors, and more who would love to work in a theater and get health insurance.

And it doesn't take a genius to know that these geniuses would improve the audience's experience.

Even Microsoft has figured it out.

September 17, 2008

Tony got another Trophy. And it's not a Tony.

The talented Tony Kushner won a brand new playwriting prize this week, which put $200,000 in his bank account. As **this** NY Times article states, the $200k purse is a fat one, compared to the $50k Pritzker or the $10k Pulitzer.

Nothing like trouncing the other big prizes with a few more zeros to show how important the subject matter, writing for the stage, truly is.

And for that, I'm uber grateful to the uber generous Harold and Mimi Steinberg Charitable Trust. The Steinberg's dedication to the theater is unprecedented.

But if I had a couple hundred Gs to give away? With all due respect to Mr. K, I wouldn't give him a G.

Why? It certainly isn't because he doesn't deserve it.

It's because the $200k wouldn't make much of a difference to the man who "has spent much of his time in recent years writing Hollywood scripts."

But put $200k into an account of a kid who is still working on his *Angels in America* while working at a diner at the same time?

That would make a difference.

I'd give the green to a rookie of the year. A promising playwright. Someone on his or her way up that could use a little less worrying about his or her electric bill, and a little more worrying about Act II.

But it wouldn't be that easy. Oh no. As a Producer you never want to give away something without a guarantee of something in return. My $200k would come with a catch. You gotta have a play in one year's time. Not saying it has to be good, but it has to be done.

Or maybe it would be $100k in cash and $100k in production costs. Some kind of split that would give the playwright what most of them want even more than a trophy, or $200k; to see their show up.

For years we've all griped about how we've lost our best writers to Hollywood (including Mr. Kushner, according to the article).

Big prizes and notoriety for the young ones would not only help keep the ones we've got, but they might also reverse the flow, and send us some of what the West Coast has to offer.

So, when $200k feels like $20 bucks, make the biggest difference you can when you dole it out.

Just imagine how getting that money would make you feel.

September 18, 2008

My response to the current Wall St. woes.

I got an email from a **_13_** investor yesterday who thanked me for giving him the opportunity to get in, because if he hadn't sunk money into the show, he would have sunk it in a stock . . . and that stock would have sunk and sunk and stunk.

All of a sudden, investing in a Broadway show doesn't seem as risky, does it?

It's a hard time to raise money, but as a Producer it's your job to demonstrate why a dip in one market means it could be time to go shopping in another.

September 19, 2008

What kind of pitcher are you?

I can hear the groans from my staff already . . . "Another baseball analogy?"

Yep, another baseball analogy.

Obviously I have some unresolved issues with my all-too-short baseball career, and I'm taking it out on all of you. Like Roger Clemens, all that I can say is that I'm sorry.

And, like Roger Clemens, I'm really not sorry.

Ok then . . . This Tuesday I've been asked to do some batting practice for some up and coming pitchers at the TRU "Art of the Pitch" seminar.

Both myself and Cheryl Wiesenfeld will be stepping up to the plate, letting some of the mentees in the TRU Producer Mentorship program show us their stuff. They'll be throwin' whatever projects they are working on at us and Cheryl and I will give them some tips.

Want to come and watch? I asked TRU for some passes for my peeps and they agreed. So, email me and I'll set you up. The passes are very limited. Here's the skinny:

Tuesday, 9/23 at 7:30 PM
Roy Arias Theater
300 West 43rd St. 5th Floor

Perfecting your pitch is not as important in theater as it is for the movie industry, as not many people buy product in our biz without seeing at least a script first. And in our business, we don't need a studio to get our project off the ground.

But learning to summarize your show in a succinct way also helps you sell your show to everyday people (your audience) as well as to potential partners. It makes you focus on the three most important questions that you have to answer before getting a commercial theater project off the ground:

- What is your show about?

- Why are people going to want to see it?

- Why are they going to want to recommend it to their friends *before they recommend other shows?*

Answer these, and you've got yourself a 100 mile-an-hour fastball.

Where the baseball analogy goes bust? When throwing this kind of pitch, you *want* the guy to get a hit.

- - - -

I deliberately posted this <u>photo</u> and not a photo of Roger Clemens in order to wean myself off the baseball analogies. I'm trying. E-Hold my hand and I'll get through it.

September 22, 2008

<u>Has the economy affected Broadway sales?</u>

Broadway? I don't think Broadway has seen any major downturn that can be directly attributed to the current economic situation . . . yet.

But frankly, it's too early to tell.

When there's a drought or a famine, the first ones to go aren't the rich folks on the hill in their big houses. Oh no, the first to go are the smaller, the weaker . . . the poor.

In the past three months, three of the longer running Off-Broadway shows have announced their closing: *I Love You, You're Perfect, Now Change, My Mother's Italian, My Father's Jewish and I'm in Therapy* and (I still can't believe it) *Forbidden Broadway.*

I Love You ran for over 12 years, *My Mother's Italian* for 2 and *Forbidden Broadway* has been running for 26 years (at almost as many theaters).

In those many years, these shows have seen a lot: a dot-com bubble-busting, a black Monday, and the obvious day in September.

And they got through it all.

And they're not getting through this.

So, either this drought is different from the rest, or expenses have inflated more than prices, so shows can't tighten their belts as tight as they used to.

My feeling? It's a bit of both.

Will the drought ever reach those rich fat-cat Broadway shows on the hill?

Well, let's hope that something settles soon, because I think it's creeping closer. . . and closer (think it's a coincidence that both of these "closers" are basically big Off-Broadway shows?)

Does that mean you should run for this hills if you're looking to put up a show in the next 12 months? Nope, but like the modern consumer, you have to be more discerning with where you spend you money and what you spend your money on.

September 23, 2008

A pisser of a show.

I snapped this shot in the bathroom of the Lyceum Theater tonight.

Yep, some guy left more than his dinner drinks in this john.

Some guy left a postcard advertising his show.

Gotta give the guy (a reasonable assumption) a lot of credit:

- He advertised to a targeted audience (anyone in the WC at the Lyceum is going to be a theatergoer).

- He advertised to a captive audience (no explanation needed).

and

- He had postcards with him everywhere he *went.*

So, for all of the above, I'm giving the show a shout out:

Michael Horn & The Michael Chekhov Theatre Co. Present
Sam Shepard's
EYES FOR CONSUELA
9/15 - 10/13
Tix at smarttix.com or 212-868-4444
www.chekhovtheatre.com

If you go see the show, tell the Producer that someone in his show has a lot of (clears throat).

September 24, 2008

Let someone else play with your play.

When I saw the Mexican production of *My First Time* earlier this month, I remembered something: there are ideas other than my own . . . and some of them are good!

When you create something and work on it closely, it's easy to get tunnel vision, even if that tunnel is taking you to great places.

So here's a kooky developmental idea:

Got a new show that you have been working on with your team? Let another team take a shot at it. That's right. Leave your baby with a babysitter . . . for the whole weekend!

Seriously, give it to a new director or a new group of actors or both, and see what they come up with. Don't give them stage directions, don't give them the benefit of seeing earlier readings, just give up control (you control freak, you) and see what they do.

Do it in a living room, or at a small community theater out of state that would kill for a shot at a new show, or do it in Mexico (but wherever you do it, make sure it's somewhere risk-free, away from the mainstream).

You may hate half of it. Or you may hate all of it.

But I guarantee that a different take will make you get out of the tunnel and just may help you see the light.

September 25, 2008

A market correction.

It happened.

An unexpected closing. Our version of a market correction.

Ok, so most folks knew that *Blonde's* roots were showing, but most were betting on it getting through to January, until the Jets and the Sharks rumbled their way into the Palace.

And I would argue that in another market, it would have.

Is this an omen? A harbinger of doom? A sign of a market collapse?

Not likely. In fact, this sort of correction eases some of the pressure on the other shows that are struggling right now.

Think about it. *Blonde* has been grossing in the $400s lately. If it goes away, that $400k per week doesn't go away with it. Over 50% of Broadway theatergoers are from out of town. You think they all of a sudden just don't want to go see a show?

Most of that money will still go in the market. It will just be dispersed to other shows (which shows will benefit depends on the demo - I doubt you'll see *The Seagull* get a bump).

In other words, same amount of food, one less kid to feed.

That's a harsh analogy, but I picked it for a reason. No one in this community likes to see a show close. It's a sad day. Jobs are lost. Investor money is lost.

So let's just hope that this correction keeps another show from having to do the same.

September 26, 2008

Why can't I get a pony too?

Ever get jealous of something someone else got and you didn't?

Even though you thought you deserved it more?

That's how I and so many other Broadway and Off-Broadway producers felt after reading this article about tax credits for the television industry (to accompany those already received by the film industry).

It makes sense.

City wants money.

City uses tax breaks as bait.

Hollywood bites (you can read that both ways).

City gets the added benefit of free advertising by getting its streets and monuments in front of millions of people.

And it's working. The article reports that the economic impact from "city based shoots" has doubled in the last six months to almost 1 billion bucks!

I'm happy for the city. And the TV/film producers. I really am.

At the same time, I can't help feeling a bit slighted. After all, Broadway alone contributed 5.1 billion in '06-07.

Take that film and TV! Hi-yah!

And do our investors get tax breaks? What about relief for plays or musicals that take place in New York City?

Or what about a break for shows by career Producers, who qualify by producing a certain number of shows over a certain number of years. If they left the market, they might take some of that economic impact with them. Should we give them a break to inspire them to keep on keeping on, and to give other producers a reason to do more shows?

Noooooooo.

We don't get the same special treatment as our 2-dimensional sister industries.

Why not? Because the city doesn't have to give us jack. They know Broadway isn't going anywhere, whereas film and TV production is centered in LA, but can go to Vancouver, Toronto, and other cities offering similar incentives. And they know that the advertising and marketing benefits don't come with helping out $5 billion dollar Broadway.

So TV shows get the pony, and we pony up.

And don't even get me started on how much the city and state pitch in for new sports stadiums.

Well two can play at that game.

Calling all states . . . give us some big tax breaks and maybe we can come tryout our shows in your big cities, rather than spend the money elsewhere.

You'd get $$$, press, and some culture cred.

Or NYC can stop nibbling on one of the biggest hands that feeds it and give us a "break".

We sure deserve it.

September 27, 2008

Special Saturday post: Because he deserves it.

The trick of living is to slip on and off the planet with the least fuss you can muster. I'm not running for sainthood. I just happen to think that in life we need to be a little like the farmer, who puts back into the soil what he takes out.
                                        - Paul Newman (1925 - 2008)

We lost a true gentleman today.

And a funny one.

If you'd like to honor him by giving to one of his many charities, click here.

Paul, enjoy the Heavyside Layer.

September 29, 2008

WWYD with TOS?

Remember when we talked about the concept of a Broadway to Off-Broadway transfer?

Title of Show is as close to a perfect candidate as you can get for this experimental idea. Shoot, give me 24 hours, a u-haul, and a collaborative team (and unions) and I could have a version of that show up somewhere else in the city.

The one flaw from our original concept is that *TOS* hasn't benefited from any Tony publicity yet. And then there's the question . . . would they even be eligible if they downsized before the Tonys? Would they be eligible for Off-Broadway and Broadway awards (Broadway shows that have moved from Off-Broadway are eligible for both)?

Lots of questions . . . but the most important question is:

What would you do if you were the Producers of TOS?

Comment away with your thoughts. Luckily, this is Fantasy Broadway, where you make the call, but no real dollars are won or lost.

Which means you have no excuse not to play. So think about it. Because when your real dollars are at stake, and they will be soon . . . you'll have wished you practiced more.

September 30, 2008

These people are officially not allowed to complain.

On BestOfOffBroadway.com, we have a weekly news feature called "Look Who's Off-Broadway" that puts the online spotlight on important folks treading the Off-Broadway boards. By showing our visitors that since television, film and Broadway stars are willing to take a chance Off-Broadway, the ticket-buyers should as well, at the same time hoping to increase the perceived value of Off-Broadway.

It's a simple 10 question interview that can be done over email and has no deadline.

As Off-Broadway shows scream for attention from the media or even the guy on the street, you would think that any Off-Broadway show would kill for a shot to be featured for free on the most heavily trafficked site that caters specifically to Off-Broadway ticket buyers.

And you would be wrong.

Over the past few weeks, we've reached out to the following shows and given them all a chance for their shows and actors to be featured:

Three Changes
Fifty Words
Boys' Life
Fela!
Forbidden Broadway
The Tempest
What's That Smell?
Kindness

What have we been told?

"Sorry, he is not available."

"Unfortunately, due to the rehearsal/performance schedule and other demands at this time, we are going to have to pass on this request."

"He is not doing interviews."

And my favorite response?

No response.

Yep, that's right. Three shows didn't even return our calls and emails.

Oooohhhhh, I have so many questions:

- Are all of these shows really doing so well that they can afford to say no to offers like this or any others?

- How can actors not do press?

- How can people not return phone calls?

And most importantly . . .

- If the star really was too busy (!), why wouldn't the Press Agent offer us another actor or creative team member or janitor or anyone involved with the show to try and still get the media attention?

Look, every show and every star has a choice. And if you want to be picky about your press, that's your prerogative.

But when you refuse opportunities like this, you also lose your whining-privileges, so I don't want to hear from any of the above or their people that it's hard to market your show Off-Broadway.

The sad part is that I bet the Producers were never even made aware of this offer.

In which case, they should remind their people that in the Off-Broadway environment, where recoupment is as rare as a unicorn holding a four-leaf-clover, it's important to take advantage of every free opportunity you can to speak to your buyers.

Oh, and get your stars on board.

OCTOBER 2008

October 01, 2008

An article about me shopping.

Portfolio.com did an article on me browsing through the aisles of NYMF, looking to see if I'd pick up a new show or two.

I didn't find anything my size.

October 02, 2008

Mmmm, M&M. My favorite.

Music and Marketing.

Those 2 Ms go together better than chocolate and peanut butter, Siegfried and Roy, Jonas and Brothers..

Think about it . . .

If I told you I could give you a three-and-a-half minute marketing message that elicited an emotional response in its audience, you'd jump all over it, right?

Now, what if I told you that one message would be accompanied by twelve or so other messages of the same type, and that if they were high enough quality, those messages might be heard multiple times a day . . . for weeks!

Those are some super-sized impressions, no?

And what if I said that your audience would <u>pay</u> to listen to these messages?

As you can probably guess, I just described a cast recording, one of the greatest weapons in our marketing war chest.

Cast recordings, demos, etc. are the purest form of using content to market your production. They don't seem like advertising, but surprise, surprise, they are everything you dream about in an ad: emotional, viral, and they encourage the audience that has seen your show to want to see it again, as well as inspire new audiences to want to see it for the first time.

They can even make some <u>shows</u> seem better than they were.

In one of the fastest turnarounds in musical history, **Ghostlight Records** had the *13* cast recording on the online shelves in only 4 weeks. And in one day the album was #2 on the iTunes soundtrack charts and #38 in overall albums sold!

There is no print ad, no radio spot, no billboard, no nothing other than the show itself, that can drive our marketing message deeper into the hearts of our customers right now.

And for any musical, there is no better time to have your music out in the world than at the beginning of a run or even before your run begins - one of many reasons the British poperas of the 80s (*Phantom, Les Miz, Saigon*, etc.) started out with such a bang here in the States is that the London recordings were already on a lot of people's CD players before the shows arrived.

Are you doing a musical? What sort of music do you have available that can help put your marketing hooks into the hearts of your fans? Got a demo? If not, get one. (And while you're at it, get a "name" singer to sing it - fans of the singer will become fans of the show.)

Is your music online? Can it be downloaded? Shared?

Like Etymology, it's all about the roots. When the root word of musical is music, what you do with that music is fortissimo important..

So, *13* got the recorded music out fast . . . what other type of music marketing could we do? I've got an idea. Stay 'tuned' (bad pun intended).

October 03, 2008

Do you have debate fever?

Maybe it's the ol' debate-club nerd in me, but these debates have got me hot. They're so . . . old school.

Parliamentary Style, Extemp., Oh yessss!

And regardless of which candidate you favor, you gotta love the process of putting two people protected only by a pedestal (and a few hundred hours of boot camp-like preparation) in front of the people and letting them duke it out over the big issues facing us today.

I've learned something at every debate I've ever watched. I've also been inspired by every debate I've ever watched.

Debates encourage people to get involved, to learn, and can motivate change.

So forget Presidential debates, I'm proposing some Producer debates! Here are a few that I'd like to see:

Shubert's vs. Nederlander's (Possible topics: Facility Fees, Ticketmaster vs. Telecharge, etc.)

A Shubert or a Nederlander vs. a Producer (Topics: Whose customer is it?, Control of the Advance, etc.)

Serino vs. Spotco (Topics: Value of NY Times advertising, Photos vs. Illustrations in art, etc.)

Or let's do it Perot-style and throw up three industry big-wigs and let them go at it on a myriad of subjects like:

- Is there too high a price for theater tickets?

- The APC: Antiquated or Essential?

- Do NY Times reviews matter?

- To publish our grosses or not publish or grosses?

We'd all learn a great deal about how we differed on our issues. But just like the Presidential debates, we'd also learn that our primary goal is the same.

A successful and strong theater is what we all want. We just differ on the ideas that will get us there.

Any industry leaders out there ready to go a few rounds?

Email me. I'll play Don King and set this sucker up!

October 06, 2008

"The economy will collapse."

Believe it or not, that's a quote from *Speed The Plow*, written in the '80s, about the end of the world.

Want another?

"Everyone says, 'I'm a maverick' but we're, you know that, just one part of the whole. Nobody's a maverick"

We started previews on Friday, and it's obvious that this play is a lot more timely than ever before.

I've got a special discount for my readers. If you want it, drop me a f***ing email (sorry, channeling Mamet there for a second).

October 07, 2008

Favorite Quotes: Volume X

Fooled you.

No inspirational quotes from Presidents today No quick missives on how to not have to advertise.

Today's edition of 'Favorite Quotes' is sponsored by *13*; And you don't get just one quote, you're gonna get a whole bunch of 'em.

Click below to be the one of the very first to see two versions of monster post-opening *13* quote ads for this Sunday's newspapers.

We had a choice:

Version #1

Version #2

So, you know the game . . . what would you have done? Pretend you were in that ad meeting. Which one would you have run?

Comment below with your choice.

But I'm not gonna tell you the answer.

Pick up a Sunday NY Times, Newsday, Bergen Record, Star Ledger or Journal News to find out what we did.

October 08, 2008

The web is a time machine.

It allows you to go back through the years and dig up old articles that talk about some of the same problems we're talking/blogging about today.

Re-reading these articles gives us a chance to take a self-test to see how we did.

Did we solve any of these problems? Did our ideas work? Are we still faced with the same problems? Are they worse?

Here are a couple of classic articles from more than 10 years ago:

Marketing Broadway as a Cool Spot - April 14, 1996 (right before the opening of *Rent*)

Big Bucks on Broadway Marketing Survey Shows Audiences Older & Richer - March 7th, 1997

Broadway Mounts A Brand-New Production - June 29, 1995

How do you think we're doing?

October 09, 2008

"Hi. My name is Ken. Would you like to buy a knife?"

A reader from Austin asked me what I considered to be the best training for a Producer.

I rolled back through the years to see what I thought was most valuable to me:

Was it Company and General Management?

Was it NYU?

Was it being in the ensemble of *The Fantasy Spectacular* at Carousel Dinner Theater?

The truth is, it was all of those things. Throw all those experiences in the blender known as life, put it on puree, and pour yourself a Producing smoothie. Mmmm, mmmm, good.

But there's one secret ingredient in my smoothie that I recommend you all try (in fact, I recommend it much more than singing "Your Cheatin' Heart" on stage at the Carousel Dinner Theater).

Sell knives.

In 1991, Massachusetts was in a recession and jobs were scarce for us college kids home from school so I responded to an newspaper ad from Vector Marketing and got the gig! My first marketing job! Of the "finest cutlery in the world".

And that's when I first learned that marketing really meant **sales**.

I was an old fashioned salesman, but I was being trained (without pay and with a mandatory $99 fee for a sales kit) by one of the largest direct marketing firms out there who had spent millions perfecting how to sell.

I learned how to pitch, cold call, close a sale, find leads, advertise, negotiate, and more. I learned that back-end incentives and commission drove me (and the rest of the team) to work harder.

And I learned how believing in a product made it much easier to get out of bed in the morning.

So if you've never sold Cutco or Mary Kay or Tupperware, give it a shot, or let someone who sells this stuff pitch to you. See what tips you can pick up for talking to investors, or pricing your tickets, or ...

. . . here's an idea for someone looking to create the next Vector Marketing:

We hire reps to hold ticket parties, where instead of Tupperware, we sell Broadway tickets to a whole different bunch of shows at a discount.

I wonder if I've got my old Cutco training manual . . .

October 10, 2008

Where did that come from? Oh wait, I put it there.

I was doing a detailed audit of the weekly costs on one of my shows recently, and I stumbled upon a small expense for a service that I implemented over a year ago. Because the expense was so small, and because the day-to-day auditing of the expenses had changed hands a few times during that year, the value of the service wasn't questioned.

10 minutes and 3 questions later, we deemed the expense no longer valid, and we cut it, saving the show some moolah.

It could have been done earlier, but we made the mistake of many shows. We fell into an expense comfort zone. You've been doing the same thing for the same money for so long, it seems like you just have to keep doing it the same way, right?

Wrong-o.

You probably do this with your own budget. Ever stop reading a magazine but it keeps showing up? Ever order a pay cable station but never watch it? Ever get your hair cut at the same place every month, even though you don't love it

. . . but it's what you're used to and you don't want to take the time to look somewhere else?

Don't beat yourself up. It happens to everyone.

Which is why I'm introducing a new Super Hero to the scene.

Duh-dah-dah! It's Efficiency Expert Man!

Our industry needs third party consultants to come in, spend 1-2 weeks analyzing all of our expenses and provide us with a detailed list on what we can do to trim down (new vendors, questioning services, etc.)

Why would we pay for such a superhero? Here's how it would work:

Hire Efficiency Expert Man to come in and pay him only if he finds savings, and only what he could save you over 1 month. The other 11 months of the year become super savings.

Or trade it.

You be the Super Hero for a peer's show and let him/her be the Super Hero for yours.

You've got nothing to lose but unnecessary expenses.

October 13, 2008

And I would make the check payable to . . .? ME!

It ain't easy being self-employed.

As a writer or painter or anyone trying to create something from nothing, it's hard to churn stuff out without a boss giving you guidelines, deadlines . . . and a paycheck.

One of the first practical lessons they give you as self-employed artist is to give yourself guidelines and deadlines (write a scene a week, or write between the hours of 9 - 10 AM every weekday) . . . so why not give yourself a paycheck, too?

Yep, I'm telling you to pay yourself, because you'd probably never tell yourself that.

Give yourself an hourly wage, weekly wage, or a wage-per-page . . . and at the end of each week, literally give yourself that money.

And blow it on yourself like you're a playa in Vegas, yo.

You can spend it each week, or save it up. But eventually spend it on something you wouldn't normally buy, but something that makes you feel great: a pedicure, a steak, a trip to St. Croix.

You don't have to pay yourself a lot of money, just something.

Besides, if *you* don't feel like you're worth a few bucks, how can you expect anyone else to think you're worth *more* than a few bucks?

ABOUT THE AUTHOR

Recently hailed as the "P.T. Barnum of Off-Broadway" in the New York Times, featured on a <u>national commercial for the iPhone</u>, and named one of <u>Crain's Magazine's 40 Under 40</u> for 2008, Ken is the only independent producer to have three shows running simultaneously Off-Broadway: *Altar Boyz, The Awesome 80s Prom* and *My First Time*. Ken also produced the Broadway productions of *13, Speed The Plow* starring Jeremy Piven, Will Ferrell's *You 're Welcome America. A Final Night With George W Bush* and *Blithe Spirit* with Angela Lansbury. Prior to his career as a Producer, Ken was a Company Manager and General Manager for many Broadway productions and National Tours including: *Gypsy, Thoroughly Modern Millie, Chicago, Jekyll & Hyde, Cinderella, Ragtime, Showboat, Candide*, and many others. Ken has had the pleasure of being asked to speak to a variety of organizations on theatrical marketing and producing including the Center for Communication Studies, The Commercial Theater Institute, The Independent Presenter's Network, Yale University, The American Theatre Wing, The TAMY Awards, Columbia University's Graduate Program for Theatre Management and Arts Administration, and others. Ken also runs a number of theatrical websites including BestOfOffBroadway.com, DidHeLikeIt.com, the new social networking site, BroadwaySpace.com. His blog, on which this book is based, has been featured in *Vanity Fair, New York Magaizine, The Gothamist* and many other online and print publications. Ken is currently adapting the novel and film *Somewhere in Time* into a Broadway musical and filming a documentary on one of the top unsigned rock bands in the country, *Red Wanting Blue*. For more info, visit www.DavenportTheatrical.com.

—